First World War
and Army of Occupation
War Diary
France, Belgium and Germany

3 CAVALRY DIVISION
Divisional Troops
4 Brigade Royal Horse Artillery
1 October 1914 - 10 June 1919

WO95/1146/1

The Naval & Military Press Ltd
www.nmarchive.com
Published in association with The National Archives

Published by

The Naval & Military Press Ltd

Unit 10 Ridgewood Industrial Park,

Uckfield, East Sussex,

TN22 5QE England

Tel: +44 (0) 1825 749494

www.naval-military-press.com

www.nmarchive.com

Contents

Document type	Place/Title	Date From	Date To
Heading	WO95/1146/1 3 Cavalry Division Divisional Troops. 4 Brigade Royal Horse Artillery Oct 1914-June 1919		
Heading	4th Bde R.H.A. Oct 1914-June 1919		
Heading	4th Bde R.H.A. 3rd Cavalry Division. Vol I. 1.10-31.12.14 to Dec 1918		
War Diary	Windmill Hill Camp	01/10/1914	06/10/1914
War Diary	Southampton	07/10/1914	07/10/1914
War Diary	Ostend	08/10/1914	10/10/1914
War Diary	Oostkamp	10/10/1914	13/10/1914
War Diary	Iseghem	14/10/1914	14/10/1914
War Diary	Wytschaete	14/10/1914	16/10/1914
War Diary	Passchendaele	16/10/1914	25/11/1914
War Diary		00/12/1914	00/12/1914
Heading	War Diary of C.R.A. 3rd Cavalry Division Jany to Feby-1915		
Heading	C.R.A. 3rd Cavalry Division Vols. II III. 1.1-28.2.15		
War Diary		00/01/1915	00/01/1915
War Diary		07/02/1915	07/02/1915
Heading	War Diary of Hd Qrs R.H.A 3rd Cavalry Division March-1915		
Heading	Hd Qrs. R.H.A. 3rd Cavalry Division Vol IV 1-31.3.15		
War Diary	Hazebrouck	01/03/1915	31/03/1915
Heading	3rd Cavalry Division 4th 15th Bde R H A. Vol I. 1-30.4.15		
War Diary		01/04/1915	30/04/1915
Heading	3rd Cavalry Division 4th Bde. R.H.A. Vol II 1-31.5.15		
War Diary	Kemmel.	01/05/1915	31/05/1915
Heading	3rd Cavalry Division. 4th Bde. R.H.A. Vol III 1-30.6.15		
War Diary	Kemmel	01/06/1915	08/06/1915
War Diary	Renescure.	18/06/1915	30/06/1915
Heading	3rd Cavalry Division IVth Bde. R H A. Vol IV 5-27-7-15		
War Diary	Renescure.	05/07/1915	27/07/1915
War Diary	Bilques	06/08/1915	06/08/1915
War Diary	Wandonne	07/08/1915	29/08/1915
Heading	4th Bde R H A 3 Cav Div. Sep 1915		
Miscellaneous	Headquarters Cavalry Divn 4th Corps	17/10/1914	17/10/1914
War Diary	Wandonne	01/09/1915	03/09/1915
War Diary	Hinges	04/09/1915	16/09/1915
War Diary	Wandonne	17/09/1915	21/09/1915
War Diary	Bois Des Dames	22/09/1915	26/09/1915
War Diary	Mazingarbe.	26/09/1915	26/09/1915
War Diary	Quality Street	27/09/1915	28/09/1915
War Diary	Labuissiere	29/09/1915	30/09/1915
Heading	4th Bde R H A Oct 1915		
War Diary	Labuissiere	01/10/1915	03/10/1915
War Diary	Ecquedecques.	04/10/1915	04/10/1915
War Diary	Saint-Hilaire	11/10/1915	16/10/1915
War Diary	Matringhem.	17/10/1915	18/10/1915

War Diary	Fruges	19/10/1915	30/10/1915
Heading	4th Bde R.H.A. Nov 1915 Vol VIII		
War Diary	Fruges	01/11/1915	30/11/1915
Heading	4th Bde. R.H.A. Dec 1915 Vol IX		
War Diary	Fruges	01/12/1915	31/12/1915
War Diary	Bois Jean	15/12/1915	29/12/1915
War Diary	Neuville-St-Vaast.	18/12/1915	31/12/1915
Heading	4th Bde R.H.A Jan 1916 Vol X		
War Diary	Fruges	01/01/1916	01/01/1916
War Diary	Estree Blanche	02/01/1916	05/01/1916
War Diary	Vermelles	06/01/1916	22/02/1916
Heading	4 Bde R H a Vol XII March 1916 April 1916		
War Diary	Fruges	01/03/1916	30/06/1916
Miscellaneous	Warning Order App V	17/06/1917	17/06/1917
Miscellaneous	Warning Order. Appendix VI	20/06/1917	20/06/1917
Miscellaneous	Appendix VII	24/06/1917	24/06/1917
Miscellaneous	Royals Raid.	23/06/1917	23/06/1917
Operation(al) Order(s)	3rd Cavalry Divisional Artillery Operation Order No. 2	25/06/1917	25/06/1917
Miscellaneous	Royals Raid Barrage Table 3rd Cavalry Divisional Artillery.		
Miscellaneous	Royals Raid Barrage Table 2nd Cavalry Divisional Artillery.		
Miscellaneous	Royals Raid Barrage Table 35th Divisional Artillery.		
Miscellaneous	Royals Raid Barrage Table Heavy Artillery.		
Miscellaneous	Warning Order Appendix VIII	28/06/1917	28/06/1917
Operation(al) Order(s)	3rd Cavalry Divisional Artillery Operation Order No. 3	29/06/1917	29/06/1917
Miscellaneous	Night Firing 29th/30th June By 3rd Cavalry Divisional Arty.		
Miscellaneous	3rd Cavalry Divisional Artillery. Intelligence Summary. 6.0 p.m. 31st to 6.0 p.m. 1st.	02/05/1917	02/05/1917
Miscellaneous	3rd Cavalry Divisional Artillery. Intelligence Summary. 6.0 p.m. 1st to 6.0 p.m. 2nd.	03/06/1917	03/06/1917
Miscellaneous	3rd Cavalry Divisional Artillery. Intelligence Summary. 6.0 p.m. 2nd to 6.0 p.m. 3rd.	04/06/1917	04/06/1917
Miscellaneous	3rd Cavalry Divisional Artillery. Intelligence Summary. 6.0 p.m. 3rd to 6.0 p.m. 4th.	05/06/1917	05/06/1917
Miscellaneous	3rd Cavalry Divisional Artillery. Intelligence Summary. 6.0 p.m. 4th to 6.0 p.m. 5th.	06/06/1917	06/06/1917
Miscellaneous	3rd Cavalry Divisional Artillery. Intelligence Summary. 6.0 p.m. 5th to 6.0 p.m. 6th.	07/06/1917	07/06/1917
Miscellaneous	3rd Cavalry Divisional Artillery. Intelligence Summary. 6.0 p.m. 6th to 6.0 p.m. 7th.	08/06/1917	08/06/1917
Miscellaneous	3rd Cavalry Divisional Artillery. Intelligence Summary. 6.0 p.m. 7th to 6.0 p.m. 8th.	09/06/1917	09/06/1917
Miscellaneous	3rd Cavalry Divisional Artillery. Intelligence Summary. 6.0 p.m. 8th to 6.0 p.m. 9th.	10/06/1917	10/06/1917
Miscellaneous	3rd Cavalry Divisional Artillery. Intelligence Summary. 6.0 p.m. 9th to 6.0 p.m. 10th.	11/06/1917	11/06/1917
Miscellaneous	3rd Cavalry Divisional Artillery. Intelligence Summary. 6.0 p.m. 10th to 6.0 p.m. 11th.	12/06/1917	12/06/1917
Miscellaneous	3rd Cavalry Divisional Artillery. Intelligence Summary. 6.0 p.m. 11th to 6.0 p.m. 12th.	13/06/1917	13/06/1917
Miscellaneous	3rd Cavalry Divisional Artillery.	13/06/1917	13/06/1917
Miscellaneous	3rd Cavalry Divisional Artillery. Intelligence Summary. 6.0 p.m. 12th to 6.0 p.m. 13th.	14/06/1917	14/06/1917

Miscellaneous	3rd Cavalry Divisional Artillery. Intelligence Summary. 6.0 p.m. 13th to 6.0 p.m. 14th.	15/06/1917	15/06/1917
Miscellaneous	3rd Cavalry Divisional Artillery. Intelligence Summary. 6.0 p.m. 14th to 6.0 p.m. 15th.	16/06/1917	16/06/1917
Miscellaneous	3rd Cavalry Divisional Artillery. Intelligence Summary 6 p.m. 15th to 6 p.m. 16th.	17/06/1917	17/06/1917
Miscellaneous	3rd Cavalry Divisional Artillery. Intelligence Summary. 6.0 p.m. 16th to 6.0 p.m. 17th	18/06/1917	18/06/1917
Miscellaneous	3rd Cavalry Divisional Artillery. Intelligence Summary. 6.0 p.m. 17th to 6.0 p.m. 18th.	19/06/1917	19/06/1917
Miscellaneous	3rd Cavalry Divisional Artillery. Intelligence Summary 6.0 p.m. 10th to 6.0 p.m. 19th	20/06/1917	20/06/1917
Miscellaneous	3rd Cavalry Divisional Artillery.	20/06/1917	20/06/1917
Miscellaneous	3rd Cavalry Divisional Artillery. Intelligence Summary. 6.0 p.m. 19th to 6.0 p.m. 20th.	21/06/1917	21/06/1917
Miscellaneous	3rd Cavalry Divisional Artillery. Intelligence Summary. 6.0 p.m. 20th to 6.0 p.m. 21st.	22/06/1917	22/06/1917
Miscellaneous	Night Firing 29th/30th By 3rd Cavalry Divisional Arty.		
Miscellaneous	3rd Cavalry Divisional Artillery. Intelligence Summary. 6.0 p.m. 21st to 6.0 p.m. 22nd.	23/06/1917	23/06/1917
Miscellaneous	3rd Cavalry Divisional Artillery. Intelligence Summary. 6.0 p.m. 22nd to 6.0 p.m. 23rd.	24/06/1917	24/06/1917
Miscellaneous	3rd Cavalry Divisional Artillery. Intelligence Summary. 6.0 p.m. 23rd to 6.0 p.m. 24th.	25/06/1917	25/06/1917
Miscellaneous	3rd Cavalry Divisional Artillery. Intelligence Summary. 6.0 p.m. 24th to 6.0 p.m. 25th	26/06/1917	26/06/1917
Miscellaneous	3rd Cavalry Divisional Artillery. Intelligence Summary. 6.0 p.m. 25th to 6.0 p.m. 26th	27/06/1917	27/06/1917
Miscellaneous	3rd Cavalry Divisional Artillery. Hostile shelling report for week ending Tuesday, June, 26th, 1917.	27/06/1917	27/06/1917
Miscellaneous	3rd Cavalry Divisional Artillery. Intelligence Summary. 6.0 p.m. 26th to 6.0 p.m. 27th.		
Miscellaneous	3rd Cavalry Divisional Artillery. Intelligence Summary. 6.0 p.m. 27th to 6.0 p.m. 28th	29/06/1917	29/06/1917
Miscellaneous	3rd Cavalry Divisional Artillery. Intelligence Summary. 6.0 p.m. 28th to 6.0 p.m. 29th	30/06/1917	30/06/1917
Miscellaneous	3rd Cavalry Divisional Artillery. Intelligence Summary. 6.0 p.m. 29th to 6.0 p.m. 30th.	01/07/1917	01/07/1917
War Diary	Laneuville	01/07/1917	04/07/1917
War Diary	Hallencourt	05/07/1917	08/07/1917
War Diary	Daours	09/07/1917	31/07/1917
War Diary	Daours Le Quesnoy	01/08/1917	02/08/1917
War Diary	Gapennes	03/08/1917	03/08/1917
War Diary	Ligescourt	04/08/1917	05/08/1917
War Diary	Crequy	06/08/1917	10/09/1917
War Diary	Dompierre	11/09/1917	11/09/1917
War Diary	Conteville	12/09/1917	12/09/1917
War Diary	Belloy	13/09/1917	13/09/1917
War Diary	Daours	14/09/1917	15/09/1917
War Diary	Laneuville	16/09/1917	16/09/1917
War Diary	Daours	17/09/1917	21/09/1917
War Diary	Crouy	22/09/1917	22/09/1917
Miscellaneous	Frohen le Grand	23/09/1917	30/09/1917
War Diary	Mouriez	01/10/1917	18/10/1917
War Diary	Bois Jean	19/10/1917	21/10/1917
War Diary	Le Ponchel & Willencourt	22/10/1917	29/10/1917

War Diary	Mesnil	29/10/1917	24/11/1917
War Diary	Bois Jean.	01/12/1917	30/12/1917
Miscellaneous	Headquarters 3rd Cavalry Division.	09/02/1917	09/02/1917
War Diary		01/01/1917	31/01/1917
War Diary		11/01/1917	26/01/1917
War Diary	Verchocq	01/02/1917	14/03/1917
War Diary	Merlimont	20/03/1917	31/03/1917
War Diary		22/03/1917	26/03/1917
War Diary	In the Field	01/04/1917	25/05/1917
Operation(al) Order(s)	Cavalry Corps Artillery Operation Order No.4. Appendix I	12/05/1917	12/05/1917
Operation(al) Order(s)	2nd Cavalry Divisional Artillery Order No.1. Appendix II.	16/05/1917	16/05/1917
Miscellaneous	Reference 42nd Divisional Artillery Order No.10 and 2nd Cavalry Division Order No.20. Appendix III.	20/05/1917	20/05/1917
Miscellaneous	2nd Cavalry Divisional Artillery. Disposition of Batteries. Appendix IV.	22/05/1917	22/05/1917
Miscellaneous	2nd Cavalry Divisional Artillery. Intelligence Summary. 6.0 p.m. 20th to 6.0 p.m. 21st.	22/05/1917	22/05/1917
Miscellaneous	2nd Cavalry Divisional Artillery. Intelligence Summary.		
Miscellaneous	2nd Cavalry Divisional Artillery. Intelligence Summary. 6.0 p.m. 22nd to 6.0 p.m. 23rd.	24/05/1917	24/05/1917
Miscellaneous	2nd Cavalry Divisional Artillery. Intelligence Summary. 6.0 a.m. 23rd to 6.0 a.m. 24th.	25/05/1917	25/05/1917
Miscellaneous	3rd Cavalry Divisional Artillery. Intelligence Summary. 6.0 p.m. 24th to 6.0 p.m. 25th.	26/05/1917	26/05/1917
Miscellaneous	3rd Cavalry Divisional Artillery. Intelligence Summary. 6.0 p.m. 25th to 6.0 p.m. 26th.	27/05/1917	27/05/1917
Miscellaneous	3rd Cavalry Divisional Artillery. Intelligence Summary. 6.0 p.m. 26th to 6.0 p.m. 27th.	28/05/1917	28/05/1917
Miscellaneous	3rd Cavalry Divisional Artillery. Intelligence Summary. 6.0 p.m. 27th to 6.0 p.m. 28th.	28/05/1917	28/05/1917
Miscellaneous	3rd Cavalry Divisional Artillery. Intelligence Summary. 6.0 p.m. 28th to 6.0 p.m. 29th.	30/05/1917	30/05/1917
Miscellaneous	3rd Cavalry Divisional Artillery. Intelligence Summary. 6.0 p.m. 29th to 6.0 p.m. 30th.	31/05/1917	31/05/1917
Miscellaneous	3rd Cavalry Divisional Artillery. Intelligence Summary. 6.0 p.m. 30th to 6.0 p.m. 31st.	01/06/1917	01/06/1917
War Diary		01/06/1917	29/06/1917
Miscellaneous	3rd Cavalry Divisional Artillery. Disposition of Batteries. Appendix I.		
Miscellaneous	Appendix II Warning Order.	30/05/1917	30/05/1917
Miscellaneous	Appendix III	10/06/1917	10/06/1917
Miscellaneous	6/296 Battery, R.F.A. O.O. 295th Brigade, R.F.A. 3rd Cavalry Division.	10/06/1917	10/06/1917
Miscellaneous	O.C. "C" Battery R.H.A.	08/06/1917	08/06/1917
Miscellaneous	Appendix IV. Herewith location Statement and amended Table A. IV of Defence Scheme 3rd Cavalry Divisional Artillery.	12/06/1917	12/06/1917
Miscellaneous	Table A.I. Appendix IV.		
Miscellaneous	Table A.IV. (A) Support For 2nd Cavalry Division By Artillery of 3rd Cavalry Division.		
War Diary		01/07/1917	18/07/1917
Operation(al) Order(s)	Northern Group 2nd Cavalry Divisional Artillery Operation Order No.5.	02/07/1917	02/07/1917
Miscellaneous	Relief Table.		

Miscellaneous	3rd Cavalry Divisional Artillery. Intelligence Summary. 6.0 p.m. 30th to 6.0 p.m. 1st.	02/07/1917	02/07/1917
Miscellaneous	3rd Cavalry Divisional Artillery. Intelligence Summary. 6.0 p.m. 1st. to 6.0 p.m. 2nd.	03/07/1917	03/07/1917
Miscellaneous	3rd Cavalry Divisional Artillery. Intelligence Summary. 6.0 p.m. 2nd to 6.0 p.m. 3rd.	04/07/1917	04/07/1917
Miscellaneous	3rd Cavalry Divisional Artillery. Intelligence Summary. 6.0 p.m. 3rd to 6.0 p.m. 4th.	05/07/1917	05/07/1917
Miscellaneous	3rd Cavalry Divisional Artillery. Intelligence Summary. 6.0 p.m. 4th to 6.0 p.m. 5th.	06/07/1917	06/07/1917
Miscellaneous	3rd Cavalry Divisional Artillery. Intelligence Summary. 6.0 p.m. 5th to 6.0 p.m. 6th.	07/07/1917	07/07/1917
Miscellaneous	3rd Cavalry Divisional Artillery. Intelligence Summary. 6.0 p.m. 6th to 6.0 p.m. 7th.	08/07/1917	08/07/1917
War Diary	In the Field	01/08/1917	31/08/1917
War Diary	Lapierriere	01/09/1917	02/09/1917
War Diary	Lamiquellerie	06/09/1917	30/11/1917
Operation(al) Order(s)	R.H.A.Group-Order No. 3	09/12/1917	16/12/1917
Miscellaneous	4th Bde R.H.A Vol 36		
Miscellaneous	4th Bde R H A Vol 37		
War Diary	4th Brigade, R.H.A Vol 38	01/03/1918	13/03/1918
Operation(al) Order(s)	Operations Carried Out By 4th Brigade, R.H.A. Between 21st March And 10th April, 1918.	10/04/1918	10/04/1918
Heading	Headquarters, 4th Brigade, R.H.A. April 1918.		
War Diary		04/04/1918	16/12/1918
War Diary		01/01/1919	31/01/1919
Miscellaneous			
War Diary		11/03/1919	11/03/1919
War Diary	Chokier	01/04/1919	10/06/1919

1

WO 95/1146

3 Cavalry Division
Divisional Troops

4 Brigade Royal Horse
Artillery

Oct 1914 - June 1919.

1914-1918

3RD CAVALRY DIVISION

4TH BDE R.H.A.

OCT 1914-~~DEC 1918~~ JUNE 1919

121/4196

4th Bde RHA. 3rd Cavalry Division.

Vol I. 1.10 — 31.12.14

to

Dec 1918

Instructions regarding War Diaries and Intelligence Summaries are contained in F. S. Regs., Part II. and the Staff Manual respectively. Title pages will be prepared in manuscript.

WAR DIARY
or
INTELLIGENCE SUMMARY
(Erase heading not required.)

Army Form C. 2118.

Hour, Date, Place	Summary of Events and Information	Remarks and references to Appendices
Oct 1st 1914 WINDMILL HILL CAMP	Lt Col C H de Rougemont as C.R.A 3rd Cavalry Division formed the headquarters of the 15th Brigade RHA with Capt E.O Lewin RHA as his adjutant, 2Lt J d'Arcy as orderly officer: Lt T.O Thompson as medical officer, & Lt J.A. Ward as veterinary officer were attached. Although there were 2 Cavalry Brigades (6th & 7th) in the Division there was only one Battery RHA detailed to go to France with it, the intention being to allot 'J' Battery to the Division on arrival in France, that Battery having already proceeded there. The Battery now present is 'K' Battery RHA, commanded by Major G H.A White with Captain A.H. Bridges, and Lts R.C.F Maitland, E.C. Fleming and N.M. McLeod as his officers. Lt. Vicomte E.E. de Satge de St Jean was attached to Hq as Interpreter.	[illegible]
Oct 2nd – 5th	These days were spent in collecting horses & forming a headquarter staff, & an ammunition column. The latter was commanded by Lt R H Walsh, with Lts E.P. Almack and G.O.S. Smyth as his officers. It was impossible to think of conditioning the horses for the work they were about to do, as they only arrived for the headquarters & Ammunition Column 48 hours before entraining. 'K' Battery were rather better off in this respect, having been in camp some little time: however even some of their horses only arrived just before we moved to SOUTHAMPTON.	[illegible]
Oct 6th	We entrained in the early hours without any hitch &	

1247 W 3299 200,000 (E) 8/14 J.B.C. & A. Forms/C. 2118/11.

Instructions regarding War Diaries and Intelligence Summaries are contained in F. S. Regs., Part II. and the Staff Manual respectively. Title pages will be prepared in manuscript.

WAR DIARY
or
INTELLIGENCE SUMMARY
(Erase heading not required.)

Army Form C. 2118.

Hour, Date, Place	Summary of Events and Information	Remarks and references to Appendices
	and proceeded to SOUTHAMPTON, embarking at once on our various transports.	
Oct 7th SOUTHAMPTON	We sailed at 1 am & steamed East, anchoring off the DOWNS at 7pm; at 7.30 we received directions to take us through the mine fields and reached OSTEND early next morning.	Jol
Oct 8th 4 am OSTEND	We disembarked, but owing to the want of arrangements for unloading horses were not finished till late at night. Bivouacked on the Race Course with the exception of the Ammunition Column which stayed on the Quay.	Jol
Oct 9th 11 am.	Marched to BRUGES	Jol
" 4.30 pm.	Billeted in an 'abattoir' near the Station.	
" 10th midday	Marched for OEDELEM, but en route our destination was changed to OOSTKAMP.	Jol
" 4 pm. OOSTKAMP	Went into Billets.	
" 11th	Headquarters to THOROUT. 'K' Battery and Ammunition column to RUDDERVOORDE.	Jol
" 12th	Marched to ROULERS and billeted near level crossing by station.	Jol
" 13th	Marched to YPRES — MENIN — YSEGHEM. On arrival at MENIN we came into touch with some Uhlans, and again on the way to ISEGHEM in semi darkness we saw some more. Into billets at 10.30pm.	Jol
" 14th 5 am. ISEGHEM	Marched via YPRES and KEMMEL to WYTSCHAETE. South of KEMMEL the Germans were in position, NEUVE EGLISE being held by them. 1 section of 'K' Battery was sent forward	Jol

1247 W 3299 200,000 (E) 8/14 J.B.C. & A. Forms/C. 2118/11.

Instructions regarding War Diaries and Intelligence Summaries are contained in F. S. Regs., Part II. and the Staff Manual respectively. Title pages will be prepared in manuscript.

WAR DIARY
or
INTELLIGENCE SUMMARY
(Erase heading not required.)

Army Form C. 2118.

Hour, Date, Place	Summary of Events and Information	Remarks and references to Appendices
	forward to assist the Cavalry, but no attack took place	
Oct 14 WYTSCHAETE	& we moved into billets.	JSL
	We joined hands with 2nd Cavalry Division today.	JSL
Oct 15th "	Remained in billets.	JSL
" 16th 7am	Marched via YPRES to POELCAPELLE.	JSL
	7th Cav: Bde with 'K' Battery moved in the afternoon towards WESTROOSEBEKE where a small action was fought: the battery was not brought into action but was kept rather dangerously close to the village where the 7th Cav Bde were engaged with the Germans.	
PASSCHENDAELE	'K' Battery billet in PASSCHENDAELE.	
	Headquarters & Ammtn: Column near ZONNEBEKE.	
Oct 17th "	'K' Bty stays in its billets.	JSL
	Hq, & Ammtn Column move into ZONNEBEKE.	
" 18	7th Brigade with 'K' Bty to WESTROOSEBEKE	JSL
" 19th	7th Bde were engaged with enemy about DUIVELHOCKSKEN, while 7th Bde were engaged against infantry moving on ROULERS – MENIN road. 'K' were in action N.E of MOORSLEDE. The first position being considered too exposed, a more covered position West of the MOORSLEDE – ROULERS road was occupied: very shortly after the move a very heavy fire from guns was directed by the enemy on the position first occupied: as no aeroplanes were seen it is surmised that spies reported the first position. ~~[illegible]~~	~~[illegible]~~

1247 W 3299 200,000 (E) 8/14 J.B.C. & A. Forms/C. 2118/11.

WAR DIARY
or
INTELLIGENCE SUMMARY
(Erase heading not required.)

Army Form C. 2118.

Hour, Date, Place	Summary of Events and Information	Remarks and references to Appendices
Oct 19th (contd)	'C' Battery joined on this day, & were attached to the 6th Brigade. Major Lamont commanded with Captain J.L. Philips & Lts G.G. Fitze, E.L. Talbot, & C.E.D. Bridge as his officers. The 6th Brigade with 'C' Battery operated about ST. PIERRE towards LEDEGHEM. One section was detached to assist the Cavalry in attacking LEDEGHEM, but not being required was sent to help Commander Samson RN near the ST PIERRE cross roads, to shell a farm. Common shell from the Naval guns cleared the enemy out of the farm, & shrapnel from the 13 prs was used with great effect on them as they retired, Lt Bridge was in command of this section. Lt Fitze took one gun on to LEDEGHEM & shelled the retiring Germans with effect. The enemy's strength led to our retiring about 5 pm to the line WESTROOSEBEKE - PASSCHENDAELE - X roads E of ZONNEBEKE. 'C' came into action on the way back but did little firing, & the attack was not pressed. K lost 1 man killed & 4 wounded (1 of these died on 20th): also 1 horse killed & 3 destroyed after being wounded. 'C' billet for night near POELCAPELLE, & K in ZONNEBEKE.	
Oct 20th.	The Division being on the line WESTROOSEBEKE—PASSCHENDAELE with the 7th Brigade on the right & the 6th on the left, 'C' Battery	

Instructions regarding War Diaries and Intelligence Summaries are contained in F. S. Regs., Part II. and the Staff Manual respectively. Title pages will be prepared in manuscript.

WAR DIARY
or
INTELLIGENCE SUMMARY

(Erase heading not required.)

Army Form C. 2118.

Hour, Date, Place	Summary of Events and Information	Remarks and references to Appendices
Oct. 19 (contd)	A heavy fire was brought to bear, late in the day, on the battery, & the teams, & when the time came to withdraw, the battery was extricated with difficulty under fire. Fortunately the German shrapnel were comparatively ineffective, & the casualties were few. The G.O.C. 3 Cav Div made special mention of the valuable support rendered by K Battery in this action.	[illegible]

1247 W 3299 200,000 (E) 8/14 J.B.C. & A. Forms/C. 2118/11.

Instructions regarding War Diaries and Intelligence Summaries are contained in F. S. Regs., Part II. and the Staff Manual respectively. Title pages will be prepared in manuscript.

WAR DIARY or INTELLIGENCE SUMMARY

(Erase heading not required.)

Army Form C. 2118.

Hour, Date, Place	Summary of Events and Information	Remarks and references to Appendices
Oct 20th (contd)	came into action W of the road & S by W of WESTROOSEBEKE, & fired a considerable number of rounds at the advancing Germans. 'K' were also west of the road, but close to PASSCHENDAELE: the battery was about 600x behind the crest the O.C being on a haystack in the firing line. This part of the firing line was held by French Territorials, & as these were being moved away gradually, an escort was asked for from G.O.C. 7th Cav Bde who sent a troop of the R.H.G. Towards midday a strong attack developed against PASSCHENDAELE, the lines of Germans offering excellent objectives for fire: effective fire was brought to bear on these lines, but communication with the Battery was much interfered with by a break in the telephone wire: this was mended under a heavy gun fire which also much interfered with the observation. The attack developed with great rapidity, & there were signs of the line giving way. An officer was sent to Headquarters to explain the somewhat critical situation & ask for orders. The O.C of the Battery seeing that the Germans had entered PASSCHENDAELE rejoined his Battery & prepared to receive the Germans as they reached the crest some 600x away. Not being aware that the left of the line were retiring he decided to do his utmost to prevent the centre being pierced. Orders to retire were brought him just in time, he limbered up & galloped out of action under rifle fire from the Germans who were now only 500x away. Nothing was lost in this retirement, but while in action	

Instructions regarding War Diaries and Intelligence Summaries are contained in F. S. Regs., Part II. and the Staff Manual respectively. Title pages will be prepared in manuscript.

WAR DIARY
or
INTELLIGENCE SUMMARY
(Erase heading not required.)

Army Form C. 2118.

Hour, Date, Place	Summary of Events and Information	Remarks and references to Appendices
	the wagon line lost through rifle & gun fire, 2 men killed and 2 wounded, also 2 horses killed & 7 destroyed after being wounded: 1 man was missing. This retirement was covered by fire from a French Battery in action about 1 mile west of PASSCENDAELE.	
	'K' Battery came into action again at a range of about 2300x & shelled the Germans as they came out of the village, thereby helping to check their advance. They again retired, & billeted for the night at FREZENBURG.	
	When the left of the line was threatened the 6th Brigade & with it 'C' Battery. The Battery came into action S of POELCAPELLE, & again S of LANGEMARCK against advancing Germans, & finally billeted for the night at PILKEM.	
Oct 21st	'C' Battery moved with the 6th Cav Bde to YPRES & thence along the MENIN road, moving down to Canal between VERBRANDEN MOLEN, & HOLLEBEKE where 4 guns were placed in action firing in a SE direction: 1 gun was taken E of railway to fire in direction of Chateau of HOLLEBEKE. Late in the day they moved to ZANDVOORDE where they billeted.	
	'K' Battery moved with the 7th Brigade to ZONNEBEKE & came into action S of the town firing in an Easterly direction, with	

Instructions regarding War Diaries and Intelligence Summaries are contained in F. S. Regs., Part II. and the Staff Manual respectively. Title pages will be prepared in manuscript.

WAR DIARY
or
INTELLIGENCE SUMMARY
(Erase heading not required.)

Army Form C. 2118.

Hour, Date, Place	Summary of Events and Information	Remarks and references to Appendices
Oct 21st (contd)	the O.C in a house on the outskirts of the town, whence he could observe the fire. In the afternoon they moved to VOORMEZEELE where they billeted.	SCL
Oct 22nd	'C' Battery had 2 Sections in action just N of the ZANDVOORDE ridge, where they were shelled throughout the day, but not very accurately: fire was directed on various objectives in a Southerly & S Easterly direction. 'K' Battery with 7th Cav Bde were in reserve at HOOGE & moved into action near KLEIN ZILLEBEKE at about 2pm, firing towards HOUTHEM and KORTEWILDE. the battery was withdrawn at dusk.	SCL
Oct 23rd	'C' as for 22nd; German fire more severe. Lt E.L. Talbot wounded by shell & died on his way to YPRES. 'K' in action about same place as on 22nd.	SCL
Oct 24th	'C' withdrawn to a position 1200x from crest as they were unable to clear the crest at short ranges & the forward position held no compensating advantages. 'K' as for 23rd.	SCL
Oct 25th	As for 24th. Both Batteries withdrawn at dusk & billeted near level crossing, 1/2 mile S.W of ZILLEBEKE; Ammunition Column there also.	SCL

1247 W 3299 200,000 (E) 8/14 J.B.C. & A. Forms/C. 2118/11.

Instructions regarding War Diaries and Intelligence Summaries are contained in F. S. Regs., Part II. and the Staff Manual respectively. Title pages will be prepared in manuscript.

WAR DIARY or INTELLIGENCE SUMMARY

(Erase heading not required.)

Army Form C. 2118.

Hour, Date, Place	Summary of Events and Information	Remarks and references to Appendices
Oct 26th	Both Batteries were in action by dawn in the same places as on 25th. Advance of Cavalry Corps in direction of HOUTHEM planned, & arrangements made to support with Artillery fire: this advance was cancelled as the 22nd Brigade 7th Division was pushed back from KRUISEIK. Both batteries placed under CRA who had orders to cover the retirement of 22nd Brigade. The 7th Cav Brigade made a demonstration towards HOUTHEM supported by the fire of 2 guns of 'K' Battery: G.O.C. 7th C.B. expected more gun support, but orders had been given to CRA to fire in direction of KRUISEIK.	
~~Oct 27~~ [illegible]	'C', 'F', 4 guns of 'K' & 12th Battery RFA were all in line covering the retirement of 22nd Brigade. 1 man of 'C' Battery wounded on this day	[illegible]
Oct 27	'C' Battery in action at dawn, firing in direction of KRUISEIK, with the O.C. observing on forward slope of ridge NE of ZANDVOORDE. 'K' Battery in readiness. A quiet day.	[illegible]
Oct 28th	as for 27th. Lt Fitze of 'C' Battery was sent to reconnoitre a position for a gun near village of ZANDVOORDE: he was never seen again. B.C. & B.S.M. searched the village but found no trace of him.	

1247 W 3299 200,000 (E) 8/14 J.B.C. & A. Forms/C. 2118/11.

Instructions regarding War Diaries and Intelligence Summaries are contained in F. S. Regs., Part II. and the Staff Manual respectively. Title pages will be prepared in manuscript.

WAR DIARY
or
INTELLIGENCE SUMMARY
(Erase heading not required.)

Army Form C. 2118.

Hour, Date, Place	Summary of Events and Information	Remarks and references to Appendices
Oct 28th (Contd)	Both Batteries withdrawn at dusk.	
Oct 29th	'C' Battery in same place. 'K' Battery sent up to a position close to 'C', with O.C in a pit close to O.C of 'C' Bty. Both Batteries firing throughout the day in support of an infantry attack on KRUISEIK ridge, which was occupied at about 3.30 pm. Batteries withdrawn at dusk. During the 27th, 28 & 29th O.C 'C' Battery was able to bring effective fire on reserves which were being collected, dispersing them: the fire he brought to bear also caused two trenches to be evacuated	
Oct 30th	Both Batteries in action at dawn ~~..~~ in same places as on 29th Enemy started a violent bombardment of ZANDVOORDE & at about 8 am blew in the trenches forcing the 7th Cav. Bde to retire. Both Batteries had therefore to fall back. They came into action again N & S of the road junction close to the Estaminet of KLEIN ZILLEBEKE. Both positions rather exposed, but at first no other positions available. The German attack was accompanied by very heavy shell fire: on this way back Lt J. D'Arcy was badly wounded while riding alongside ~~the~~ Colonel de Rougemont, his horse being killed & the Colonel's wounded.	

Instructions regarding War Diaries and Intelligence Summaries are contained in F. S. Regs., Part II. and the Staff Manual respectively. Title pages will be prepared in manuscript.

WAR DIARY
or
INTELLIGENCE SUMMARY
(Erase heading not required.)

Army Form C. 2118.

Hour, Date, Place	Summary of Events and Information	Remarks and references to Appendices
Oct 30: (contd)	A Field Battery, which was in action in a covered position close to 'K' Battery having received orders to move, 'K' at once occupied the vacated position; a German aeroplane had however marked down the first position occupied by 'K' Battery, & no sooner had they moved to the second position than the first came under an exceedingly heavy fire. Both Batteries were very lucky in escaping the shell fire, which was a slightly longer range than their positions. The Batteries kept up a lively fire throughout the midday & afternoon, the Battery Commanders being in a forward observation post. Orders were issued that under no circumstances would a further retirement take place, but fortunately the German attack was not further pressed, & darkness brought relief from a critical situation. Both Batteries were withdrawn. O.C. 'C' Battery claims to have put a German Battery out of action as it unlimbered at the W. end of ZANDVOORDE ridge Casualties were comparatively very small. 'C' Battery 2 men wounded.	[illegible]

1247 W 3299 200,000 (E) 8/14 J.B.C. & A. Forms/C. 2118/11.

Instructions regarding War Diaries and Intelligence Summaries are contained in F. S. Regs., Part II. and the Staff Manual respectively. Title pages will be prepared in manuscript.

WAR DIARY
or
INTELLIGENCE SUMMARY
(Erase heading not required.)

Army Form C. 2118.

Hour, Date, Place	Summary of Events and Information	Remarks and references to Appendices
Oct 30 – (contd)	K Battery had an entire limber blown up by 1 shell, & the Staff horses, 7 in number, killed by another. Their total casualties were 3 men, & 11 horses killed 7 men wounded, & 1 rendered useless through shock. Headquarters lost Lt D'Arcy wounded, 1 horse killed & 2 wounded.	[initials]
Oct 31st	'C' Battery remained in billets until ordered to join 6th Cav: Bde. which moved to HOOGE; Battery came into action near W of WESTHOEK but did not fire. Casualties 1 horse killed. K' Battery with 7th Cav: Bde to ST ELOI but not being wanted there, came back to VERBRANDEN MOLEN where it came into action late in the afternoon, & was withdrawn at dusk.	H.Q. R.H.A. 3rd Div. [initials]
Nov 1st	The Division was not engaged on this day K' had 2 men wounded by stray shell, 1 of which died: C had 1 man wounded.	[initials]
Nov 2nd	at 3 pm 1 section of K went into action near ~~[illegible]~~ ZWARTOLEEN, till dusk	[initials]

1247 W 3299 200,000 (E) 8/14 J.B.C. & A. Forms/C. 2118/11.

Instructions regarding War Diaries and Intelligence Summaries are contained in F. S. Regs., Part II. and the Staff Manual respectively. Title pages will be prepared in manuscript.

WAR DIARY
or
INTELLIGENCE SUMMARY
(Erase heading not required.)

Army Form C. 2118.

Hour, Date, Place	Summary of Events and Information	Remarks and references to Appendices
Nov. 3rd, 4th, 5th	In reserve & not wanted.	
Nov 6th	When the 7th Brigade were called upon to counterattack against the German advance on ZWARTELEEN, K battery went into action ½ mile N of ZILLEBEKE and supported them with fire, being withdrawn for the night. Casualties 2 men killed, 1 died of wounds.	
Nov 7th	'K' Battery were in action again in the same place as on 7th, all day, firing in direction of ZWARTOLEEN.	H.Q. R.H.A. 3rd ...
Nov 8th & 9th	In reserve. on 9th K lost 1 man missing.	
Nov 10th	Both Batteries went into action close to railway N. of HOOGE Chateau, firing in direction of GHELUVELT, ready to repel any attack from that direction. K had 1 man wounded.	
Nov. 11th	'K' occupied position C was in on 10th, with an observing officer in front infantry trenches: long telephone line worked well. C in reserve.	
Nov 12th	as for 11th	

1247 W 3299 200,000 (E) 8/14 J.B.C. & A. Forms/C. 2118/11.

Instructions regarding War Diaries and Intelligence Summaries are contained in F. S. Regs., Part II. and the Staff Manual respectively. Title pages will be prepared in manuscript.

WAR DIARY
or
INTELLIGENCE SUMMARY
(Erase heading not required.)

Army Form C. 2118.

Hour, Date, Place	Summary of Events and Information	Remarks and references to Appendices
Nov 13th 14th & 15th	In reserve. On 13th Headquarters lose 1 horse killed.	
Nov 16th	In reserve	
Nov. 17th	"C" lose 11 horses during night, from shell fire. 1 man wounded.	
" 18th 19th	Both Batteries in action S of HALTE, on YPRES-MENIN road, firing towards ZWARTOLEEN.	
" 20th	Division goes to rest at HAZEBROUCK.	
" 21 - 30th	Resting & refitting.	
Nov. 25th	"G" Battery RHA joins the Division from the 8th Division	H. Q. R.H.A. 3rd Div
	Major H.M. Dawson Commanding	
	Maj N.H.C. Sherbrooke	
	Capt. J.K.L. Fitzwilliams.	
	" C.H.T. Broad	
	" S.C. Rait Kerr.	

1247 W 3299 200,000 (E) 8/14 J.B.C. & A. Forms/C. 2118/11.

Army Form C. 2118.

Instructions regarding War Diaries and Intelligence Summaries are contained in F. S. Regs., Part II. and the Staff Manual respectively. Title pages will be prepared in manuscript.

WAR DIARY
or
INTELLIGENCE SUMMARY
(Erase heading not required.)

Hour, Date, Place	Summary of Events and Information	Remarks and references to Appendices
December	Resting at HAZEBROUCK.	S B Lewin Major RHA Staff Capt RHA 8 Cav Bde

1247 W 3299 200,000 (E) 8/14 J.B.C. & A. Forms/C. 2118/11.

WAR DIARY

OF

C.R.A.

3RD CAVALRY DIVISION

JANY & FEBY - 1915

a.2.

121
4559

C.R.A. 3rd Cavalry Division

Vols: II & III. 1.1 — 28.2.15

Nil

Instructions regarding War Diaries and Intelligence Summaries are contained in F. S. Regs., Part II. and the Staff Manual respectively. Title pages will be prepared in manuscript.

WAR DIARY
or
INTELLIGENCE SUMMARY
(Erase heading not required.)

Army Form C. 2118.

Hour, Date, Place	Summary of Events and Information	Remarks and references to Appendices
January	C, G, & K Batteries RHA & the Ammunition Column remained in billets throughout the month. L. O. Lewin [?] Major RHA Staff Capt RA 3 Cav Div	

1247 W 3299 200,000 (E) 8/14 J.B.C. & A. Forms/C. 2118/11.

Army Form C. 2118.

Instructions regarding War Diaries and Intelligence Summaries are contained in F. S. Regs., Part II. and the Staff Manual respectively. Title pages will be prepared in manuscript.

WAR DIARY
or
INTELLIGENCE SUMMARY
(Erase heading not required.)

Hour, Date, Place	Summary of Events and Information	Remarks and references to Appendices
February 1915	'C', 'G' & 'K' Batteries RHA remained in billets throughout the month [illegible] Major RHA Staff Capt RA 3 Cav Div	[illegible]

1247 W 3299 200,000 (E) 8/14 J.B.C. & A. Forms/C. 2118/11.

WAR DIARY

OF

H^{D} Q^{RS} R.H.A.

3RD CAVALRY DIVISION

MARCH - 1915.

121/4919

Hd Qrs. R.H.A. 3rd Cavalry Division

Vol IV 1–31. 3. 15

A2
BG

Instructions regarding War Diaries and Intelligence Summaries are contained in F. S. Regs., Part II. and the Staff Manual respectively. Title pages will be prepared in manuscript.

WAR DIARY
or
INTELLIGENCE SUMMARY
(Erase heading not required.)

Army Form C. 2118.

Hour, Date, Place	Summary of Events and Information	Remarks and references to Appendices
Hazebruck March 1st to 9th	Resting at Hazebrouck with 3rd Cav Div.	
" 10th	Received orders to move next day.	
" 11th	Moved at 6 am with Cav. Div to rendezvous near LA MOTTE on MERVILLE road. Stayed here till 4 pm & went into billets – Good news of NEUVE CHAPELLE attack –	[illegible]
" 12th	Standing to ready to move.	
" 13th	Returned to Hazebrouck in the evening.	
" 15th	Orders received that RHA 3rd C.D were attached to 2nd Army.	[illegible]
" 16th	Moved towards BAILLEUL & thence South towards SAILLY SUR LA LYS – Batteries took over from a Canadian Artillery Brigade & did not get into position till late –	
" 17th	Batteries registered on the German trenches Orders received that Canadians would come back & batteries to be withdrawn by dawn	[illegible]
18th	Back into billets at HAZEBRUCK at 10 am	

1247 W 3299 200,000 (E) 8/14 J.B.C. & A. Forms/C. 2118/11.

Instructions regarding War Diaries and Intelligence Summaries are contained in F. S. Regs., Part II. and the Staff Manual respectively. Title pages will be prepared in manuscript.

WAR DIARY
or
INTELLIGENCE SUMMARY
(Erase heading not required.)

Army Form C. 2118.

Hour, Date, Place	Summary of Events and Information	Remarks and references to Appendices
March 19.	Lieut Colonel J. G. Rotton arrived from England to take over command of RHA. 3rd Cav Div	
— 20	2/Lt. Balcombe Brown arrived as Orderly Officer.	
— 21.	Received orders to relieve a Brigade of 5th Division	JMB
— 22.	C. G & K Batteries & Ammunition Column marched at 9 am via Borré, STRAZEELE & METEREN to Cross roads near St JEAN · CAPELLE. Battery Commanders with the OC went on to reconnoitre positions near KEMMEL & Batteries moved up into them after dark.	
— 23	Batteries took up concealed positions on the edge of the stream about 1 mile N of KEMMEL HILL, the Observation Stations for all batteries being on the top of KEMMEL Hill - their objective being the German trenches on the WYTSCHAETE - SPANBROCK ridge & in the PETIT BOIS due W of WYTSCHAETE Village. Registration on the trenches was carried out during the afternoon - The Bde was temporarily attached to the 5th Division	JMB

1247 W 3299 200,000 (E) 8/14 J.B.C. & A. Forms/C. 2118/11.

Instructions regarding War Diaries and Intelligence Summaries are contained in F. S. Regs., Part II. and the Staff Manual respectively. Title pages will be prepared in manuscript.

WAR DIARY

or

~~INTELLIGENCE SUMMARY~~

(Erase heading not required.)

Army Form C. 2118.

Hour, Date, Place	Summary of Events and Information	Remarks and references to Appendices
March 24th	A quiet night, weather fine & frosty with snow showers. Batteries did a little registering on German trenches	Major E. O. Lewin went to 18th Battery R.F.A. on posting to 28th Division
" 25th	Cold & frosty. Germans firing very little. Our Heavy Guns shooting during the afternoon. Capt. T. H. Carlisle arrived & took over the duties of Adjutant in place of Capt. J. L. C. White who went to "N" Battery in his place. 2Lt Balcombe Brown went to R. Flying Corps as Observation Officer.	ML
" 26th	Fine day. Aeroplanes very active & heavily shelled by Germans. Our Heavy Guns firing: Registration.	
" 27th		
" 28th	Considerable firing during night 27/28. Frosty & fine. Desultory artillery firing on both sides. A few German shell at G Battery, one of which wrecked the mess & officers billet just behind the battery. No one hurt.	
" 29th	Desultory artillery firing on both sides. G Battery's wagon line shelled at 9 am. 2 men wounded & 2 horses killed. Wagon line moved back to another farm in the evening	ML

1247 W 3299 200,000 (E) 8/14 J.B.C. & A. Forms/C. 2118/11.

Army Form C. 2118.

Instructions regarding War Diaries and Intelligence Summaries are contained in F. S. Regs., Part II. and the Staff Manual respectively. Title pages will be prepared in manuscript.

WAR DIARY
or
~~INTELLIGENCE SUMMARY~~
(Erase heading not required.)

Hour, Date, Place	Summary of Events and Information	Remarks and references to Appendices
March 30st - 31st -	Both sides very quiet, only desultory shelling. 23rd Bde R.F.A. leaving, and we are ordered to take over their areas. Bde H.Qs move down into KEMMEL Chateau tomorrow, to be near the Infantry Brigadier of 14th Inf. Bde.	[illegible]

F. W. Rotton Lt. Col. R.H.A.
Commanding Royal Horse Artillery
3rd Cavalry Division.

1247 W 3299 200,000 (E) 8/14 J.B.C. & A. Forms/C. 2118/11.

121/5140

3rd Cavalry Division

? 4th 15th Bde R H A.

Vol I. 1 – 30. 4. 15

Army Form C. 2118.

Instructions regarding War Diaries and Intelligence Summaries are contained in F. S. Regs., Part II. and the Staff Manual respectively. Title pages will be prepared in manuscript.

WAR DIARY
or
~~INTELLIGENCE SUMMARY~~

(Erase heading not required.)

Hour, Date, Place	Summary of Events and Information	Remarks and references to Appendices
April 1st	RHA Bde H.Qs moved into billets at KEMMEL Chateau. Very quiet day, hardly any shelling.	
" 2nd	Not a shot from the Germans. N. MIDland Territorial Brigade R.F.A. coming in place of 23rd Bde R.F.A. and are taking over their positions. 23rd Bde left one section of each battery who are withdrawing tomorrow night. N. MID Batteries registered their zones.	MC
(Easter Sunday) 4th	Very quiet indeed. Germans fired a few shell on our trenches during the evening.	
" 5th	14th Infantry Bde left being relieved by Notts & Derby Bde of N. MID. Terr. Division. Desultory shelling & our batteries registering.	
" 6th	G. Battery RHA & 4th North Mid Battery changed positions the range being too great for 15pr guns. A very quiet day.	
" 7th	Very quiet. N. MID Howitzer Battery came up & into action just behind 4th N MID.	
" 8th	Howitzer battery registered on WYTSCHAETE. Our zones changed to the S. Batteries registered new areas.	MC

1247 W 3299 200,000 (E) 8/14 J.B.C. & A. Forms/C. 2118/11.

Instructions regarding War Diaries and Intelligence Summaries are contained in F. S. Regs., Part II. and the Staff Manual respectively. Title pages will be prepared in manuscript.

WAR DIARY

or

~~INTELLIGENCE SUMMARY~~

(Erase heading not required.)

Army Form C. 2118.

Hour, Date, Place	Summary of Events and Information	Remarks and references to Appendices
April 9th & 10th	Positions unaltered. Very quiet. Desultory Artillery Exchanges. Weather fine & cold –	[illegible]
April 11th & 12th –	Situation unaltered, fine warm weather. Zeppelin passed over at 12 mn 11/12th & dropped bombs on Bailleul. Easily distinguishable in clear sky.	[illegible]
April 13th	Maj Gen Allenby commanding Cavalry Corps and Maj Gen Byng visited ~~the~~ Batteries –	
" 14th & 15th –	Quiet days.	
– 16th –	Quiet day. about 4pm heavy rifle & gun fire opened died down under an hour with no serious attack	[illegible]
– 17th –	7pm Mine exploded and heavy bombardment on Hill 60 – which was rushed by British – Made demonstration on our front at 7.45 pm.	
– 18th –	Fierce fighting on Hill 60. in early morning – 6pm heavy gun fire to the North on Hill 60. G. battery moved position to LINDEN HOEK. at dusk	[illegible]

1247 W 3299 200,000 (E) 8/14 J.B.C. & A. Forms/C. 2118/11.

Army Form C. 2118.

WAR DIARY
or
INTELLIGENCE SUMMARY
(Erase heading not required.)

Instructions regarding War Diaries and Intelligence Summaries are contained in F. S. Regs., Part II. and the Staff Manual respectively. Title pages will be prepared in manuscript.

Hour, Date, Place	Summary of Events and Information	Remarks and references to Appendices
April 19th	Maj Gen Sir J Byng visited batteries & horse billets	
	12 noon Germans shelled DICKEBUSH heavily	
	6pm fighting on Hill 60. Quiet on our front.	
— 20th	Very heavy shelling on Hill 60. Germans bombard	MC.
	YPRES with 17 inch mortars. Fairly quiet on zone	
— 21st	Germans shelled H2 trench for 2 hours and in evening	
	shelled G section. Our batteries replied.	
	YPRES again heavily shelled. Heard noise of shells from Kemmel.	
— 22nd	G battery shelled in afternoon, no casualties.	
	H2 & G2 trenches shelled by Germans.	
	Very heavy firing since 4pm N of YPRES. Hear	
	French driven back & Canadian left refused.	
— 23rd	Heavy fighting N of YPRES. Town of YPRES on	
	fire. Fairly quiet on our front.	
— 24th	YPRES shelled. More activity on our front. Evening	
	H3 & G2 trenches heavily shelled ~~with~~ minenwerfers	
	Several casualties. K Batt took on maxim after dark	MC

Instructions regarding War Diaries and Intelligence Summaries are contained in F. S. Regs., Part II. and the Staff Manual respectively. Title pages will be prepared in manuscript.

WAR DIARY
or
INTELLIGENCE SUMMARY
(Erase heading not required.)

Army Form C. 2118.

Hour, Date, Place	Summary of Events and Information	Remarks and references to Appendices
April 25th	Quieter to N of YPRES – Quieter in our front. Desultory shelling by Germans. K Battery upsticked maxim emplacement – & fired on it after dark.	[initials]
April 26th	V. Quiet on our front. and quiet night – Heavy firing N of YPRES from 2pm till dusk. British counter attack timed for 2pm.	
April 27th	Quiet morning – 5pm a small charge exploded at Peckham to blow in German mine shaft. Germans shelled more than usual during the afternoon. which was very misty & dull. Heavy firing N of YPRES which continued from 2pm to dusk.	[initials]
April 28th	Quiet day on our front. Hot & sunny. Burst of firing N of YPRES at 7pm.	

1247 W 3299 200,000 (E) 8/14 J.B.C. & A. Forms/C. 2118/11.

Army Form C. 2118.

Instructions regarding War Diaries and Intelligence Summaries are contained in F. S. Regs., Part II. and the Staff Manual respectively. Title pages will be prepared in manuscript.

WAR DIARY
or
INTELLIGENCE SUMMARY
(Erase heading not required.)

Hour, Date, Place	Summary of Events and Information	Remarks and references to Appendices
April 29th	Quiet in our front. Germans shelled G4 a little C Battery replying on their trenches opposite. G & K Batteries exchanged billets, to get nearer their gun lines. Col Rotton reconnoitred alternative positions for the 3 Batteries RHA.	[initials]
April. 30th	Quiet day. very hot. Crumps on Territorial battery about 11.am. In the evening our new trench mortar fired a few rounds into German trenches.	

J. F. Rotton Lt. Col R.H.A.
Commanding 15th Bde R.H.A.
3rd Cav. Div.

1247 W 3299 200,000 (E) 8/14 J.B.C. & A. Forms/C. 2118/11.

3rd Cavalry Division

121/5482

4th Bde R. H. A.

Vol II 1–31.5.15

Army Form C. 2118.

Instructions regarding War Diaries and Intelligence Summaries are contained in F. S. Regs., Part II. and the Staff Manual respectively. Title pages will be prepared in manuscript.

WAR DIARY

or

~~INTELLIGENCE~~ SUMMARY

(Erase heading not required.)

Hour, Date, Place	Summary of Events and Information	Remarks and references to Appendices
KEMMEL. May 1st	Batteries still in action in ~~the~~ same positions – Quiet day on our front, except 2pm a few shrapnel fired into KEMMEL Hill, & again at 6pm about 50 H.E. in quick succession on our F Sector trenches evidently trying to knock out our trench mortar.	MB.
May 2nd	Quiet day on our front. Very heavy firing N of YPRES about 5pm. & Chlorine gas most distinctly smelt here. G Battery moved billets – N.E wind.	
May 3rd	Very quiet, cold with East wind. 7pm our large trench mortar fired at SPANBROEK MOLEN with apparently good results. G. battery cooperated	MB
" 4th	Very quiet day. misty & raining.	
" 5th	Quiet day. Hot & misty. Batteries did not shoot. Heard Germans captured Hill 60 again –	MB

1247 W 3299 200,000 (E) 8/14 J.B.C. & A. Forms/C. 2118/11.

Instructions regarding War Diaries and Intelligence Summaries are contained in F. S. Regs., Part II. and the Staff Manual respectively. Title pages will be prepared in manuscript.

WAR DIARY
or
~~INTELLIGENCE SUMMARY~~
(Erase heading not required.)

Army Form C. 2118.

Hour, Date, Place	Summary of Events and Information	Remarks and references to Appendices
May 6th	Quiet day. Hot & misty. Heard fighting on Hill 60. Lt.Col. GHA White left K Battery on appointment to 28th Div at Ypres.	
— 7th	Hot & misty. Germans shelled more than usual during the afternoon.	
— 8th	Quiet day in our front. 3.am very heavy bombardment N.E. of YPRES again at 7.am continuing till 9.30 & at intervals all thro' the day. Heard there was heavy German attack on 5th Corps & heavy fighting continued all day.	JMC
— 9th	Quiet day. A mine successfully exploded under the German trench at Peckham. Our batteries all shelled the enemy trenches at the same moment. A crater 70 feet across made & German trench wrecked. Very hot day. One of our aeroplanes shot down a German plane near WYTSCHAETE in the evening. Heard news of French attack near ARRAS & also British attack at AUBERS.	
— 10th	Very fine & hot day. Quiet in our front except 12 m.n. Germans took E.1. trench, but it was immediately retaken by counter attack. Fighting continues round YPRES. G battery fired a few rounds about 12. m.n.	JMC

1247 W 3299 200,000 (E) 8/14 J.B.C. & A. Forms/C.2118/11.

Instructions regarding War Diaries and Intelligence Summaries are contained in F. S. Regs., Part II. and the Staff Manual respectively. Title pages will be prepared in manuscript.

WAR DIARY
or
~~INTELLIGENCE SUMMARY~~
(Erase heading not required.)

Army Form C. 2118.

Hour, Date, Place	Summary of Events and Information	Remarks and references to Appendices
KEMMEL. May 11th.	Very quiet day on our front. Hot & fine N.W. wind. YPRES burning very furiously. Intermittent artillery shooting to the North. C. Battery fired on enemy working party by night.	MC.
" May 12th	Quiet day on our front. KEMMEL village shelled a little in the evening. C & K Batts each sent one gun to Railway workshops STEENBECQUE for repair.	
" " 13th	Wet day, & no fighting on our front until evening. Germans attacked G1 & G2 trenches about 7.30pm with minenwerfer & hand bombs, damaged parapet but did not capture the trench. Quiet night. Heard heavy firing to the South. Reports of severe fighting E of YPRES.	MC.
" 14th } 15th }	Very quiet day. no shelling. cold & wet.	
" 16th	Quiet day. desultory shelling in afternoon. Our trench mortar fired on Peckham in the evening. C & K Batts cooperated. Germans reported poisoning streams with arsenic.	MC

1247 W 3299 200,000 (E) 8/14 J.B.C. & A. Forms/C. 2118/11.

Instructions regarding War Diaries and Intelligence Summaries are contained in F. S. Regs., Part II. and the Staff Manual respectively. Title pages will be prepared in manuscript.

WAR DIARY

or

~~INTELLIGENCE SUMMARY~~

(Erase heading not required.)

Army Form C. 2118.

Hour, Date, Place	Summary of Events and Information	Remarks and references to Appendices
KEMMEL. May 17th	Zeppelin seen going East about 4.30 am. Very wet day ~~&~~ bad light. Quiet day on our front. Heavy firing N of YPRES during afternoon, probably French attack.	
— 18th	Heavy burst of rifle fire during night round St. ELOI. Quiet day on our front. Wet & misty.	[initials]
— 19th	No fighting on our front. Very misty & wet.	
— 20th	Quiet morning. At 3 pm Germans blew up a mine under E1. trench, completely wrecking it & causing several casualties, they made no effort to occupy the trench. K Battery fired a few rounds in evening at enemy's sniping post.	
— 21st	At 3 am a heavy bombardment was heard to the North of YPRES, ceasing about 6 am. Misty day. Maj Gen. Briggs visited the Batteries at 11 am. 8 pm. We blew up a mine under the German trenches opposite 13 & 15.	
— 22nd	Fine day, desultory shelling in the afternoon. 10.30 pm heard heavy firing to the N. of YPRES.	[initials]

1247 W 3299 200,000 (E) 8/14 J.B.C. & A. Forms/C. 2118/11.

Instructions regarding War Diaries and Intelligence Summaries are contained in F. S. Regs., Part II. and the Staff Manual respectively. Title pages will be prepared in manuscript.

WAR DIARY
or
~~INTELLIGENCE SUMMARY~~
(Erase heading not required.)

Army Form C. 2118.

Hour, Date, Place	Summary of Events and Information	Remarks and references to Appendices
KEMMEL May 23rd	Fine hot day. Artillery activity in the morning – Evening Germans blew up a mine under their own trench opposite E sectn. Aeroplanes very busy & heavily shelled by both sides –	Mb
May 24th	Heavy bombardment to the N started at 3 am. Distinctly smelt noxious gases at 3.30 am in KEMMEL. this bombardment continued less violently all day – Fine day with an East wind. Heard the Germans had attacked again in ~~the~~ Salient helped by gas – Very quiet on our line –	
– 25th	Very quiet day on our front. Not so much shelling ~~to the North~~. Heard heavy firing to Southward – Did not fire at all during ~~the~~ day.	Mb
– 26th	Quiet day. hot & clear. German aeroplanes busy. Germans have done a lot more trench digging in their lines	
– 27th	Cold day. but quiet. Major G.R.V. Kinsman arrived from 5th Div to take command of K. Battery.	Mb
– 28th	Cold day. N.W. wind. K. Battery fired on Germans working on trench behind PECKHAM. Great activity of German working parties along our whole front.	

1247 W 3299 200,000 (E) 8/14 J.B.C. & A. Forms/C. 2118/11.

Army Form C. 2118.

Instructions regarding War Diaries and Intelligence Summaries are contained in F. S. Regs., Part II. and the Staff Manual respectively. Title pages will be prepared in manuscript.

WAR DIARY

or

~~INTELLIGENCE SUMMARY~~

(Erase heading not required.)

Hour, Date, Place	Summary of Events and Information	Remarks and references to Appendices
KEMMEL. May 29th	Fine day & good light. Howitzers shelled redoubt a S W Corner WYTSCHAETE wood. Desultory shelling by Germans. One large crump into KEMMEL Village killing 3 children	Me.
May. 30th	Very quiet. fine & hot. German working parties busy.	
May 31st	Very quiet. 2Lt. H. S. Hutchinson joined ~~the~~ Bde for duty. Received orders to rejoin 3rd Cav Div, & to withdrawn by June 3rd. being replaced by 49th Bde R.F.A. 4.5 How. 1st New Army.	Me

J. S. Rotton.
Lt. Col. R.H.A.
Commanding 4th Bde R.H.A.

1247 W 3299 200,000 (E) 8/14 J.B.C. & A. Forms/C. 2118/11.

3rd Cavalry Division

4th Bde. R. H. A.

Vol III 1 — 30. 6. 15.

Instructions regarding War Diaries and Intelligence Summaries are contained in F. S. Regs., Part II. and the Staff Manual respectively. Title pages will be prepared in manuscript.

WAR DIARY
or
INTELLIGENCE SUMMARY
(Erase heading not required.)

Army Form C. 2118.

Hour, Date, Place	Summary of Events and Information	Remarks and references to Appendices
Kemmel June 1st June 2nd	Quiet on our front. 49 Brigade RFA busy taking over from C G & K Batteries.	
June 3rd	Headquarters and C, G, K Batteries moved back to 'rest billets' near Renescure rejoining 3rd Cavalry Division. Batteries split up to Cav. Brigades as follows C to 6th G to 8th and K to 7th & placed under them for administration, being billeted with their respective Brigades at BOESEGHEM, BLARINGHEM and RACQUINGHEM.	
June 8th	3rd Cav. Div. Amm. Col. splitting up into 3 sections each joining & billeting with a battery, the remainder designated B échelon moving up to billets near Renescure.	

1247 W 3299 200,000 (E) 8/14 J.B.C. & A. Forms/C. 2118/11.

Instructions regarding War Diaries and Intelligence Summaries are contained in F. S. Regs., Part II. and the Staff Manual respectively. Title pages will be prepared in manuscript.

WAR DIARY
or
~~INTELLIGENCE SUMMARY~~
(Erase heading not required.)

Army Form C. 2118.

Hour, Date, Place	Summary of Events and Information	Remarks and references to Appendices
RENESCURE.		
June 18th –	Sir John French, inspected 3rd Cav Div. dismounted	
June 19th to 30th	Resting in billets –	

J. F. Rotton Lt. Col. RHA.
Commanding II Bde RHA.

1247 W 3299 200,000 (E) 8/14 J.B.C. & A. Forms/C. 2118/11.

3rd Cavalry Division

121
6390

IVth Bde: R H A.

Vol IV

5-27-7-15

Instructions regarding War Diaries and Intelligence Summaries are contained in F. S. Regs., Part II. and the Staff Manual respectively. Title pages will be prepared in manuscript.

WAR DIARY
or
~~INTELLIGENCE SUMMARY~~
(Erase heading not required.)

Army Form C. 2118

Hour, Date, Place	Summary of Events and Information	Remarks and references to Appendices
RENESCURE.		
July 5th	Capt. R.H. Walsh. 2Lt. Johnstone & 2Lt. Hillyard lent to 2nd Army for work with Trench Howitzer Batteries.	
July. 14th	Moved billets from RENESCURE to BILQUES.	
July. 26th	Lt. Col. J.G. Rotton. promoted Brigadier General and posted to 7th Division.	
July. 27th	Lt. Col. W.H. Kay. RHA arrived to Command RHA. 3rd Cavalry Division.	
	W.H. Kay Lt. Col RHA Commanding IV Bde RHA.	

1247 W 3299 200,000 (E) 8/14 J.B.C. & A. Forms/C. 2118/11.

1915

Instructions regarding War Diaries and Intelligence Summaries are contained in F. S. Regs., Part II. and the Staff Manual respectively. Title pages will be prepared in manuscript.

WAR DIARY

or

~~INTELLIGENCE SUMMARY~~

(Erase heading not required.)

IV Bde RHA

Army Form C. 2118.

Hour, Date, Place		Summary of Events and Information	Remarks and references to Appendices
BLEQUES	Aug 6th	3 Cav Div moved to new billeting area.	C Battery at FLECHIN
		HQ IV Bde RHA went to WANDONNE and Bde [illegible]	G " RECLINGHEM
		Amm Column to ~~[illegible]~~ COUTELLE - VIEILLE	K " DELETTE
	Aug 5th	Lieuts MacIlwaine (K Battery) and Elliott [illegible]	Temp. Lt Thomas posted IV Bde RHA
		went to 5th + 14th Divs to [illegible] [illegible] Batteries	
WANDONNE	Aug 7th	Lieut Johnson + 2/Lt Hollyard returned from [illegible]	Lieut J T [illegible]
		[illegible] from the 100th [illegible]	2/Lt [illegible]
	Aug 26th	Orders received for [illegible] [illegible]	2/Lt [illegible]
		[illegible]	2/Lt [illegible]
	Aug 29th	[illegible]	
		"C" Battery RHA [illegible]	
		[illegible]	
		[illegible]	
		6 [illegible] Howitzer [illegible].	
		Lieuts MacIlwaine + Elliot rejoined from Trench Mortar Batteries.	

Lt Col. RHA. Commanding IV Bde RHA

1247 W 3299 200,000 (E) 8/14 J.B.C. & A. Forms/C. 2118/11.

Sep. 1915

4th Bde R.H.A

3 Cav Div.

RE 9/185

44

Headquarters

Cavalry Divn 4th Corps

The following are forwarded herewith:-

G.H.Q. Summary of information about the enemy for 15th Oct.

Notes on bridges over River Lys.

Summary of information extracted from prisoners examined on 15-10-14.

Also some information from French H.Q.rs regarding a recent method of espionage.

Also a copy of G H Q telegram O A 537

C. Mey. [illegible] Capt. G.S.

Intelligence Officer, 4th Corps.

4th Corps.

17-10-14

Intelligence of 17.10.14.

Instructions regarding War Diaries and Intelligence Summaries are contained in F. S. Regs., Part II, and the Staff Manual respectively. Title pages will be prepared in manuscript.

1915

WAR DIARY
or
~~INTELLIGENCE SUMMARY~~
(Erase heading not required.)

4 Bde RHA

Army Form C. 2118.

Hour, Date, Place		Summary of Events and Information 904	Remarks and references to Appendices
WANDONNE	Sept. 1st	G. Battery, together with its Gun Sect: Small Amm Col & a section of B Echelon A.C., is detached from IV Bde RHA and marched to join IV Corps, where it went into action on Sept 2nd at LE BREBIS under the orders of the 15th Division —	
	Sept. 3rd	Remainder of IV Bde RHA and Amm Col ordered to march on Sept 3rd to HINGES where it was kept in reserve under orders of 1st Corps — A few [illegible] batteries were not allowed to [illegible] until dark — The Amm Col was billeted at GONNEHEM —	
HINGES	Sept 4th	Orders received putting remainder IV Bde RHA under 7th Division — [illegible] of the Battery [illegible] [illegible] [illegible] were shown their battery positions [illegible] W of VERMELLES — Digging parties sent out & all preparations made to render Gun positions ready for occupation —	

1247 W 3299 200,000 (E) 8/14 J.B.C. & A. Forms/C. 2118/11.

Instructions regarding War Diaries and Intelligence Summaries are contained in F. S. Regs., Part II. and the Staff Manual respectively. Title pages will be prepared in manuscript.

WAR DIARY

or

~~INTELLIGENCE SUMMARY~~

(Erase heading not required.)

Army Form C. 2118.

905

Hour, Date, Place	Summary of Events and Information	Remarks and references to Appendices
HINGES. Sept 6th	Orders received cancelling our attachment to 7th Div and keeping us still in Reserve under 1st Corps.	
Sept. 7th – 8th	Spent in digging gun pits near VERMELLES.	
Sept. 9th	Orders received (putting us into the [illegible] Batt.) under orders of Meerut Div. to go into action tomorrow, for purpose of experimental firing of H.E. Shell.	
12. M.N.	Orders cancelled placing us under Meerut Div.	
Sept 10th	Awaiting orders.	
Sept 11th	Orders again received to go into action under Meerut Div on 12th.	
Sept 12th	B.C's & O.C. R.H.A. went to Meerut Div and reconnoitred positions.	
12. Noon	Orders cancelled again.	
Sept 13th – 14th	Continued digging on gun pits at Vermelles.	

1247 W 3299 200,000 (E) 8/14 J.B.C. & A. Forms/C. 2118/11.

Instructions regarding War Diaries and Intelligence Summaries are contained in F. S. Regs., Part II. and the Staff Manual respectively. Title pages will be prepared in manuscript.

WAR DIARY

or

~~INTELLIGENCE SUMMARY~~

(Erase heading not required.)

Army Form C. 2118.

906

Hour, Date, Place		Summary of Events and Information	Remarks and references to Appendices
HINGES.	Sept 15th	Digging Gun pits. Orders received 10pm for IV Bde RHA to rejoin 3 Cav Div.	
	Sept 16th	H.Q. C & K. Batteries & Amm Col marched under Battery arrangements to rejoin 3 Cav Div. C & K. Batt. went into their old billets, and B Echelon Amm Col billetted in AUDINCTHUN.	
WANDONNE	Sept 17th	"G" Battery rejoined 3 Cav Div from 15th Division and occupied old billets at RECLINGHAM.	
	Sept 18 } 19 }	In Billets.	
	Sept 20th	Received orders for 3 Cav Div to march on 21st (less 7th Cav Bde) to bivouacs in BOIS DES DAMES.	
	Sept 21st	6th Cav Bde marched night 20/21. 8 Cav Bde & Div Troops on morning 21st 7th Cav Bde & K. Battery left on 21st. destination unknown.	
BOIS DES DAMES	Sept 22nd 23rd 24th }	Received orders on night 24th for 3 Cav Div less 7 Cav Bde to be ready saddled up at 5.30 am 25th	

Instructions regarding War Diaries and Intelligence Summaries are contained in F. S. Regs., Part II, and the Staff Manual respectively. Title pages will be prepared in manuscript.

WAR DIARY

or

~~INTELLIGENCE SUMMARY~~

(Erase heading not required.)

Army Form C. 2118.

907

Hour, Date, Place	Summary of Events and Information	Remarks and references to Appendices
8 am Sept 25th	3 Cav Div moved to VAUDRICOURT.	
11. am.	News received that HULLUCH. LOOS & hill 70 had been taken by our troops & that the Germans were withdrawing. 3 Cav Div ordered to advance to rendezvous between VERMELLES & FOSSE. 3. & await orders at 15 Div H.Q. in MAZINGARBE.	
2 pm	Orders received for 3 Cav. Div. to push on between HULLUCK and LOOS and make for the high ground between PONT a VENDIN and HARNES. 15th Div were reported being pushed back from hill 70 E. of LOOS for want of support. At same time further information of the situation arrived showing that HULLUCH was still in German hands as also a portion of first line German trench SW of HULLUCH. 3 Cav Div orders to advance were cancelled and part of 11th Corps who had meanwhile come up sent to reinforce. Situation not very clear & 3 Cav Div ordered to keep in touch with situation. No further orders received this night and Bdes. bivouaced where they were near Fosse 3.	
Sept 26th	Reports showed that 1st Corps had made little progress and had not succeeded in occupying AUCHY & HAINES.	
6. am.	8th Cav Bde put under orders of 7th Div to be used only in case of urgent necessity. During night reports	

1247 W 3260 200,000 (E) 8/14 J.B.C.& A. Forms/C. 2118/11.

Instructions regarding War Diaries and Intelligence Summaries are contained in F.S. Regs., Part II. and the Staff Manual respectively. Title pages will be prepared in manuscript.

WAR DIARY
or
~~INTELLIGENCE SUMMARY.~~
(Erase heading not required.)

Army Form C. 2118.

908

Hour, Date, Place	Summary of Events and Information	Remarks and references to Appendices
	Showed that 1st Corps had been driven back in places to their original line. British attack to commence again at 11 a.m.	
MAZINGARBE. 9 am 26th	C & G Batts withdrawn from action & placed under orders CRA 3 Cav Div to work under orders of 15th Div Artillery. Went into action just S of Fosse 3 South of VERMELLES – LENS road and fired barrages. Remained in action line during the night. 21st Div attacked during afternoon unsuccessfully.	
10 pm.	3 Cav Div went up to LOOS & manned the trench line just E of the town.	
QUALITY STREET Sept 27th	9 am. orders received for C & G Batts to move forward to a position on either side of main road just N of Fosse 7 where they dug in & fired a few rounds in the afternoon. Guards Division came up & made an attack reaching western slopes of hill 70 and a line W of point 14 bis. 15th Div Artillery fired barrages for this attack which was to have been supported by its own Div Artillery which however never came up. Batteries remained in action all night. Their wagon lines were near Fosse 3 & Amn Cols at NOYELLES & Div Amn Col at NOEUX LES MINES.	

Instructions regarding War Diaries and Intelligence Summaries are contained in F. S. Regs., Part II. and the Staff Manual respectively. Title pages will be prepared in manuscript.

WAR DIARY.

or

~~INTELLIGENCE SUMMARY~~

(Erase heading not required.)

Army Form C. 2118.

Hour, Date, Place	Summary of Events and Information	Remarks and references to Appendices
	904	
QUALITY STREET Sept 28th	Loos fairly heavily shelled. Situation known all along the line. No headway made on 1st Corps front. An attack by Guards Brigade on Puits 14 Bis during the afternoon prepared before by heavy shelling with heavy guns was not successful. C & G. Batteries fired barrages together with remainder 15 Div. Arty during the whole night, stopping at 5 am. 3 Cav Div withdrawn during night & relieved by 2nd Inf Bde. ~~Cav~~	
LABUISSIÉRE Sept. 29th	C & G. Batts withdrawn at 5.30 am & rejoined 3 Cav Div marching back to billets in BOIS DES DAMES and LABUISSIERE.	
Sept. 30th	Resting in bivouac & billets.	
	W. H. Kay Lt Col RHA Commanding IV Bde RHA.	

1247 W 3299 200,000 (E) 8/14 J.B.C. & A. Forms/C. 2118/11.

OCT - 1915

4th Bde R H A

Instructions regarding War Diaries and Intelligence Summaries are contained in F. S. Regs., Part II. and the Staff Manual respectively. Title pages will be prepared in manuscript.

WAR DIARY
or
~~INTELLIGENCE SUMMARY~~
(Erase heading not required.)

4th Bde RFA

Army Form C. 2118.

910

Hour, Date, Place		Summary of Events and Information	Remarks and references to Appendices
LABUISSIÈRE	Oct 1st } 2nd }	In Billetts.	
	3rd	3rd Cav Div moved billetts to ECQUEDECQUES – HQ IV Bde and	Amm Col in this village.
ECQUEDECQUES.	4th	"G" Batt at BURBURE & "C" Batt at CAUCHY-LA-TOUR.	
SAINT-HILAIRE.	11th to 16th	H.Q. 3 Cav Div moved billetts. H.Q. IV Bde RHA & Amm Col to SAINT	HILAIRE.
		In Billetts.	
MATRINGHEM.	17th 18th	H.Q. IV Bde & Amm Col moved to MATRINGHEM.	
FRUGES	19th	H.Q. IV Bde moved to FRUGES. Amm Col to HEZECQUES.	
	23rd	Capt's J.H. Nunn and R.C.F. Maitland ordered to England	
	26th	Capt's T.H. Carlisle and J.K.L. Fitzwilliams to 14th and 15th Divisions respectively.	
	27th	Lts H.R. Bennett RFA and F.W. Bracecamp RFA arrived to join the Brigade.	
	28th	Lt D.C. Ferguson RFA joined the Brigade	

Instructions regarding War Diaries and Intelligence Summaries are contained in F. S. Regs., Part II, and the Staff Manual respectively. Title pages will be prepared in manuscript.

WAR DIARY
or
INTELLIGENCE SUMMARY
(Erase heading not required.)

Army Form C. 2118.

Hour, Date, Place	Summary of Events and Information 911	Remarks and references to Appendices
FRUGES Oct 29th	Major A.E. Erskine joined the Brigade and took over the command of C Battery RHA.	
Oct 30	Resting in Billets	

W.H. Kay Lt Col RHA
Commanding 4th Bde RHA.

1247 W 3299 200,000 (E) 8/14 J.B.C. & A. Forms/C. 2118/11.

3rd Cavalry Division

4th Bde R.H.A.

Nov 1915

Vol VIII

B/
7871

2nd Cav

Army Form C. 2118.

Instructions regarding War Diaries and Intelligence Summaries are contained in F. S. Regs., Part II. and the Staff Manual respectively. Title pages will be prepared in manuscript.

WAR DIARY
or
INTELLIGENCE SUMMARY
(Erase heading not required.)

Hour, Date, Place	Summary of Events and Information	Remarks and references to Appendices
FRUGES Nov 1st	Resting in Billets	
Nov 12th	Major D.C. Spencer Smith took over command of K. Battery vice Kinsman to Guards Division	
Nov 15th	K. Battery moved to new billets at 'ASSONVAL' and RIMEUX	
Nov 16th	G. Battery moved into new billets at COUPELLE-VIEILLE Ammunition column also to COUPELLE-VIEILLE C. Battery moved to billets at SAINS-LES-FRESSIN.	
Nov 30th	Still in Billets.	

W.H. Kay Lt Col R.H.A.
Commanding 4th Brigade R.H.A.

1247 W 3299 200,000 (E) 8/14 J.B.C. & A. Forms/C. 2118/11.

3rd CD

4th Bde. R.H.A.

Dec 1915.

Vol IX

Instructions regarding War Diaries and Intelligence Summaries are contained in F. S. Regs., Part II. and the Staff Manual respectively. Title pages will be prepared in manuscript.

WAR DIARY
or
INTELLIGENCE SUMMARY.
(Erase heading not required.)

Army Form C. 2118.

Place	Date	Hour	Summary of Events and Information	Remarks and references to Appendices
FRUGES	Dec 1st to Dec 31st		Resting in Billets	
— " —	Dec 27th		Dismounted Division ordered to form forthwith & concentrate in billets by evening of 28th Dec.	
	Dec 30th		Received orders to march on Jan 1st 1916	

W. H. Kay Lt Col RHA
Commanding 4th Bde R.H.A.

1577 Wt. W10791/1773 500,000 1/15 D. D. & L. A.D.S.S./Forms/C. 2118.

Instructions regarding War Diaries and Intelligence Summaries are contained in F. S. Regs., Part II. and the Staff Manual respectively. Title pages will be prepared in manuscript.

WAR DIARY
or
INTELLIGENCE SUMMARY.
(Erase heading not required.)

Army Form C. 2118.

Hour, Date, Place	Summary of Events and Information	Remarks and references to Appendices
	Remounts	
BOIS JEAN – Dec 15th	Headquarters - 1. 'C' Battery - 12. 'G' Battery - 23.	
	'K' Battery - 12. Ammunition Column - 12.	
18th	Reinforcements joined Div: Amm: Col – 18.	
29th	" " " 1.	
NEUVILLE-ST. VAAST. Dec 18	K. Battery R.H.A. continued march from AUBIGNY getting into action on night 18/19 about 1 mile S.W. of NEUVILLE-ST. VAAST.	
Dec 19	Having registered in morning, assisted with covering fire the successful day light raid carried out by 3rd Canadian Division just N of ARRAS in which over 50 prisoners were taken – ammunition expended 600 rounds.	
Dec 20 to Dec 25	Registered enemy trenches on immediate front & on neighbouring fronts	
Dec 25	Observed as far as possible as a holiday – very little firing.	
Dec 27	Visibility Co.	
Dec 27-31.	Continued registration of enemy front line system.	

[illegible] Lt Col
4 Brigade RHA.

(73989) W4141—463. 400,000. 9/14. H.&J.Ltd. Forms/C. 2118/10.

3rd Cav

4th Bde R.H.A

Jan 1916

Vol V

Instructions regarding War Diaries and Intelligence Summaries are contained in F. S. Regs., Part II. and the Staff Manual respectively. Title pages will be prepared in manuscript.

WAR DIARY
or
INTELLIGENCE SUMMARY.
(Erase heading not required.)

Army Form C. 2118.

Place	Date	Hour	Summary of Events and Information	Remarks and references to Appendices
FRUGES	Jan	1st	4th Brigade moved to ESTRÉE-BLANCHE. Hdqrs Bde, C.G Btys & Ammunition Col billeted at ESTREEBLANCHE, K Bty at FLECHINELLE.	
ESTREE BLANCHE		2nd 3rd 4th 5th	Remained at ESTREE BLANCHE. 3rd Dismounted Brigade (part of 3 Cav. Div.) went into trenches night of 4th inst.	
VERMELLES		6th	1 Advanced section of each Bty C,G,K took over gun positions of the 12th 13th 14th 18th London Btys. Area taken over from G4 & 8.9 to	
	7th	5pm	2 Remaining sections of batteries took over from London Batteries. Ammunition Col. marched & billeted at FOUQUIERES. All batteries registered on trenches. C fired 31 G 38 K 34 rounds	
	8th		Quiet on our immediate front. C fired 94 G 75 K 25 rounds.	
	9th		No hostile firing worth mentioning. Batteries still registering very difficult trench line.	
	10th		C Battery placed its forward gun in action near LE RUTOIRE. FOSSE 9 was 'crumped' during the morning. Germans working hard on craters in front of the HAIRPIN.	
	11th		Front trenches, Stansfield Road and LE RUTOIRE shelled during the day otherwise fairly quiet in the Brigade Zone.	
	12th		LE RUTOIRE was heavily shelled between 9am and 11.30 by 2 guns 5.9 from the direction of AUCHY-LES-LA-BASSEE	

1577 Wt. W10791/1773 500,000 1/15 D. D. & L. A.D.S.S./Forms/C. 2118.

Instructions regarding War Diaries and Intelligence Summaries are contained in F. S. Regs., Part II. and the Staff Manual respectively. Title pages will be prepared in manuscript.

WAR DIARY
or
INTELLIGENCE SUMMARY.
(Erase heading not required.)

Army Form C. 2118.

Place	Date	Hour	Summary of Events and Information	Remarks and references to Appendices
VERMELLES	13th	1pm.	Noyelles les Vermelles cross roads shelled by Whizz Bang	
			Nothing of interest on our front.	
	14th		C Battery forward gun fired at intervals during night on trenches near BIG WILLIE trench and also every time hostile Trench Mortar opened. In consequence trenches report very quiet night.	
	15th		A good deal of hostile firing on communication trenches throughout the day. More work being done on the Crater by the Huns.	
	16th		Nothing to report.	
	17th		German aeroplanes very active all the morning. Stansfield Road communication trench and WATER TOWER neighbourhood shelled intermittently, probably on account of aeroplane observing numerous parties of men strolling about in the open. Communication trenches, front trenches and likely positions of trench mortars shelled by us during the day as retaliation.	
	18th		A fair amount of hostile fire on the communication trenches in the Bite zone in the morning. The 13th shell was not effective enough to silence this. C Battery forward gun dealt with a sniper who had been particularly busy all day.	
	19th		Hostile aeroplanes very active again especially over VERMELLES.	
	20th		A quiet day on the part of the Germans. Our 3 batteries averaged a hundred rounds apiece.	

1577 Wt. W10791/1773 500,000 1/15 D. D. & L. A.D.S.S./Forms/C. 2118.

Instructions regarding War Diaries and Intelligence Summaries are contained in F. S. Regs., Part II. and the Staff Manual respectively. Title pages will be prepared in manuscript.

WAR DIARY
or
INTELLIGENCE SUMMARY.
(Erase heading not required.)

Army Form C. 2118.

Place	Date	Hour	Summary of Events and Information	Remarks and references to Appendices
VERMELLES	21st		A large percentage of blind shell is being fired by the enemy. K Battery fired at a machine gun emplacement on the Dump. The usual targets were engaged during the day.	
	22nd		At 8.20 hostile aeroplanes were again active with the result that VERMELLES was shelled in the morning and again heavily in the afternoon.	
	23rd		On this part of the front our command of the air seems to have temporarily lapsed as German planes maintained undisputed possession of the sky practically all day.	
			'C' Battery forward gun continues to give valuable assistance to our men in the trenches. On more than one occasion today they were called upon to silence rifle grenades and trench mortar activity on the part of the 'Hun' & did so effectively.	
		6.23	At 6.23 am today we fired a defensive mine near "Hohenzollern Redoubt".	
	24th		Dull day & observation difficult	
	25th		At 12 noon C & G Batteries carried out a small organised bombardment of the enemy's front line & communication trenches. Hostile aeroplanes still active.	
	26th		About 4.30 pm Germans opened a very heavy bombardment on our front trenches. CROWN TRENCH and ALEXANDRA TRENCH were chiefly affected. The shelling was on a zone about 400 yards long by 200 deep and was very severe for about one hour. Our batteries replied firing altogether 1700 rounds.	

1577 Wt. W16791/1773 500,000 1/15 D. D. & L. A.D.S.S./Forms/C.2118.

Army Form C. 2118.

Instructions regarding War Diaries and Intelligence Summaries are contained in F. S. Regs., Part II. and the Staff Manual respectively. Title pages will be prepared in manuscript.

WAR DIARY
or
INTELLIGENCE SUMMARY.
(*Erase heading not required.*)

Place	Date	Hour	Summary of Events and Information	Remarks and references to Appendices
VERMELLES	26th	contd	Our fire was very effective as it successfully frustrated the German object and in all probability prevented their attack developing. They had obviously arranged and were trying to carry out a bomb attack from the KINK down ALEXANDRATRENCH, after their artillery preparation. Our barrage stopped this, nothing further developed and a quiet night followed.	
	27th		At 8 am the Germans again started a heavy bombardment, shelling the same neighbourhood in the same manner. The same batteries of 5.9's were probably used. The firing was very severe while it lasted but the duration was shorter than on the previous evening. Our batteries retaliated and no attack developed. A quiet night.	
	28th		There was a certain amount of hostile fire on our zone chiefly directed against the communication trenches. Just to the left of our zone very heavy firing was going on commencing about 1pm and leaving off about 4 pm. The Germans fire was directed on our front line between MINE POINT and MAD POINT and they were certainly not lacking in ammunition.	
	29th		Very quiet day & difficult for observation. C G & K Batteries fired during the night on enemy communication trenches SLAG ALLEY, ZEPPELIN PARSIVAL and CORON ALLEY's at irregular intervals.	
	30th		Very thick mist precluding any attempt at observation.	
	31st		A quiet day on our front. On our right between 4.15 pm & between 7-8 pm fairly heavy firing on the 47th Div. front.	W. A. [illegible] Lt Col Comdg 2nd [illegible]

1577 Wt. W10791/1773 500,000 1/15 D. D. & L. A.D.S.S./Forms/C. 2118.

Instructions regarding War Diaries and Intelligence Summaries are contained in F. S. Regs., Part II. and the Staff Manual respectively. Title pages will be prepared in manuscript.

WAR DIARY
or
INTELLIGENCE SUMMARY.
(Erase heading not required.)

Army Form C. 2118.

Place	Date	Hour	Summary of Events and Information	Remarks and references to Appendices
VERMELLES	February 1st		The two or three misty days at the end of last month were taken full advantage of by the Germans. All along POTSDAM Trench their saps have been very much enlarged and several new machine gun emplacements made. A fine day & very little hostile firing.	
	2nd and 3rd		'C' Battery forward gun was again doing good work last night firing on trenches North of BILL'S BLUFF and cavalry report a very quiet night in consequence. Small parties of Germans have lately been seen in the early morning walking along PEKIN TRENCH and FOSSE ALLEY. They have been fired at and dispersed on every occasion, but the next morning generally sees them at the same place. 'C' Battery have carefully registered the spot and are hoping for a good bag on the next occasion.	
	[illegible]		The Germans are using green sandbags on parts of their front line. Cyclists & motorcars were observed today behind the German lines ~~in the same locality on FOSSE ALLEY~~ on the road between HAISNES and the Dump and were fired on. A small mine was exploded at 6.15pm on the 2nd inst. at G4a6.8 and the crater was occupied by our bombers. At 8.45pm on 2nd we blew up a mine between the legs of the HAIRPIN 40 yards in front of our own front line trench and occupied and consolidated the Crater.	
	4th		C Battery forward guns fired at intervals during the night on communication trenches in the neighbourhood of the Dump. The enemy have done a considerable amount of wiring in front of the numerous saps leading out of POTSDAM Trench.	

1577 Wt. W10791/1773 500,000 1/15 D. D. & L. A.D.S.S./Forms/C. 2118.

Instructions regarding War Diaries and Intelligence Summaries are contained in F. S. Regs., Part II. and the Staff Manual respectively. Title pages will be prepared in manuscript.

WAR DIARY
or
INTELLIGENCE SUMMARY.
(*Erase heading not required.*)

Army Form C. 2118.

Place	Date	Hour	Summary of Events and Information	Remarks and references to Appendices
VERMELLES	FEBRUARY 5th		Working parties on the HAISNES AUCHY road were shot at, also two cyclists one of whom was 'knocked over'.	
	6th		LE RUTOIRE was heavily shelled with 4.2 and 5.9. Two different Hun Batteries were engaged in this short firing from different localities.	
	7th		A very quiet day. Major Mardyce took over command of the Bde during the temporary absence of Colonel Kay at the School of Instruction AIRE	
	8th } 9th		2 quiet days. Two direct hits on the Water Tower VERMELLES on 8th.	
	10th		Hostile artillery more active. From 8am – 10am a slow rate of fire was kept up on our communication trenches and after on support trenches. Our batteries retaliated. Enemy still working hard on POTSDAM trench & saps in front. Trains can be seen every day in LA BASSÉE. They run at 10 am 12 noon 1.30 and during the afternoon.	
	11th		Hostile artillery again active. Intermittent fire was kept up the whole morning on our support + communication trenches. Our Batteries retaliated on enemys comm trenches SLAG, ZEPPELIN, PARSIVAL, Alleys etc.	
	12th		At 3.30 ~~[illegible]~~ a bombardment was carried out in conjunction with 4.5 Howitzers. K. Bty fired on trenches around BILLS BLUFF and BIG WILLIE and C Battery forward guns fired between these last named. G. Bty were allotted SLAG & PARSIVAL ALLEY. This was in retaliation	K. Bty front & trenches

1577 Wt. W10791/1773 500,000 1/15 D. D. & L. A.D.S.S./Forms/C. 2118.

Instructions regarding War Diaries and Intelligence Summaries are contained in F. S. Regs., Part II. and the Staff Manual respectively. Title pages will be prepared in manuscript.

WAR DIARY
or
INTELLIGENCE SUMMARY.
(Erase heading not required.)

Army Form C. 2118.

Place	Date	Hour	Summary of Events and Information	Remarks and references to Appendices
VERMELLES	12th Feb.		for the organised bombardment carried out by the Germans on the afternoon of the 11th. When they commenced with machine gun fire + rifle grenades, went on to a heavy bombardment with aerial torpedoes, crumps + on our right blew up a mine. This activity was between 3 and 5 in the afternoon + chiefly centred around BILL'S BLUFF & the KINK	
	13th		At 4.20 the Germans opened up a very heavy bombardment with 77mm 4.2 + 5.9 shell on our front + support trenches opposite BILLS BLUFF and ALEXANDRA Trench. Our communications between Infantry + Batteries were soon cut but G.K. Batteries immediately retaliated, news of events coming from their forward O.P.'s. About 5.30 a 4th mine went up, the bombardment immediately ceased and 3 parties of Germans, each about 15 men, slipped across to our trenches. They succeeded in getting to and in some cases in our trenches but were at once ejected by our bombers. Our batteries fired a considerable amount of H.E. but the Heavies in spite of warning from us were slow in getting on + ineffective when they did commence.	
	14th		LE RUTOIRE was again shelled and three bombs were also dropped there by aeroplanes. No damage done. A continual stream of men were seen on the HAISNES-AUCHY road forward guns of C Battery successfully dealt with these. A shell was dropped v. near Chateau at NOYELLES	
	15th		A retaliatory shoot arranged for 1pm today had to be postponed owing to the gale of wind.	
	16th		Impossible day to shoot owing to exceptionally high wind.	

1577 Wt. W10791/1773 500,000 1/15 D. D. & L. A.D.S.S./Forms/C. 2118.

Army Form C. 2118.

Instructions regarding War Diaries and Intelligence Summaries are contained in F. S. Regs., Part II. and the Staff Manual respectively. Title pages will be prepared in manuscript.

WAR DIARY
or
INTELLIGENCE SUMMARY.
(Erase heading not required.)

Place	Date	Hour	Summary of Events and Information	Remarks and references to Appendices
VERMELLES	17th		The retaliatory bombardment arranged for came off today at 1 pm. The Results were as far as could be ascertained successful. BILLS BLUFF was badly knocked about. One German was seen on top of the Dump minus his head. The Howitzers were slow in getting to work but made very good shooting when they did start. C.G and K Batteries fired about 600 rounds each including a large proportion of HE. The trenches were methodically & scientifically fired on and breaches were made but the resulting damage of a single shell is extremely small. The German retaliation was very slight.	
	18th 19		Very quiet days.	
	20th		K. Battery obtained a direct hit on a trench mortar behind BILLS BLUFF Working parties were dispersed behind FOSSE 8 and a battery located and taken on by C. Battery.	
	21st.		A quiet day on our front. Heavy firing commenced at 1 pm to our South which proved to be a German Gas attack on the French positions South of the Somme. This firing continued until late in the evening. The German offensive at VERDUN commenced today. There was considerable aeroplane activity on our front 2 British machines were forced to land one behind ANNEQUIN one by FOSSE 3. On this night C Battery forward guns were taken out of action. The relieving Batteries are not finding a forward guns yet. One section of each Battery C G K are relieved tonight and return to their respective wagon lines.	

1577 Wt. W10791/1773 500,000 1/15 D. D. & L. A.D.S.S./Forms/C. 2118.

Instructions regarding War Diaries and Intelligence Summaries are contained in F. S. Regs., Part II. and the Staff Manual respectively. Title pages will be prepared in manuscript.

WAR DIARY
or
INTELLIGENCE SUMMARY.
(Erase heading not required.)

Army Form C. 2118.

Place	Date	Hour	Summary of Events and Information	Remarks and references to Appendices
VERMELLES	22nd		The remaining 2 sections of each battery were relieved by sections of the 36th Brigade of the 2nd Div. that is taking over from 4th Bde R.H.A. The relief was successfully completed by 7.30 with the exception of G. Battery whose relieving battery took a wrong turn and did not arrive until 9 pm. The Hdqrs were relieved in the morning handing over responsibility for the Brigade front at 12 noon. They marched back to rest billets at FRUGES via LABOURSE NOEUX LES MINES, BRUAY, CAMBLAIN CHATELAIN, PERNES, BOYAVAL HEURCHIN, BERGENEUSE and CRÉPY. Starting at 11 am and arriving 12 pm midnight. There were no casualties. It was a long march partly in a snowstorm and on frozen roads in the night. The Horses came very well.	
			The Batteries on being relieved marched back to their Permanent billets by night C. to SAINS LES FRESSIN G to WAILLY (near FRUGES) K to ASSONVAL. They all arrived about 10 am next day after a very long and difficult march owing to snow and frost. Route VERMELLES BEUVRY BETHUNE LILLERS ST HILAIRE FEBVIN-PALFART LAIRES.	
			The Ammunition Column was relieved on 22nd and marched back to their old billets at COUPELLE VIEILLE arriving between 11 and 12 on the morning of 23rd.	
	24th to 29th		Resting in Billets. HQrs at FRUGES. C Battery at SAINS LES FRESSIN G. Bty at WAILLY K Bty at ASSONVAL	

W. H. Kay
Lt Col Comdg IV Brigade Royal Horse Artillery

3 C

4 Bde R. H. A.

Vol XII

March 1916

April 1916

Army Form C. 2118.

WAR DIARY
or
INTELLIGENCE SUMMARY.
(Erase heading not required.)

Instructions regarding War Diaries and Intelligence Summaries are contained in F. S. Regs., Part II. and the Staff Manual respectively. Title pages will be prepared in manuscript.

Place	Date	Hour	Summary of Events and Information	Remarks and references to Appendices
FRUGES –	March 1st to 31st		Resting in Billets at FRUGES and continuing training. Batteries in same Billets, – C at SAINS LES FRESSIN G at WAILLY K at ASSONVAL.	
			Major L.W. Joyce took over command of G. Battery on 4th inst vice Major J.G.B Allardyce to 2nd Div.	
			J.M. Hillyard Lt Adjt 4th Bde RHA for Lt Col W.A. Kay Comdg. Bde.	

Instructions regarding War Diaries and Intelligence Summaries are contained in F. S. Regs., Part II. and the Staff Manual respectively. Title pages will be prepared in manuscript.

WAR DIARY
or
INTELLIGENCE SUMMARY.
(Erase heading not required.)

Army Form C. 2118.

3C

Place	Date	Hour	Summary of Events and Information	Remarks and references to Appendices
FRUGES	April 1st to 30th		Resting in Billets at and around Fruges and continuing training.	Vol XIII
			Lt Col P. WHEATLEY joined as O.C. Bde on 14th inst vice Lt Col W.H. Kay to command RA. 49th Division	
			[illegible] and Lt Adjt for O.C. 4th Bde R.F.A.	

1577 Wt. W10791/1773 500,000 1/15 D. D. & L. A.D.S.S./Forms/C. 2118.

4 Bde R.H.A. 3C

Army Form C. 2118.

Vol 14

Instructions regarding War Diaries and Intelligence Summaries are contained in F. S. Regs., Part II. and the Staff Manual respectively. Title pages will be prepared in manuscript.

WAR DIARY
or
INTELLIGENCE SUMMARY.
(Erase heading not required.)

Place	Date	Hour	Summary of Events and Information	Remarks and references to Appendices
FRUGES	May 1st to 15th		Resting in billets and around Fruges	
	15th to 21st		3rd Cavalry Division moved to St Riquier Training Area. 'C' Bty in St Riquier, 'K' Bty in Millencourt, 'G' Bty in Domvast. Headquarters in Bernatre. Divisional Training ended.	
	21st to 30th		Batteries and Headquarters moved into St Riquier to continue Battery Training; driving drill, signalling etc.	
	30th		Batteries and Headquarters moved back to permanent billets in Fruges and around Fruges.	
			Major H. J. R. Scarlett joined as O.C. 'C' Bty on the 28th May vice Major A. E. Erskine as Brigade Major to 20th Division	
			L. R. Galsworthy 2nd Lt R.H.A. for Lt Col G. Wheatley Comd 4th Bde R.H.A.	

1577 Wt. W10791/1773 500,000 1/15 D. D. & L. A.D.S.S./Forms/C. 2113.

3 C

4 Bde RHA

Vol 15

Army Form C. 2118.

Instructions regarding War Diaries and Intelligence Summaries are contained in F. S. Regs., Part II. and the Staff Manual respectively. Title pages will be prepared in manuscript.

WAR DIARY
or
INTELLIGENCE SUMMARY.
(*Erase heading not required.*)

Place	Date	Hour	Summary of Events and Information	Remarks and references to Appendices
FRUGES	June 1st to 6th		Billets in Fruges	
	7th		Hdqrs 4th Bde R.H.A. moved to CRÉQUY	
	24th		3rd Cavalry Division marched to new billetting area by night. RHA HQ first night to FONTAINE-S-MAYE 2nd night to DOMART PONTHIEU 3rd night to LA NEUVILLE close to CORBIE Batteries followed their Brigades.	
	27th		3 Cavalry Division concentrated and bivouacking in the area between BONNAY and LA NEUVILLE	
	28th 29th 30th		Waiting & concentrated as above. Capt R.L. Palmer joined the Brigade and took over command of K. Bty vice Major D.C. Spencer Smith to be Bde Major 4th Div.	

R.W. Leathe[?] Lt Col R.H.A.
Commanding 4th Bde R.H.A.

1577 Wt. W10791/1773 500,000 1/15 D. D. & L. A.D.S.S./Forms/C. 2118.

APP: V

S E C R E T. C.R.A./945.

O.C. "C" Battery, R.H.A.
O.C. "G" Battery, R.H.A.
O.C. "K" Battery, R.H.A.
O.C. B/296 Battery, R.F.A.
O.C. C/296 Battery, R.F.A.
O.C. D/296 Battery, R.F.A.
2nd Cavalry Divisional Arty:
Heavy Artillery (for information).

W A R N I N G   O R D E R

1. An enterprise will probably be undertaken by the 3rd Cavalry Division shortly.

2. Artillery Barrages for your Unit will probably be as in attached tables.

3. "K" Battery, R.H.A. and C/296 Battery, R.F.A. will come into action on night of 18th/19th and register on 19th instant C/296 Battery to their former position in F.8.a., "K" Battery (less Section in action) to a position at F.8.Central.
These two Batteries can leave their guns under a guard on night of 18th/19th and 19th/20th if more conveinent.

4. Batteries at present in action will endeavour to get their Barrages registered before night of 18th so as to leave new Batteries free to register on 19th.

5. Sufficient ammunition for the enterprise will be drawn by Batteries in excess of their normal dump of 300 rounds per gun.

6. Detailed Operation Orders will be issued in due course.

E.T. Boylan.

R.A. Headquarters. Lieutenant, R. H. A

17th June, 1917. Adjutant 3rd Cavalry Divisional Artillery.

APPENDIX VI

SECRET.

C.R.A./961.

O.C. "C" Battery, R.H.A.
O.C. "G" Battery, R.H.A.
O.C. "K" Battery, R.H.A.
O.C. B/293 Battery, R.F.A.
O.C. C/293 Battery, R.F.A.
O.C. D/293 Battery, R.F.A.
Headqrs: 293 Brigade, R.F.A.)
Headqrs: 'D' Sector.) For information.
3rd Cavalry Division.)
Cavalry Corps, R.A.)

WARNING ORDER.

Reference my C.R.A./945 - The operation referred to therein is postponed.

Another enterprise is under consideration to take place about night 24th/25th June, when is it proposed to raid the enemy's trenches about X.24.a.& c.

1. In consequent the following moves will take place on night 22nd/23rd -

"K" Battery, R.H.A. (less two guns in action) from reserve to a position in X.25.b.

C/293 Battery, R.F.A. from reserve to old position in F.2.a.

From 6 p.m. 23rd June until further orders C/293 Battery, R.F.A. will be responsible for S.O.S. Barrage as under -

from X.30.c.5.4. to X.30.c.5.0. to F.6.a.4.2.

On night 23rd/24th Detached Section "G" Battery, R.H.A. from position in F.2.a. to rejoin "G" Battery, R.H.A. in action in X.30.b.

2. From night 23rd Liaison Officer to D.1. Headquarters will be found as follows:-

June 23rd	-	"C" Battery, R.H.A.
24th	-	C/293 Battery, R.F.A.
25th	-	"C" Battery, R.H.A.
26th	-	Detached Section "K" R.H.A.
27th	-	"C" Battery, R.H.A.

3. Probable Barrage for your Unit as on attached slip. Registration should be completed by night of 23rd instant as far as possible.

4. Batteries at present in the line will arrange to dump sufficient ammunition at gun positions in excess of their 300 rounds per gun.

5. Arrangements will bo made to dump ammunition at positions for Batteries now in reserve.
These Batteries will bring sufficient ammunition for rogistration.

6. Operation Orders and Zero Hour will be forwarded lator.

7. Acknowledge.

E. F. Boylan.

R.A. Hoadquarters. Lieutenant, R. H. A.

20th June, 1917. Adjutant 3rd Cavalry Divisional Arty:

APPENDIX VII

S E C R E T.
= = = = = =

C.R.A./961/8.

O.C. "C" Battery, R.H.A.
O.C. "G" Battery, R.H.A.
O.C. "K" Battery, R.H.A.
O.C. B/296 Battery, R.F.A.
O.C. C/296 Battery, R.F.A.
O.C. D/296 Battery, R.F.A.
Cavalry Corps Heavy Arty:
Colonel WORMALD.
'D' Sector.
3rd Cavalry Division.
Cavalry Corps R.A.

Owing to attached ADDENDA to Instructions for Royals Raid the following amendments to 3rd Cavalry Divisional Arty: Operation Order No.2 and Barrage Tables have been found necessary -

(A) Page 1. para.3 line 5.

for "Zero + $6\frac{1}{2}$" read "Zero + $7\frac{1}{2}$".

line 7

for "Zero + 17" read "Zero + 18"

line 8

for "Zero + 30" read "Zero + 31"

(B) Pages 5 and 6, in column 1 - "TIME"

for "0 + $4\frac{1}{2}$ to 0 + $6\frac{1}{2}$" read "0 + $4\frac{1}{2}$ to 0 + $7\frac{1}{2}$"
Period 2 mins. Period 3 mins.

for "0 + $6\frac{1}{2}$ to 0 + $17\frac{1}{2}$" read "0 + $7\frac{1}{2}$ to 0 + $18\frac{1}{2}$"

for "0 + $17\frac{1}{2}$ to 0 + $25\frac{1}{2}$" read "0 + $18\frac{1}{2}$ to 0 + $26\frac{1}{2}$"

for "0 + $25\frac{1}{2}$ to 0 + $30\frac{1}{2}$" read "0 + $26\frac{1}{2}$ to 0 + $31\frac{1}{2}$".

(C) Page 5, column 3 - " "G" Battery, R.H.A."

line 6

for "X.24.a.9.3." read "X.24.a.8.5."

(D) Page 9. "Heavy Artillery"

Column 1, Time.

for "Zero to 0 + $6\frac{1}{2}$" read Zero to 0 + $7\frac{1}{2}$"

for "0 + $6\frac{1}{2}$ to 0 + $30\frac{1}{2}$" read "0 + $7\frac{1}{2}$ to 0 + $31\frac{1}{2}$.

R.A. Headquarters.
24th June, 1917.

E. T. Boylan
Lieutenant, R. H. A.
Adjutant 3rd Cavalry Divisional Arty:

S E C R E T.   C.R.A./961/7.

O.C. "C" Battery, R.H.A.
O.C. "G" Battery, R.H.A.
O.C. "K" Battery, R.H.A.
O.C. B/296 Battery, R.F.A.
O.C. C/296 Battery, R.F.A.
O.C. D/296 Battery, R.F.A.
Lieut: Col: WORMALD.
Headqrs: 'D' Sector.
3rd Cavalry Division.
Cavalry Corps R.A.

ROYALS RAID.

Reference 3rd Cavalry Divisional Artillery Operation Order No.2.

Liaison duties for the raid will be carried out on night 24th/25th June as follows -

Major H. YOUNG, D.S.O.,R.H.A. will be in liaison with the directing Officer Lieutenant Colonel WORMALD at X.22.d.7.7½.

He will have a wire from this point to 'K' Post and thence to "G" Battery, R.H.A., a wire will also be laid by Signal Officer Q.F. from D/296 Battery O.P. to X.22.d.7.7½.

All wires will be kept clear of ordinary messages from Zero - 15 to Zero - 45.

Call of Station at X.22.d.7.7½ will be B.Z.

E. T. Boylan

Lieutenant, R. H. A.
Adjutant 3rd Cavalry Divisional Arty:

R.A. Headquarters.
23rd June, 1917.

War Diary

S E C R E T. - ROYALS RAID. Copy No. 22

3rd CAVALRY DIVISIONAL ARTILLERY OPERATION ORDER No.2.

Reference 1/20,000 LE CATELET, Sheet III, Edition 2, corrected to 25/5/1917.

1. The attached Barrage Tables are for co-operation with the Cavalry of the 3rd Division in a raid on the enemy's trenches in X.24.a.& c. to take place on night 24th/25th June, 1917.

2. The trenches will be raided from X.24.a.2.4. to X.24.c.05.70. The wire will be penetrated by raiding columns -

   a) Between X.24.a.2.3. and X.24.a.2.4.
   and
   b) Between X.24.c.0.7. and X.23.d.8.4.

3. At Zero hour Raiding Parties start and Barrage opens 100 yards short of wire - The Barrage reaches wire at Zero + 1 minute.
The wire cutters reach Barrage at Zero + 4½ minutes when Barrage lifts at once ~~on the~~ off places of entry.
Wire should be open by Zero + 3½ at which time Barrage lifts off trenches to be raided
The raiding party leaves trenches at Zero + 17 for return journey.
The operation is to be completed by Zero + 30 mins

4. All Batteries will 'stand to' 15 minutes before Zero and will remain standing to for 1 hour after Zero + 30, except "K" Battery, R.H.A. which will withdraw on termination of Barrage to F.8.Central.

5. Fire will be directed into enemy works within the limits of the Barrage and will not be arbitary straight lines.

6. Watches will be syncronized by a watch sent round from Divisional Artillery Headquarters at 9 p.m. ~~and 12 mid-night~~ on night of raid.

7. Zero hour will be notified later.

8. Prior to operation and immediately after raid "S.O.S." Barrages if asked for will be those normally in use - except C/293 Battery, R.F.A. which will take over the Barrage normally supplied by Detached Sections "K" R.H.A. and "G" R.H.A. vide my O.R.A./961.

9. Orders as to Liaison for the operations will be forwarded separately.

10. Acknowledge.

Issued at 9 0 am.

E. V. Boylan.

R.A. Headquarters. Lieutenant, R. H. A.

25 June, 1917. Adjutant 3rd Cavalry Divisional Artillery.

Copy No.1 "C" Battery, R.H.A.
No.2 "G" Battery, R.H.A.
No.3 "K" Battery, R.H.A.
No.4 "K" Battery, R.H.A. - Detached Section.
No.5 B/293 Battery, R.F.A.
No.6 C/293 Battery, R.F.A.
No.7. D/293 Battery, R.F.A.
No.8 2nd Cavalry Divisional Arty:
No.9 " " " "
No.10 " " " "
No.11 " " " "
No.12 35th Divisional Artillery.
No.13 " " "
No.14 " " "
No.15 " " "
No.16 Cavalry Corps Heavy Artillery
No.17 C.O. 1st Royal Dragoons
No.18 Headquarters 'D' Sector
No.19 3rd Cavalry Division
No.20 Cavalry Corps, R.A.
No.21)
No.22) War Diary
No.23 File

S E C R E T.

ROYALS RAID - BARRAGE TABLE.

3rd CAVALRY DIVISIONAL ARTILLERY.

T I M E	BATTERY & TARGET	BATTERY & TARGET	BATTERY & TARGET	R E M A R K S
	B/296 Battery, R.F.A.	"C" Battery, R.H.A.	"K" Battery, R.H.A.	
Zero to 0+½ min. Period - 30 Secs.	X.24.a.1.9. to X.24.a.0.4. Rate - 5 rounds per gun per minute.T.S.	X.23.b.9.4. to X.23.d.8.7. Rate - 3 rounds per gun per minute. T.S.	4 guns - X.23.d.8.7. to X.23.d.8.4. 2 guns - X.24.c.5.6. ~~to~~ and X.24.c.5.9. Rate - 4 rounds per gun per minute. T.S.	Barrage 100 yards short of wire.
0+½ min. to 0+1 min. Period - 30 Secs.	X.24.a.1.9. to X.24.a.4.9. to X.24.a.2.4. Rate - 3 rounds per gun per minute. T.S.	X.24.a.2.4. to X.24.c.1.7. Rate - 5rounds per gun per minute. T.S.	4 guns - X.24.c.1.7. to X.23.d.9.4. 2 guns - X.24.c.5.6. ~~to~~ and X.24.c.5.9. Rate - 4 rounds per gun per minute. T.S.	Barrage lifts at rate 100 yards in 30 secs. Reaching wire at Zero+1 minute.
0+1 min. to 0+4½ min. Period - 3½ minutes.	As above Rate - 4 rounds per gun per minute. T.S.	As above Rate - 4 rounds per gun per minute. T.S.	As above Rate - 4 rounds per gun per minute. T.S.	Barrage wire and trenches.

ROYALS RAID - BARRAGE TABLE.

3rd CAVALRY DIVISIONAL ARTILLERY.

TIME	BATTERY & TARGET	BATTERY & TARGET	BATTERY & TARGET	REMARKS
	"J" Battery, R.H.A.	C/293 Battery, R.F.A.	D/293 Battery, R.F.A.	
Zero to 0 + ½ min. Period - 30 secs.	2 guns - N. edge OSSUS WOOD. X.29.b.7.7. to X.24.c.5.3. 2 guns - X.23.d.8.3. to X.24.c.0.0. 2 guns - X.30.a.1.9. to X.30.a.4.6. Rate - 2 rounds per gun per minute. H.E.	X.30.a.4.3. to X.30.c.6.6. Rate - 3 rounds per gun per minute. H.E.	1 How. X.24.c.5.3. 1 How. X.24.c.5.9. 1 How. X.24.a.5.5. 1 How. X.24.a.3.8. Rate - 2 rounds per How:	
0 + ½ min to 0 + 1 min Period - 30 secs.	As above Rate - 3 rounds per gun per minute. H.E.	As above Rate - 3 rounds per gun per minute. H.E.	As above. Rate - 2 rounds per How:	
0 + 1 min to 0 + 4½ min Period - 3½ minutes.	2 guns - X.29.b.8.8. to X.24.c.5.3. 2 guns - X.23.d.8.3. to X.24.c.0.0. 2 guns - X.30.a.1.9. to X.30.a.4.6. Rate - 4 rounds per gun per minute. P.S.	As above Rate - 4 rounds per gun per minute. H.E.	As above Rate - 2 rounds per How: per min.	

S E C R E T.

ROYALS RAID - BARRAGE TABLE.

3rd CAVALRY DIVISIONAL ARTILLERY.

T I M E	BATTERY & TARGET	BATTERY & TARGET	BATTERY & TARGET	REMARKS
	B/293 Battery, R.F.A.	"G" Battery, R.H.A.	"K" Battery, R.H.A.	No fire between X.24.A.24 and X.24.a.3.7
0+4½ to 0+6½ Period - 2 minutes.	X.24.a.1.9. to X.24.A.48.8 X.24.a.65.95. to X.24.a.6.5. Rate - 4 rounds per gun per minute. T.S.	X.24.a.2.4. to X.24.c.1.7. Rate - 4 rounds per gun per minute. T.S.	4 guns - X.23.d.9.2. to X.24.c.0.0. 2 guns - X.24.c.5.9. to and X.24.c.5.6. Rate - 4 rounds per gun per minute. T.S.	No fire between X.24.c.1.7. and X.23.d.9.2. (Barrage lifts off these places of entry)
0+6½ to 0+17½ Period - 11 minutes	2 guns - X.24.a.1.9. to X.24.a.65.95. H.E. 2 guns - X.24.a.3.8. to X.24.a.7.9. P.S. 2 guns - X.24.a.6.8. to X.24.a.3.5. H.E. Rate - 4 rounds per gun per minute H.E.	X.24.a.9.3. to X.24.c.9.6. to S.19.d.2.9. Rate - 4 rounds per gun per minute. H.E.	As above Rate - 4 rounds per gun per minute. T.S.	Barrage lifts. off trenches to be raided.
0+17½ to 0+25½ Period - 8 minutes.	As above Rate - 3 rounds per gun per minute. P.S	As above Rate - 3 rounds per gun per minute. H.E.	As above Rate - 3 rounds per gun per minute. T.S.	
0+25½ to 0+30½ Period - 5 minutes.	As above Rate - 1 round per gun per minute. H.E.	As above Rate - 1 round per gun per minute. H.E.	As above Rate - 1 round per gun per minute. H.E.	

<u>S E C R E T.</u>

ROYALS RAID – BARRAGE TABLE.
****

3rd CAVALRY DIVISIONAL ARTILLERY.
****

T I M E	BATTERY & TARGET	BATTERY & TARGET	BATTERY & TARGET	REMARKS
	<u>"C" Battery, R.H.A.</u>	<u>C/298 Battery, R.F.A.</u>	<u>D/298 Battery, R.F.A.</u>	
0 + 4½ to 0 + 6½ Period – 2 minutes	3 guns – X.29.b.9.9. to X.24.c.9.5. 3 guns – X.30.a.1.9. to X.30.a.4.6. Rate – 3 rounds per gun per minute. T.S.	X.30.a.4.6. to X.30.c.6.6. [handwritten: 0.] Rate – 3 rounds per gun per minute. H.E.	1 How. S.19.d.0.5. 1 How. S.19.d.20.90. 1 How. S.19.d.5.8. 1 How. S.19.b.5.5. Rate – 2 rounds per How. per minute.	
0 + 6½ to 0 + 17½ Period – 11 minutes.	As above Rate – 3 rounds per gun per minute. H.E.	As above Rate – 5 rounds per gun per minute. H.E.	1 How. S.19.d.[5.8.] 0.5 1 How. S.19.[b.5.5.] d.0.6. 1 How. S.20.a.4.8. 1 How. S.20.a.1.8. Rate – 2 rounds per How. per minute.	
0 + 17½ to 0 + 25½ Period – 8 minutes.	X.29.b.7.7. to X.24.c.9.5. Rate – 5 rounds per gun per minute. H.E.	As above Rate – 2 rounds per gun per minute. H.E.	As above Rate – 2 rounds per How. per minute.	
0 + 25½ to 0 + 30½ Period – 5 minutes.	As above Rate – 1 round per gun per minute. H.E.	As above Rate – 1 round per gun per minute. H.E.	As above Rate – 1 round per How. per minute.	

S E C R E T.

ROYALS RAID - BARRAGE TABLE.

2nd CAVALRY DIVISIONAL ARTILLERY.

T I M E	BATTERY & TARGET	BATTERY & TARGET	BATTERY & TARGET	REMARKS
	Battery	Battery	D/210 Battery, R.F.A.	
Zero to 0 +10 Period - 10 minutes	X.30.c.55.70 to A.1.b.35.40 Rate - 2 rounds per gun per minute.	F.6.a.5.7. to F.3.c.9.6. Rate - 2 rounds per gun per minute.	1 How. S.25.d.8.8. 1 How. S.25.d.9.3. Rate - 1 round per How. per minute.	
0 + 10 to 0 + 20 Period - 10 minutes.	As above Rate - 5 rounds per gun per minute.	As above Rate - 5 rounds per gun per minute.	As above Rate - 2 rounds per How. per minute.	
0 + 20 to 0 + 30 Period - 10 minutes.	As above Rate - 1 round per gun per minute.	As above Rate - 1 round per gun per minute.	As above Rate - 1 round per How. per minute.	

S E C R E T.

ROYALS RAID - BARRAGE TABLE.

35th DIVISIONAL ARTILLERY.

T I M E	BATTERY & TARGET	BATTERY & TARGET	BATTERY & TARGET	REMARKS
	Battery, R.F.A.	Battery, R.F.A.	Battery, R.F.A.	
Zero to 0+10	X.18.c.3.5 to X.18.c.7.0. Rate - 2 rounds per gun per minute.	X.17.b.9.4. to X.18.a.9.0 Rate - 1 round per gun per minute.	1 How. BOSQUET FARM. 1 How. E. end of CANAL WOOD in X.18.c. Rate - 2 rounds per gun per minute.	
0+10 to 0+20	As above Rate - 3 rounds per gun per minute	As above Rate - 2 rounds per gun per minute.	As above Rate - 2 rounds per gun per minute.	
0+20 to 0+50	As above Rate - 1 round per gun per minute	As above Rate - 1 round per gun per minute.	As above Rate - 1 round per gun per minute.	

ROYALS RAID - BARRAGE TABLE.

HEAVY ARTILLERY

T I M E	BATTERY & TARGET	BATTERY & TARGET	BATTERY & TARGET	BATTERY & TARGET
	Siege Battery, R.G.A.	Siege Battery, R.G.A.	Heavy Battery, R.G.A.	Heavy Battery, R.G.A.
Zero to 0+6½	1 How. S.19.b.3.7. 1 How. S.19.b.5.0. 1 How. S.20.a.4.2. 1 How. S.26.a.1.8. Rate - 3 rounds per How.	2 Hows. S.26.c.0.0. to S.25.d.9.5. 2 Hows. DE-LA-L'EAU S.23.b.6.7. to S.23.b.~~20.00~~. 9.2 Rate - 3 rounds per How.		
0+6½ to 0+30½	As above Rate - 10 rounds per How.	COUNTER BATTERY	COUNTER BATTERY	Roads & Tracks between S.20.a.3.1. and Quarry S.14.c.9.1. Rate - 10 rounds per gun.

APPENDIX ~~IX~~ VIII

S E C R E T.

C.R.A./999.

O.C. FRANK.
O.C. FRENCH.
O.C. U. K. A.
O.C. GAY.
O.C. GWEN

WARNING ORDER.

Information having been received that the Germans are relieving on the front tomorrow night, Cavalry Corps have ordered night firing to take place tomorrow night 29th/30th June.

Approximate number of rounds required -

128 rounds per 13 & 18 pounder gun.

64 rounds por 4.5" Howitzer.

Further details later.

R.A. Headquarters.
28th June, 1917.

Lieutenant, R. H. A.
Adjutant 3rd Cavalry Divisional Artillery.

4

S E C R E T.

3rd CAVALRY DIVISIONAL ARTILLERY OPERATION ORDER No.3

Reference 1/20,000 paper map LE CATELET, Sheet III, corrected to 25/5/1917.

1. Night Firing will take place on the night 29th/30th as per attached Barrage Tables - the object being to disturb the enemy during a Divisional Relief.

2. Watches will be synchronized by a watch sent round from this office at 7 p.m. 29th instant.

3. Times will be strictly adhered to throughout.

4. Ammunition for this shoot to be drawn surplus to normal dumps at guns.

Time____ m.

R.A. Headquarters.

29th June, 1917.

E. J. Boylan

Lieutenant, R. H. A.

Adjutant 3rd Cavalry Divisional Arty:

SECRET.

NIGHT FIRING 29th/30th June by 3rd CAVALRY DIVISIONAL ARTY:

TIME	BATTERY	SERIES	TASK	RATE	REMARKS.
10-45 p.m. to 10-49 p.m.	B/296 Battery, R. F. A.	I	Tracks near banks X.24.a.5.5. to X.18.c.8.4.	4 rounds per gun per minute T. S.	Searching by 25 yards between rounds and sweeping from end to end.
11-30 p.m. to 11-34 p.m.	-do-	II	Tracks S.20.a.4.3. to S.14.c.5.1.	-- do --	--- do ---
11-50 p.m. to 11-54 p.m.	-do-	III	Road X.24.c.8.7. to X.24.a.7.7.	4 rounds per gun per minute H. E.	--- do ---
12-10 a.m. to 12-14 a.m.	-do-	IV	As in I.	4 rounds per gun per minute H. E.	As in I.
1-0 a.m. to 1-4 a.m.	-do-	V	As in III	4 rounds per gun per minute H. E.	
1-15 a.m. to 1-19 a.m.	-do-	VI	As in I	4 rounds per gun per minute T. S.	
2-5 a.m. to 2-9 a.m.	-do-	VII	Streets of OSSUS S19d0.6 to S19b6.0	4 rounds per gun per minute H. E.	
3-0 a.m. to 3-4 a.m.	-do-	VIII	As in II	4 rounds per gun per minute T. S.	

SECRET.

NIGHT FIRING 29th/30th BY 3rd CAVALRY DIVISIONAL ARTILLERY.

TIME	BATTERY	SERIES	TASK	RATE	REMARKS
10-45 p.m. to 10-49 p.m.	"G" R. H. A. 4 Guns.	I	Tracks from Bridges East of OSSUS to ~~S.20.a.4.5.~~ S.19.B.6.0 to S.20.a.99.92.	4 rounds per gun per minute. H.E.	Sweep 75 yards after 1st minute.
11-30 p.m. to 11-34 p.m.	-do-	II	Road X.24.c.1.4. to X.24.c.80.75. Road X.24.a.1.0. to X.24.c.80.75.	4 rounds per gun per minute. T.S.	--- do ---
11-50 p.m. to 11-54 p.m.	-do-	III	AS in I ~~Roads in OSSUS VILLAGE leading to Bridges at S.19.d.5.8, S.19.d.50.99, and S.19.b.5.2.~~	4 rounds per gun per minute. T.S.	--- do ---
12-10 a.m. to 12-14 a.m.	-do-	IV	As in II	4 rounds per gun per minute. T.S.	
1-0 a.m. to 1-4 a.m.	-do-	V	X.24.c.3.0 to S.19.d.35.00 ~~As in III~~	4 rounds per gun per minute. T.S.	
1-15 a.m. to 1-19 a.m.	-do-	VI	As in I	4 rounds per gun per minute. H.E.	
2-5 a.m. to 2-9 a.m.	-do-	VII	Road X.24.c.8.7. to S.~~19.d.1.6.~~ 20.a.99.99.	4 rounds per gun per minute. H.E.	Searching by 25 yards between rounds. Sweeping from end to end.
3-0 a.m. to 3-4 a.m.	-do-	VIII	As in I.	4 rounds per gun per minute. H.E.	

S E C R E T.

NIGHT FIRING 29th/30th BY 3rd CAVALRY DIVISIONAL ARTY:

TIME	BATTERY	SERIES	TASK	RATE	REMARKS
10-45 p.m. to 10-49 p.m.	"C" Battery, R. H. A.	I	Sunken Road & Banks with Tracks. X.30.a.85.99. to X.30.a.5.0.& S.25.b.1.3.	4 rounds per gun per minute. H.E.	Searching by 25 yards between rounds. Sweeping from end to end.
11-30 p.m. to 11-34 p.m.	-do-	II	Tracks X30c 7.9 to S25 b4.1 ~~Road A.1.b.5.5. to A.2.a.30.99.~~	4 rounds per gun per minute. T.S.	Sweeping 75 yards after first minute.
11-50 p.m. to 11-54 p.m.	-do-	III	Road S.25.d.9.5. to S.25.b.2.3.	4 rounds per gun per minute. H.E.	Searching by 25 yards between rounds. Sweeping from end to end.
12-10 a.m. to 12-14 a.m.	-do-	IV	As in I	4 rounds per gun per minute. H.E.	
1-0 a.m. to 1-4 a.m.	-do-	V	As in II	4 rounds per gun per minute. H.E.	
1-15 a.m. to 1-19 a.m.	-do-	VI	Tracks to Bridges at S.25.b.7.3. ~~& S.25.b.6.8.~~ along N of Canal to S25a9.6	4 rounds per gun per minute. T.S.	Sweeping 75 yards after first minute.
2-5 a.m. to 2-9 a.m.	-do-	VII	Street in V[illegible]UILE in S.26.c.	4 rounds per gun per minute. H.E.	
3-0 a.m. to 3-4 a.m.	-do-	VIII	Road S.26.a.9.9. to S.20.c.5.5.	4 rounds per gun per minute. H.E.	Searching by 21 yards between rounds and sweeping from end to end.

S E C R E T.

NIGHT FIRING 29th/30th BY 3rd CAVALRY DIVISIONAL ARTY.

T I M E	BATTERY	SERIES	T A S K	R A T E	R E M A R K S
10-45 p.m. to 10-49 p.m.	Section "C" R. H. A.	I	Road A.2.c.5.3. to A.2.a.9.9.	4 rounds per gun per minute. T.S.	Searching by 25 yards between rounds and sweeping from end to end.
11-30 p.m. to 11-34 p.m.	-do-	II	Road F.3.a.9.3. to A.1.b.5.5.	4 rounds per gun per minute. T.S.	Searching by 25 yards between rounds and sweeping from end to end.
11-50 p.m. to 11-54 p.m.	-do-	III	Road F.6.a.9.9. to A.1.b.65.60.	4 rounds per gun per minute. T.S.	Sweeping 75 yards after first minute.
12-10 a.m. to 12-14 a.m.	-do-	IV	As in II	4 rounds per gun per minute. T.S.	
1-0 a.m. to 1-4 a.m.	-do-	V	As in I	4 rounds per gun per minute. T.S.	
1-15 a.m. to 1-19 a.m.	-do-	VI	As in III	4 rounds per gun per minute. H.E.	
2-5 a.m. to 2-9 a.m.	-do-	VII	Track A.2.a.2.4. to A.2.a.8.7.	4 rounds per gun per minute. H.E.	
3-0 a.m. to 3-4 a.m.	-do-	VIII	As in VII	4 rounds per gun per minute. H.E.	

SECRET.

NIGHT FIRING 29th/30th BY 3rd CAVALRY DIVISIONAL ARTY:

TIME	BATTERY	SERIES	TASK	RATE	REMARKS
10-45 p.m. to 10-49 p.m.	Section "K" R. H. A.	I	Banks and Track A.1.d.5.3 to A.2.a.2.5.	4 rounds per gun per minute. T.S.	Searching by 25 yards between rounds and sweeping from end to end.
11-30 p.m. to 11-34 p.m.	-do-	II	Track A.2.c.20.99 to A.2.c.1.0. to A.2.a.8.3.	4 rounds per gun per minute. T. S.	Searching by 25 yards between rounds and sweeping from end to end.
11-50 p.m. to 11-54 p.m.	-do-	III	Road F.6.a.9.3. to A.1.b.5.5.	4 rounds per gun per minute. H.E.	Searching by 25 yards between rounds and sweeping from end to end.
12-10 a.m. to 12-14 a.m.	-do-	IV	Road F.6.a.7.9. to S.25.d.6.7.	4 rounds per gun per minute. H.E.	Sweeping 75 yards after first minute.
1-0 a.m. to 1-4 a.m.	-do-	V	As in I	4 rounds per gun per minute. T.S.	
1-15 a.m. to 1-19 a.m.	-do-	VI	As in II	4 rounds per gun per minute. T.S.	
2-5 a.m. to 2-9 a.m.	-do-	VII	As in I	4 rounds per gun per minute. H.E.	
3-0 a.m. to 3-4 a.m.	-do-	VIII	Road A.2.a.4.7. to A.2.b.0.3.	4 rounds per gun per minute. H.E.	Searching by 25 yards between rounds and sweeping from end to end.

3rd Cavalry Divisional Artillery.

INTELLIGENCE SUMMARY. **6.0 p.m. 31st to 6.0 p.m. 1st.**

1. OUR FIRE.

TIME	PLACE SHELLED	NATURE OF SHELL	DIRECTION	NUMBER OF ROUNDS	REMARKS.
6.15 p.m.	S.20.c.8.7.	13 pdr.	-	50	Registration & Calibration.
9.0 a.m.	S.28.c.1.9. S.28.a.2.5.	4.5. How.	-	30	Punishment fire.
10.0 a.m.	S.26.d. central	18 pdr.	-	17	-
1.0 p.m.	OSSUS	"	-	10	-
1.15 p.m.	X.30.a.2.7.	"	-	9	-
1.30 p.m.	DE LA LEAU	4.5 How.	-	12	Punishment fire.
2.0 p.m.	S.27.c.5.9.	"	-	9	-
2.30 p.m.	X roads S.14.a.7.6.	18 pdr.	-	27	-
4.0 p.m.	S.20.a.	13 pdr.	-	10	Registration & Calibration.

2. HOSTILE SHELLING.

5.0 a.m. to 6.30 a.m.	LITTLE PRIEL FARM	4.2	-	20	-
6.30 a.m. to 8.30 a.m.	RONSSOY WOOD	5.9.	HONNECOURT LA TERRIERE	100	-
7.45 a.m. to 8.30 a.m.	RONSSOY WOOD	4.2	LE CATELET	6	-
5.45 a.m. to 7.0 a.m.	N.W. RONSSOY WOOD.	5.9	HONNECOURT	18	-
9.30 a.m. to 9.50 a.m.	F.27.c.2.8.	4.2	LE CATELET	20	-
12 noon to 12.35 p.m.	X.27. central	77 mm	VENDHUILE	20	-
1.30 p.m.	EPEHY	4.2	LA TERRIERE	18	-

2. HOSTILE SHELLING. (continued).

TIME	PLACE SHELLED.	NATURE OF SHELL	DIRECTION	NUMBER OF ROUNDS	REMARKS
1.30 p.m. to 2.30 p.m.	F.27.c.2.8.	4.2	LE CATELET	50	-
4.20 p.m.	F.5.a.2.4.	4.2	LA TERRIERE	8	-

3. GENERAL.

Entrance to a dug-out was spotted on VENDHUILE - LA TERRIERE road at S.21.a.8.3. From this spot fifteen Germans were seen going singly to and from VENDHUILE - LA TERRIERE. One man seen leading a black dog to VENDHUILE at 7.20 p.m. This is apparently a Battalion Headquarters.

1.30 p.m. to 8.30 p.m. Men seen working at earthwork in F.6.a.8.2.
Group of horses being held at S.28.d.8.8.

4. HOSTILE AIR ACTIVITY.

5.45 a.m. to 2.0 p.m. Balloon rose from S.E. edge of BASKETT WOOD.
HOstile aeroplane up - appeared to be observing for 5.9 battery shelling RONSSOY WOOD.

R.A. Headquarters. Sgd. H. R. BENNETT, Lieutenant, R. H.A.
2nd MAY, 1917. R.O. 3rd Cavalry Divisional Artillery.

3rd Cavalry Divisional Artillery.

INTELLIGENCE SUMMARY. 6.0 p.m. 1st to 6.0 p.m. 2nd.

1. OUR FIRE.

TIME	PLACE SHELLED	NATURE OF SHELL	DIRECTION	NUMBER OF ROUNDS	REMARKS
6.30 p.m. to 8.30 p.m.	F.6.a.9.3. F.6.a.5.9.	18 pdr.	-	37	With balloon observation.
4.0 a.m.	X.24.d.50.	13 pdr.	-	8	Punishment fire
4.15 a.m.	X.24.d.5.2.	"	-	8	-
5.30 a.m.	X.24.c.5.0.	"	-	20	-
8.0 a.m.	A.4.a.3.4.	4.5 How.	-	5	Transport.
9.30 a.m. to 11.30 a.m.	A.8.b.4.3.	18 pdr.	-	18	With balloon observation.
10.15 a.m. to 10.30 a.m.	Trench Mortars in CANAL WOOD.	13 pdr.	-	15	Punishment fire. T.M. ceased firing.
10.30 a.m.	F.6.a.	"	-	8	Working party.
1.30 p.m.	Trench Mortars in CANAL WOOD	"	-	10	Punishment fire. T.M. ceased firing.
2.0 p.m.	VENDHUILE	4.5 How.	-	7	Punishment fire.
2.20 p.m.	X.30.a & c.	13 pdr.	-	20	-do-
5.30 p.m.	A.3.a.9.3.	18 pdr.	-	20	With balloon observation.

2. **HOSTILE FIRE.**

TIME	PLACE SHELLED	NATURE OF SHELL	DIRECTION	NUMBER OF ROUNDS	REMARKS
9.30 p.m. to 1.0 a.m.	N. of RONSSOY	8" H.V. gun.	?	10	-
5.0 a.m.	LITTLE PRIEL FARM	77 mm	-	12	-
7.45 a.m. to 8.40 a.m.	"M" Post and road in rear	"	HONNECOURT	15	-
8.0 a.m. to 8.50 a.m.	X.2.b.	"	-do-	15	-
10.15 a.m. to 10.45 a.m.	X.23.a.7.9.	"	-do-	26	-
10.15 a.m. to 10.30 a.m.	Outposts near CANAL WOOD	T.M.	CANAL WOOD	12	Bursts very light.
11.0 a.m.	F.14	5.9	LA TERRIERE	6	-
1.45 p.m. to 2.20 p.m.	"M" Post	77 mm	HONNECOURT	20	-
2.15. p.m. to 2.35 p.m.	Trenches in X.21.b.	"	-do-	26	-
3.20 p.m.	"M" Post	"	-do-	7	Apparently fired at horse grazing near this point.
3.30 p.m.	CANAL WOOD	"	OSSUS	10	-

3. **GENERAL.**

8.30 a.m. Cloud of smoke seen rising from buildings near LES-TRENCHEES - this lasted for about a quarter of an hour.

8.32 a.m. Fired two rounds at a wagon on the LE CATELET - VENDHUILE Road causing the horse to bolt, There was a great deal of movement in this roadcduring the morning.

Six black mounds seen in sunken road S.30 .b. whi ch might possibly be a battery position.

4. **HOSTILE AIR ACTIVITY.**

Normal.

R.A. Headquarters. Lieutenant, R. H. A.

3rd JUNE, 1917. R.O. 3rd Cavalry Divisional Artillery.

3rd Cavalry Divisional Artillery.

INTELLIGENCE SUMMARY. 6.0 p.m. 2nd to 6.0 p.m. 3rd.

1. OUR FIRE.

TIME	PLACE SHELLED	NATURE OF SHELL	DIRECTION	NUMBER OF ROUNDS	REMARKS
10.35 p.m.	OSSUS WOOD	18 pdr.	-	6	Punishment fire
10.55 p.m.	-do-	"	-	15	-do-
11.30 p.m.	-do-	4.5 How.	-	6	-do- requested by Cavalry.
4.0 a.m.	Sunken road in X.30.c.	18 pdr.	-	5	Punishment fire.
9.30 a.m.	S.14.a.7.7.	13 pdr.	-	36	Registration.
10.0 a.m.	LA TERRIERE	18 pdr.	-	6	Punishment fire.
10.30. a.m.	Quarries S.14.d.	4.5 How.	-	14)	
	VENDHUILE	"	-	15)	
	BONY	"	-	32)	-do-
	HARGIVAL FARM and DUMP.	"	-	49)	
2.30 p.m.	OSSUS WOOD	13 pdr.	-	11	Registration with balloon observation.
3.0 p.m.	VENDHUILE	"	-	10	Punishment fire.
3.55 p.m.	Wood in S.8.c & d.	18 pdr.	-	17	-do-

2. HOSTILE FIRE.

TIME	PLACE SHELLED	NATURE OF SHELL	DIRECTION	NUMBER OF ROUNDS	REMARKS
5.0 a.m.	No.4 Post	4.2	HONNECOURT	5	-
9.0 a.m. to 2.30 p.m.	EPEHY	8"	LE CATELET	150	-
10.0 a.m.	EPEHY STN.	"	-do-	10	-
2.0 p.m.	F.4.b.8.3.	77 mm	?	5	Two rounds contained an explosive smelling of phosphorus.
2.30 p.m.	LITTLE PRIEL FARM	4.2	?	4	-
3.30 p.m.	X.17.d.1.7. to X.16. central	"	?	12	-

3. GENERAL.

Party seen carrying planks into VENDHUILE.

Four Germans seen coming out of the wood in S.14.a. and walked towards the Quarry, they appeared to be patrolling telephone wires.

RONSSOY and RONSSOY WOOD were heavily shelled during the morning with 5.9 and 4.2.

4. HOSTILE AIR ACTIVITY.

Hostile aeroplanes active during the morning but were driven off by our A.A. Guns.

R.A. Headquarters.
4th JUNE, 1917.

Lieutenant, R. H. A.
R.O. 3rd Cavalry Divisional Artillery.

3rd Cavalry Divisional Artillery.

INTELLIGENCE SUMMARY. 6.0 p.m. 3rd to 6.0 p.m. 4th.

1. OUR FIRE.

TIME	PLACE SHELLED	NATURE OF SHELL	DIRECTION	NUMBER OF ROUNDS	REMARKS
7.30 p.m.	VENDHUILE	4.5 How.	-	14	Punishment fire.
7.30 p.m.	Bridge at A.3.a.9.3.	18 pdr. H.E.	-	18	Registration.
8.0 p.m.	Road in S.27.d.1½.5.	18 pdr.	-	16	-do-
7.15 a.m.	Cross roads S.14.a.7.7.	13 pdr.	-	19	-do-
9.0 a.m.	Sunken road in X.30.a.6.1.	"	-	8	Punishment fire for T.M.
12.30 p.m.	CANAL WOOD	"	-	8	Registration.
3.30 p.m.	Quarry S.14.d.	"	-	20	-do-

2. HOSTILE FIRE.

TIME	PLACE SHELLED	NATURE OF SHELL	DIRECTION	NUMBER OF ROUNDS	REMARKS
8.45 p.m.	W.30.b.	8"	LE CATELET	3	-
7.0 a.m. to 8.30 a.m.	X.23.c. central	77 mm	S.6	20	-
8.0 a.m. to 8.15 a.m.	"G" Post	4.2	VENDHUILE	10	-
8.0 a.m.	LITTLE PRIEL FARM	"	-do-	8	-
11.0 a.m. to 12.22 p.m.	ST. EMELIE)	5.9	-do-	4.	-
	MALASSISE FARM)	4.2	-do-	4	-
11.30 a.m. to 12.30 p.m.	Road, outposts and Quarry X.17.c.)	77 mm	HONNECOURT	20	-
1.30 p.m. to 2.30 p.m.	Railway Line W.23.central	4.2	?	8	-
3.42 p.m.	Railway Line W.23.central	"	?	3	-

3. GENERAL.

10.45 p.m. False gas alarm.

A rocket was sent up from 35th Division's front bursting into silver spray.

From 2nd Cavalry Division's front, one rocket bursting into silver spray; two green lights and four rockets each bursting into on red light.

Strombos Horn was heard on the 35th Division's front.

11.1[illegible] p.m. Rocket bursting into silver spray was again seen on 35th Divisional Front.

Enemy searchlight seen in the direction of HONNECOURT.

Very little movement seen.

4. HOSTILE AIR ACTIVITY.

9.30 p.m. Three hostile planes crossed our lines but weredriven off by our A.A. guns.

R.A. Headquarters.
5th JUNE, 1917.

Lieutenant, R. H. A.
R.O. 3rd Cavalry Divisional Artillery.

3rd Cavalry Divisional Artillery.

INTELLIGENCE SUMMARY. 6.0 p.m. 4th to 6.0 p.m. 5th.

1. OUR FIRE.

TIME	PLACE SHELLED	NATURE OF SHELL	DIRECTION	NUMBER OF ROUNDS	REMARKS
7.0 p.m.	F.6.a.8.3.	18 pdr.	-	13	Registered by balloon.
7.30 p.m.	F.6.c.9.0.	"	-	20	-do-
5.30 a.m.	OSSUS WOOD	"	-	9	Punishment fire
6.0 a.m.	Sunken road in X.30.a. & c.	13 pdr.	-	30	Punishment fire for T.M.
9.40 a.m.	Quarry S.14.c.	"	-	4	Movement seen
12.15 p.m.	S.14.a.25.70.	" H.E.	-	56	Suspected telephone exchange.
12.40 p.m.	S.15.a.7.8.	13 pdr.	-	7	Registration.
2.40 p.m.	X roads S.14.a.7.7.	18 pdr.	-	13	-do-
4.0 p.m.	X.23.d.7.0.	4.5 How. H.E.	-	40	Registration of M.G.
4.30 p.m.	Road at A.1.a.2.5.	13 pdr.	-	30	Calibration.
5.30 p.m.	OSSUS WOOD	"	-	30	Registration.

2. HOSTILE FIRE.

TIME	PLACE SHELLED	NATURE OF SHELL	DIRECTION	NUMBER OF ROUNDS	REMARKS
6.0 a.m.	BIRDCAGE trench	T.M.	OSSUS	7	-
7.0 a.m.	HEUDECOURT	5.9	?	4	Too hogh for effect.
9.0 a.m.	RONSSOY LEMPIRE	4.2 5.9.	? ?	100	-
10.15 a.m. to 10.45 a.m.	LITTLE PRIEL FARM	77 mm	?	29	-
10.30 a.m.	-do-	5.9	VENDHUILE	9	-
9.58 a.m. to 11.32 a.m.	Ridge from X.17.a.6.2. to X.11.c.5.2.	4.2	HONNECOURT	22	One round every four minutes.
10.0 a.m.	CATELET COPSE	"	LA TERRIERE	12	-

2. **HOSTILE FIRE.** (continued)

TIME	PLACE SHELLED	NATURE OF SHELL	DIRECTION	NUMBER OF ROUNDS	REMARKS
10.45 a.m. to 11.0 a.m.	BIRDCAGE	77 mm	OSSUS	9	-
11.40 a.m.	X.17.a.	77 mm H.E.	S.23	13	-

3. **GENERAL.**

9.40 a.m. Slight movement seen at the Quarry in S.14.c.

Telephone pole seen above house in Quarry S.14.a.2.5; suspected telephone exchange.

5.30 p.m. One of our Batteries in X.20.b.4.0. shelled with 10 rounds 4.2 from the direction of HONNECOURT. No damage done and no casualties.

7.30 p.m. A small fox was seen between MAY COPSE and OLD COPSE.

4. **HOSTILE AIR ACTIVITY.**

6.0 a.m. to 8.0 a.m. Enemy planes were active but did not succeed in crossing our line.

R.A. Headquarters. Lieutenant, R. H. A.

6th JUNE, 1917. R. O. 3rd Cavalry Divisional Artillery.

3rd Cavalry Divisional Artillery.

INTELLIGENCE SUMMARY. 6.0 p.m. 5th to 6.0 p.m. 6th.

1. **OUR FIRE.**

TIME	PLACE SHELLED	NATURE OF SHELL	DIRECTION.	NUMBER OF ROUNDS	REMARKS
6.30 p.m. to 8.30 p.m.	LA TERRIERE and CANAL WOOD	18 pdr.	-	36	Registration.
-do- / -do-	X.18.c.3.2. to X.24.a.5.0. / Trench in X.24.a.2.3.	18 pdr. H.E.	-	45	Registration by balloon observation.
7.0 p.m.	CANAL WOOD	13 pdr.	-	16	-
8.10 p.m.	Trench at F.6.a.7.3.	"	-	5	Germans seen above trench.
11.30 p.m.	Sunken road in X.30.a.8.5.	" H.E.	-	20	Punishment fir for T.M.
7.5 a.m.	CANAL WOOD to S.13.	13 pdr.	-	28	Punishment fire.
9.45 a.m.	Road in S.8.c.6.1.	"	-	19	Sniping.
12.45 p.m.	OSSUS WOOD	18 pdr.	-	9	-
2.0 p.m. to 2.30 p.m.	S.27.c.5.9.	4.5 How.	-	3	Sniping.
3.0 p.m.	Quarry in S.14.a.2.7.	13 pdr.	-	14	-
3.45 p.m.	Junction of road and trench F.6.a.9.3.	"	-	27	Calibration.
4.30 p.m. to 5.0 p.m.	LA TERRIERE Wood in S.8.c. & d.	18 pdr.	-	18	Registration of forward guns.
5.40 p.m.	S.20.b.	13 pdr.	-	6	Sniping.

2. HOSTILE FIRE.

TIME	PLACE SHELLED	NATURE OF SHELL	DIRECTION	NUMBER OF ROUNDS	REMARKS
7.0 a.m.	X.22	77 mm	LA TERRIERE	18	-
7.20 a.m. to 7.35 a.m.	PIGEON RAVINE	4.2	?	10	-
7.30 a.m.	LITTLE PRIEL FARM	77 mm	LA TERRIERE	3	-
9.0 a.m.	-do-	"	-do-	10	-
9.45 a.m. to 10.0 a.m.	Road in X.14.d.6.2.	4.2	North of HONNECOURT	10	-
9.50 a.m.	X.14.d.	15 cm	RANCOURT FARM	3	-
10.15 a.m.	"G" Post	4.2	LA TERRIERE	4	-
10.15 a.m.	X.14.d.	15 cm	RANCOURT FARM	5	-
10.25 a.m.	X.14.a.	"	-do-	12	-

3. GENERAL.

11.30 p.m. Trench Mortar active from OSSUS WOOD.

11.0 a.m. Several Germans seen on the LE CATELET - VENDHUILE Road. Between 12 mid-day and 1.0 p.m. several of the enemy, 14 at one time, wereseen on the same road, between 30 and 40 passed altogether.

Small working party seen in HINDENBURG LINE at S.21 central. There appears to be new wire in this line at S.9.c.

4. AIR ACTIVITY.

One of our aeroplanes was brought down in flames and crashed at about A.8. or A.9. It was reported to hame been brought down by an enemy plane but a later report says by Anti-Aircraft guns.

R.A. Headquarters.
7th JUNE, 1917.

Lieutenant, R. H. A.
R.O. 3rd Cavalry Divisional Artillery.

3rd Cavalry Divisional Artillery.

INTELLIGENCE SUMMARY. 6.0 p.m. 6th to 6.0 p.m. 7th.

1. OUR FIRE.

TIME	PLACE SHELLED	NATURE OF SHELL	DIRECTION	NUMBER OF ROUNDS	REMARKS
6.15 p.m. to 7.45 p.m.	F.6.a.9.3.	18 pdr.	-	15	Registration.
9.15 a.m.	OSSUS VILLAGE	4.5 How.	-	21	Punishment fire.
9.30 a.m.	Sunken road X.30.a.	13 pdr. H.E.	-	10	Punishment fire for T.M.
11.0 a.m.	OSSUS WOOD	"	-	4	-
2.15 p.m.	F.6.a.8.2.	13 pdr.	-	7	Registration.
5.15 p.m.	KNOLL to F.6.a.	" H.E.	-	10	Movement seen.
6.0 p.m.	A.4.a.3.4.	4.5 How.	-	3	-

2. HOSTILE FIRE.

TIME	PLACE SHELLED	NATURE OF SHELL	DIRECTION	NUMBER OF ROUNDS	REMARKS
8.0 p.m.	X.22.c.2.0.	77 mm	LA TERRIERE	12	-
8.0 p.m.	X.14.d.	15 cm H.E.	RANCOURT FARM	6	-
8.30 p.m.	X.15.c.	10.5 cm	?	10	-
8.50 p.m.	X.17.c.	" H.E.	?	4	-
5.20 a.m.	LEMPIRE	4.2	?	6	-
6.30 a.m.	X.15.b.	77 mm	LA TERRIERE	10	-
7.0 a.m.	X.14.d.	77 mm	-do-	5	-
7.0 a.m. to 7.20 a.m.	LITTLE PRIEL FARM and TOMBOIS FARM)	"	OSSUS	10	-
8.15 a.m.	X.21.c.	"	LA TERRIERE	4	-
8.20 a.m.	X.23.a.5.0.	"	-do-	4	-
8.30 a.m. to 3.0 p.m.	ST. EMELIE	5.9	?	28	Intermittent.
4.45 p.m. to 5.30 p.m.	TOMBOIS FARM	77 mm	OSSUS	12	-
4.45 p.m.	Road in X.14.d.5.0.	"	?	6	-

3. GENERAL.

Visibility poor.

There seems to be one 77 mm gun in the Western outskirts of LA TERRIERE. It has not yet been accurately located.

5.20 p.m. Parties of Germans were seen in the trench between the "KNOLL" and F.6.a., several groups were also seen in shell holes in front of the ternch baling out water. These appeared to be Machine Gun emplacements weallhidden by the long grass.

R.A. Headquarters.
8th JUNE, 1917.

Lieutenant, R. H. A.
R.O. 3rd Cavalry Divisional Artillery.

3rd Cavalry Divisional Artillery.

INTELLIGENCE SUMMARY. 6.0 p.m. 7th to 6.0 p.m. 8th.

1. OUR FIRE.

TIME	PLACE SHELLED	NATURE OF SHELL	DIRECTION	NUMBER OF ROUNDS	REMARKS
7.0 p.m.	S.14.a.8.0.	13 pdr.	-	11	Registration.
8.0 p.m.	S.19.d.7.8.	4.5 How. H.E.	-	13	Aeroplane observing.
10.0 a.m.	VENDHUILE	"	-	20	Punishment fire for shelling of EPEHY.
10.30 a.m.	Quarry in S.13.d.8.1.	"	-	10	Punishment fire.
11.15 a.m. to 11.45 a.m.	Zero lines.	18 pdr.	-	23	Check calibration
5.0 p.m.	Quarry in S.13.d.8.1.	4.5 How. H.E.	-	16	Aeroplane observing.
6.0 p.m.	OSSUS WOOD	18 pdr. H.E.	-	5	M.G. firing at our aeroplane. Result effective.

2. HOSTILE FIRE.

TIME	PLACE SHELLED	NATURE OF SHELL	DIRECTION	NUMBER OF ROUNDS	REMARKS
6.30 a.m. to 9.5 a.m.	VILLERS GUISLAIN	77 mm	HONNECOURT	20	-
5.30 a.m. to 6.30 a.m.	TOMBOIS FARM	"	VENDHUILE	15	-
9.0 a.m. to 11.0 a.m.	W.30.a. & b.	4.1 H.V. gun	182° true	50	-
9.30 a.m.	EPEHY	10 cm gun	VENDHUILE	40	-
10.0 a.m.	VILLERS GUISLAIN	77 mm	HONNECOURT	8	-
10.0 a.m.	VILLERS FAUCON	8"	LE CATELET	52	-
10.30 a.m.	LITTLE PRIEL FARM and	4.2	VENDHUILE	2	-
	TOMBOIS FARM	4.2	-do-	10	-

3. GENERAL.

6.45 p.m. to 7.0 p.m. Our artillery shelled RANCOURT FARM and set it on fire.

11.45 a.m. An enemy party seen working in front of BASKETT WOOD on what appears to be a light railway.

Two 5.9 Hows. were seen firing in VENDHUILE this morning, they are not yet accurately located.

Movement very much less than during the last two days.

1.30 a.m. and 2.30 a.m. "Golden Rain" rockets were sent up, the first to the North of DI Sector, the second to the South.

4. HOSTILE AIR ACTIVITY.

10.30 a.m. One of our bombing squadrons crossed the german lines but met a squadron of about 15 enemy planes (Albatross and Aviatik) and were forced to return - all machines returned safely.

R.A. Headquarters.
9th JUNE, 1917.

Lieutenant, R. H. A.
R.O. 3rd Cavalry Divisional Artillery.

3rd Cavalry Divisional Artillery.

INTELLIGENCE SUMMARY. 6.0 p.m. 8th to 6.0 p.m 9th.

1. OUR FIRE.

TIME	PLACE SHELLED	NATURE OF SHELL	DIRECTION	NUMBER OF ROUNDS	REMARKS
6.5 p.m.	OSSUS WOOD	18 pdr.	-	17	Calibration.
2.45 p.m. to 3.15 p.m.	S.20.a. & c.	13 pdr.	-	38	-
4.30 p.m.	Quarry in S.30.d.7.7.	18 pdr.	-	28	-
4.45 p.m. to 5.0 p.m.	S.14.a.	"	-	17	Calibration.
5.30 p.m.	Crossing of road and trench X.23.d.9.4.	13 pdr. H.E.	-	10	Registration.
5.30 p.m.	Quarry in S.14.a.3.7.	18 pdr. H.E.	-	7	-
5.45 p.m.	Quarry in S.30.d.7.7.	18 pdr.	-	10	-

2. HOSTILE FIRE.

TIME	PLACE SHELLED	NATURE OF SHELL	DIRECTION	NUMBER OF ROUNDS	REMARKS
6.30 a.m. to 7.30 a.m.	LITTLE PRIEL FARM	77 mm	VENDHUILE	15	-
7.30 a.m. to 8.30 a.m.	-do-	4.2	?	15	-
7.45 a.m.	X.17.d.	" cm	VENDHUILE	3	-
8.15 a.m.	LITTLE PRIEL FARM	77 mm	LA TERRIERE	8	-
8.30 a.m.	Quarry at X.29.d.2.2.	4.2 cm	?	3	-
12 noon to 1.0 p.m.	X.29.d.1.3.	"	LA TERRIERE	4	-

2. **HOSTILE FIRE.** (continued)

TIME	PLACE SHELLED	NATURE OF SHELL	DIRECTION	NUMBER OF ROUNDS	REMARKS
1.15 p.m. to 4.45 p.m.	LITTLE PRIEL FARM	4.2	?	10	-
2.30 p.m. to 2.55 p.m.	"M" Post	77 mm	?	15	-
2.30 p.m.	BIRDCAGE TRENCH	10 cm	?	3	-

3. **GENERAL.**

Visibility bad, quiet on the front all day.

4. **HOSTILE AIR ACTIVITY.**

2.30 p.m. Two enemy planes flew over our outpost line and disappeared in S.E. direction.

R.A. Headquarters.
10th JUNE, 1917.

Lieutenant, R. H. A.
R. O. 3rd Cavalry Divisional Artillery

SB/30

3rd Cavalry Divisional Artillery.

INTELLIGENCE SUMMARY. 6.0 p.m. 9th to 6.0 p.m. 10th.

1. OUR FIRE.

TIME	PLACE SHELLED	NATURE OF SHELL	DIRECTION	NUMBER OF ROUNDS	REMARKS
8.30 p.m.	House at X.21.c.8.7.	18 pdr.	-	20	Registration.
11.30 a.m.	OSSUS WOOD	18 pdr.	-	27	-do-
12 noon	Working party N. of OSSUS WOOD at X.24.c.1.8.	"	-	8	Fire effective
4.0 p.m.	F.8.c.9.1.	"	-	12	Check registration.
4.0 p.m.	Trench in A.1.c.8.8.	"	-	4	-do-

2. HOSTILE ARTILLERY.

12 noon to 12.30 p.m.	LITTLE PRIEL FARM	77 mm	N.E. LA TERRIERE	20	-
3.40 p.m.	-do-	77 mm	-do-	10	-
3.45 p.m.	"O" Post	-do-	-do-	12	-
3.50 p.m.	No. 12 COPSE	-do-	-do-	5	All "duds"

3. GENERAL.

Observation bad all the morning owing to thick mist.

Front very quiet all day and very little movement seen.

R.A. Headquarters.

11th JUNE, 1917.

Lieutenant, R. H. A.

B.M. 3rd Cavalry Divisional Artillery.

2. <u>HOSTILE FIRE.</u> (continued)

TIME	PLACE SHELLED	NATURE OF SHELL	DIRECTION	NUMBER OF ROUNDS	REMARKS
8.0 a.m. to 8.45 a.m.	CATELET COPSE	4.2	LA TERRIERE	3	-
8.30 a.m. to 10.15 a.m.	"L" Post	"	?	12	-
8.40 a.m. to 9.15 a.m.	LITTLE PRIEL FARM	"	BASKETT WOOD	14	-
8.40 a.m.	X.29.a. & b.	4.2 or 5.9	VENDHUILE	8	-
8.55 a.m. to 10.20 a.m.	GREEN LINE	4.2	LA TERRIERE	18	-
9.0 a.m. 1 to 10.20 a.m.	No. 13 COPSE	"	-do-	27	-
9.12 a.m.	F.4.a.8.8.	5.9	LE CATELET	11	-
9.30 a.m. to 10.15 a.m.	Road from X.28.a. to X.28.b.	77 mm	LA TERRIERE	12	-
9.30 a.m. to 10.15 a.m.	F.9.	4.2	BASKETT WOOD	30	-
9.55 a.m. to 11.15 a.m.	GREEN LINE	"	LA TERRIERE	8	-
11.0 a.m. to 11.15 a.m.	LITTLE PRIEL FARM and "G" Post.	"	BASKETT WOOD	17	-
11.0 a.m. to 12 noon	X.20.a.	"	HONNECOURT	20	-
11.5 a.m.	X.28.b.	"	?	6	-
11.50 a.m. to 12.15 p.m.	"G" Post and LITTLE PRIEL FARM	77 mm	BONY	7	-

3rd Cavalry Divisional Artillery.

INTELLIGENCE SUMMARY. 6.0 p.m. 10th to 6.0 p.m. 11th.

1. OUR FIRE.

TIME	PLACE SHELLED	NATURE OF SHELL	DIRECTION	NUMBER OF ROUNDS	REMARKS
10.40 p.m.	A.2.a.5.0. to A.2.a.8.8. A.2.a.9.6. to A.2.b.1.9.	18 pdr.	-	182	Counter-preparation to the Div: on the right.
10.55 p.m. to 11.15 p.m.	CANAL WOOD and X.30.a.8.8. to X.30.a.9.0.	18 pdr.	-	170	-do-
10.45 p.m.	X.18.c.9.1. X.30.a.9.9. E. & W. exits of VENDHUILE.	4.5 How.	-	64	-do-
11.15 p.m.	S.&S.E. exits of VENDHUILE Valley in A.2.a. and A.1.d.	"	-	78	-do-
11.30 p.m.	X.30.a.6.9. to S.25.b.0.0. to S.25.d.0.0. A.2.a.0.0. A.8.b.4.3. A.8.b.5.1.	13 pdr.	-	147	Punishment Fire.
11.30 p.m.	A.1.b.0.7. to A.1.c.0.1. OSSUS WOOD	"	-	50	-do-
12.10 a.m.	X.25.d.9.0. to F.6.c.9.5.	18 pdr.	-	105	-do-
11.30 a.m.	Junction of road and trench at F.6.a.8.2.	13 pdr.	-	26	Registration.
11.45 a.m.	X.29.a.9.8. F.6.a.9.6.	"	-	45	Snipers post and M.G.
1.15 p.m.	Trench in S.20.a. & c.	"	-	18	Registration.
4.15 p.m.	Road at F.6.a.5.9.	"	-	17	-do-

2. HOSTILE FIRE.

TIME	PLACE SHELLED	NATURE OF SHELL	DIRECTION	NUMBER OF ROUNDS	REMARKS.
10.40 p.m. to 11.30 p.m.	Division on right and "D.L. Sector.	5.9.) 4.2) 77 mm)	?	?	Bombardment.
11.45 a.m.	CATELET COPSE	4.2	LA TERRIERE	6.	-
12.15 p.m.	LITTLE PRIEL FARM	5.9.	?	6	-
12.20 p.m.	-do-	77 mm	LA TERRIERE	15	-
2.0 p.m. to 3.0 p.m.	Trenches in X.22.a.	"	?	6	-
2.15 p.m.	LITTLE PRIEL FARM	4.2	?	12	-
2.30 p.m.	-do-	77 mm	LA TERRIERE	9	-
2.30 p.m.	"G" Post	"	MACQUINCOURT FARM	9	-
3.5 p.m. to 5.30 p.m.	X.23.c.)	4.2	?	3	F.O.O. reports this gun to be close up but does not know position yet.
	X.22.c.)	4.2	?	2	
5.30 p.m.	X.22.c.	77 mm	LA TERRIERE	10	-

3. GENERAL.

10.45 p.m. S.O.S. signal sent up on the 2nd Cavalry Divisional Front.

Batteries fired in support as in para 1.

Thick haze all morning and visibility poor all day.

A.A. Guns in LE CATELET were active during the afternoon.

4. HOSTILE AIR ACTIVITY.

4.45 p.m. Two enemy planes crossed over our lines.

No. observation balloons up.

R.A. Headquarters. Sgd, H.R. BENNETT, Lieutenant,,R. H. A.

12th JUNE, 1917. R.O. 3rd Cavalry Divisional Artillery.

SB/23

3rd Cavalry Divisional Artillery.

INTELLIGENCE SUMMARY. 6.0 p.m. 11th to 6.0 pm 12th.

1. OUR FIRE.

TIME	PLACE SHELLED	NATURE OF SHELL	DIRECTION	NUMBER OF ROUNDS	REMARKS
7.30 p.m.	CANAL WOOD	18 pdr.	-	6	Punishment fire.
9.0 p.m.	VENDHUILE	4.5 How.	-	31	-do-
9.15 a.m.	S.27.c. X roads	"	-	8	-
9.30 a.m.	A.4.a.3.4.	"	-	2	Sniping.
12 noon to 1.45 p.m. 4.30 p.m.	Trench in X.24.a.2.3. to X.24c.0.8.	18 pdr.	-	~~42~~ 100	Wire cutting.
1.45 p.m.	Trench crossing road X.30.c.6.0. F.6.c.8.3.	18 pdr.	-	18	Registration.
2.35 p.m.	VENDHUILE	4.5 How.	-	6	Punishment fire for shelling of GREEN LINE.
2.45 p.m.	S.19.d.	18 pdr.	-	11	-
6.0 p.m.	S.26.a.5.2.	4.5 How.	-	12	Aeroplane Observing
6.0 A.m. to 6.0 p.m.	X. 23. d. 9. 8.	18 pdr.		100	Wire cutting

2. HOSTILE FIRE.

TIME	PLACE SHELLED	NATURE OF SHELL	DIRECTION	NUMBER OF ROUNDS	REMARKS
7.30 p.m.	X.23.a.	77 mm	?	3	-
~~[illegible]~~	~~[illegible]~~	8"	?	[illegible]	-
6.30 a.m. to 7.30 a.m.	F.14. d.	8"	LE CATELET	50	-
7.15 a.m.	"G" Post	77 mm	VENDHUILE	4	-
7.30 a.m.	[illegible] FARM	21 cm	LE CATELET	4	-
8.30 a.m.	LITTLE PRIEL FARM	4.2	-do-	5	-
8.45 a.m. to 10.15 a.m.	No. 12 & 13 Copses	4.2	-do-	25	-
9.30 a.m. to 10.30 a.m.	"G" & "H" Post	4.2	VENDHUILE	7	-
10.30 a.m.	LITTLE PRIEL FM.	77 mm	?	8	-

2. HOSTILE FIRE. (continued)

TIME	PLACE SHELLED	NATURE OF SHELL	DIRECTION	NUMBER OF ROUNDS	REMARKS
10.0 a.m. to 5.15 p.m.	Trenches near VILLERS GUISLAIN	4.2	?	100	-
11.0 a.m. to 12 noon	LITTLE PRIEL FARM	77 mm	?	10	-

3. GENERAL.

5.0 a.m. Two hostile planes were observing the fire of one of our Batterys' in F.14.

Rounds fired into VENDHUILE by the 4.5. Hows. were seen to be effective - the road being littered with rubbish.

Enemy were firing shells set at percussion at an aeroplane these fell near EPEHY.

12.30 p.m. Flashes of an A.A. Gun were seen in FRANQUI WOOD about S.3.d.5.0 and another seen in VENDHUILE.

R.A. Headquarters.

13th JUNE, 1917.

Lieutenant, R. H. A.

R.O. 3rd Cavalry Divisional Artillery.

3rd Cavalry Divisional Artillery.

Hostile shelling report for week ending TUESDAY, JUNE 12th. 1917.

DATE.	PLACES SHELLED.	NATURE OF SHELL	DIRECTION.	NUMBER OF ROUNDS.
JUNE 7th.	X.22.c.2.0.	77 mm	LA TERRIERE	12
	X.14.d.	15 cm H.E.	BANCOURT FARM.	6
		77 mm	LA TERRIERE	12
	X.15.c & b.	4.2	?	10
		77 mm	LA TERRIERE	10
	X.17.c.	4.2	?	4
	LEMPIRE	4.2	?	6
	LITTLE PRIEL FARM and TOMBOIS FARM.	77 mm	OSSUS	22
	X.21.c.	77 mm	LA TERRIERE	4
	X.23.a.6.0.	77 mm	-do-	4
	ST. EMILIE	5.9	?	28
JUNE 8th.	VILLERS GUISLAIN	77 mm	HONNECOURT	28
	TOMBOIS FARM	77 mm	VENDHUILE	15
	LITTLE PRIEL FARM	4.2	-do-	12
	W.30.a & b.	4.1 H.V. gun	162° true	50
	EPEHY	4.2	VENDHUILE	40
	VILLERS-FAUCON	8"	LE CATELET	52

DATE.	PLACE SHELLED.	NATURE OF SHELL.	DIRECTION.	NUMBER OF ROUNDS.
JUNE 9th.	LITTLE PRIEL FARM.	77 mm	VENDHUILE) LA TERRIERE)	28
	-do-	4.2	?	25
	X.17.d.	4.2	VENDHUILE	3
	Quarry X.29.d.2.4.	4.2	?	3
	X.29.d.1.3.	4.2	LA TERRIERE	4
	"M" Post	77 mm	?	15
	BIRDCAGE.	4.2	?	3
JUNE 10th.	LITTLE PRIEL FARM	77 mm H.E.	LA TERRIERE	30
	"G" Post	77 mm	-do-	13
	No. 13 COPSE	77 mm	-do-	5
JUNE 11th.	GATELET COPSE	4.2	LA TERRIERE	6
	LITTLE PRIEL FARM	5.9	?	6
	-do-	77 mm	LA TERRIERE	25
	-do-	4.2	?	12
	X.22.a.	77 mm	?	6
	"G" Post.	77 mm	MACQUINCOURT FARM	9
	X.22.c.	77 mm	LA TERRIERE	12

DATE.	PLACE SHELLED.	NATURE OF SHELL.	DIRECTION.	NUMBER OF ROUNDS.
JUNE 12th.	X.26.a.	77 mm	?	3
	P.14.d.	8"	LE CATELET	50
	"G" Post and "H" Post	77 mm	VENDHUILE	4
		4.2	-do-	7
	MALASSIS FARM	8"	LE CATELET	4
	LITTLE PRIEL FARM	4.2	-do-	4
	-do-	77 mm	?	18
	No. 12 & 13 COPSES	4.2	LE CATELET	25
	Trenches near VILLERS GUISLAIN	4.2	?	100

R.A. Headquarters.

13th JUNE,1917.

~~Lieutenant~~, R. H. A.

R.O. 3rd Cavalry Divisional Artillery.

SB/23

3rd Cavalry Divisional Artillery.

INTELLIGENCE SUMMARY. 6.0 p.m 12th to 6.0 p.m. 13th.

1. OUR FIRE.

TIME	PLACE SHELLED	NATURE OF SHELL	DIRECTION	NUMBER OF ROUNDS	REMARKS
6.5 p.m.	S.20.c.	18 pdr.	-	24	Movement seen
7.30 p.m.	X.24.c.$\frac{1}{2}$.9$\frac{1}{2}$.	"	-	12	-do-
7.45 p.m.	S.15.a.2.5.	"	-	21	Registration
8.0 p.m.	S.15.c.	"	-	6	Movement seen
6.0 a.m. to 6.0 p.m.	X.24.a.2.6. X.24.a.5.8.	18 pdr.	-	77	Wire cutting
6.0 a.m. to 6.0 p.m.	X.24.d.9.8.	18 pdr.	-	170	-do-
8.5 a.m.	X.23.d.8$\frac{1}{2}$.3.	"	-	13	Registration
9.30 a.m.	MACQUINCOURT FARM	4.5 How.	-	8	Punishment fire.
9.30 a.m.	VENDHUILE	"	-	4	-do-
12.30 p.m.	OSSUS WOOD	"	-	5	-do-
12.30 p.m.	S.22.d.	"	-	12	-do-
12.30 p.m.	X.30.a.	18 pdr.	-	68	-do-
12.30 p.m.	X.30.a.4.7.	"	-	20	-do-
12.45 p.m.	F.6.c.2.9.	"	-	20	Calibration
2.30 p.m.	S.14.a.6.6.	"	-	15	Registration
2.30 p.m.	CANAL WOOD	18 pdr.H.E.	-	8	~~Wire cutting~~
3.30 p.m.	OSSUS WOOD	18 pdr.	-	18	Registration
4.30 p.m.	X.30.a.4.7.	"	-	63	Wire cutting
5.15 p.m.	F.6.a.6.4.	"	-	9	-do-

2. HOSTILE FIRE.

TIME	PLACE SHELLED	NATURE OF SHELL	DIRECTION	NUMBER OF ROUNDS	REMARKS
7.10 a.m.	GREEN LINE	4.2	?	4	-
7.15 a.m.	X.27.c.3.6.	"	LE CATELET	7	-
8.5 a.m.	"L" Post	"	-do-	15	-
8.15 a.m.	X.22.c.	"	?	12	-
9.20 a.m.	CATELET COPSE	77 mm	VENDHUILE	12	-
9.25 a.m.	X.29	"	A.17	12	-
9.30 a.m.	LITTLE PRIEL FARM	"	VENDHUILE	20	-
9.35 a.m.	-do-	77 mm) 4.2)	?	30	-
10.35 a.m. to 10.50 a.m.	-do- and Sector H.Q.	77 mm	VENDHUILE	?	Intermittent.
11.0 a.m. to 12 noon	LITTLE PRIEL FARM	"	-do-	21	-
11.0 a.m. to 12 noon	F.29) F.5.)	"	LE CATELET	25	-
2.30 p.m.	F.10.a. (road)	4.2 or 5.9	-do-	12	-
2.30 p.m. to 5.30 p.m.	X.21.a.7.9.	4.2	?	(approx) 30	-
2.40 p.m.	Trenches between "K" & "L"Posts	77 mm	?	15	-

3. GENERAL.

Hostile artillery more active shelling the front line.

6.5 p.m. Movement seen in S.20.c., party dispersed.

7.30 p.m. Two Germans seen to enter shell hole in X.24.c.½.9½. who after being fired on returned to trenches in rear.

Visibility ~~good~~ fair.

4. HOSTILE AIR ACTIVITY.

7.0 a.m. Two enemy planes flew over our lines but were driven off by A.A. Guns.

R.A. Headquarters. Lieutenant, R. F. A.

14th JUNE, 1917. R.O. 3rd Cavalry Divisional Artillery.

3rd Cavalry Divisional Artillery.

INTELLIGENCE SUMMARY. 6.0 p.m. 13th to 6.0 p.m. 14th.

1. OUR FIRE.

TIME	PLACE SHELLED	NATURE OF SHELL	DIRECTION	NUMBER OF ROUNDS	REMARKS
7.0 p.m.	X.24.c.5.0.	13 pdr.	-	12	-
8.15 a.m.	VENDHUILE	4.5 How.	-	5	Punishment fire.
8.40 a.m.	A.4.a.	"	-	6	Sniping.
9.0 a.m.	VENDHUILE	"	-	4	Punishment fire.
10.0 a.m.	-do-	"	-	4	-do-
11.15 a.m.	A.4.a.	"	-	2	Caused two casualties.
3.0 p.m.	X.27.b.3.0. (3)	13 pdr.	-	34	Registration.
3.30 p.m.	F.6.a.6.3.	"	-	33	-do-
4.0 p.m.	F.6.a.5.8.	"	-	6	-do-
4.30 p.m. to 5.30 p.m.	X.30.a.8.8. X.30.c.9.0.	18 pdr.	-	18	-do-
5.0 p.m.	S.26.a.1.7.	4.5 How.	-	6	Aeroplane observing.
5.15 p.m.	S.20.c.4.1.	"	-	10	-do-
1.30 p.m.	VENDHUILE	"	-	5	Punishment fire.

2. HOSTILE FIRE.

TIME	PLACE SHELLED	NATURE OF SHELL	DIRECTION	NUMBER OF ROUNDS	REMARKS
4.55 a.m. to 5.5 a.m.	TOMBOIS FARM.	77 mm	LE CATELET	6	-
7.15 a.m. to 9.30 a.m.	"H" Post and LITTLE PRIEL FARM.	"	LA TERRIERE	15	-
7.45 a.m.	CATELET COPSE	"	LE CATELET	8	-
7.50 a.m.	X.27.a.1.0. to X.27.b.9.9.	"	-do-	6	-
8.0 a.m. to 8.20 a.m.	LITTLE PRIEL FARM	4.2	AUBEMCHEUL	8	-

3. GENERAL.

Movement below normal.

77 mm gun firing from BONY is reported to be a new position and is enfilading ourtrenches betwe n "G" Post and "H" Post.

A suspicious character wasreported walking round the front line. He was reported to be a Gunner Major with no steel hat or smoke helmet and no orderly, wearing a red band on his arm. No further particulars up to dark.

4. HOSTILE AIR ACTIVITY.

9.0 p.m. Hostile aeroplane over our front line.

R.A. Headquarters. Lieutenant, R. H. A.

15th JUNE, 1917. R.O. 3rd Cavalry Divisional Artillery.

3rd CAVALRY DIVISIONAL ARTILLERY.

INTELLIGENCE SUMMARY. 6 p.m. 14th to 6 p.m. 15/6/1917.

1. OUR ARTILLERY.

TIME	PLACE SHELLED	NATURE OF SHELL	DIRECTION	NUMBER OF ROUNDS	REMARKS.
9-30 a.m.	FRANQUE WOOD	18 pdr.	-	24	Punishment fire.
10-30 a.m.	S.14.c.	13 pdr.	-	14	Sniping.
11-40 a.m.	VENDHUILE	13 pdr.	-	21	-
1-0 p.m.	X.30.c.5.4.	13 pdr.	-	20	Suspected O. P.
1-0 p.m. to 2-0 p.m.	X.24.c.8.7.)) X.24.a.0.1.)	13 pdr.	-	?	Registratio with Aeroplane.
4-30 p.m.	Trenches in X.30.a & c.	13 pdr.	-	30	Movement seen.
5-30 p.m.	F.3.a.9.5.	13 pdr.	-	66	Calibration and Registratio

2. HOSTILE FIRE.

TIME	PLACE SHELLED	NATURE OF SHELL	DIRECTION	NUMBER OF ROUNDS	REMARKS.
9-30 a.m. to 10-30 a.m.	TOMBOIS FARM	77 m.m.	VENDHUILE	11	-
9-45 a.m.	F.4.a.	77 m.m.	LE CATELET	15	-
10-30 a.m.	F.11.a.	4.2	VENDHUILE	17	-
10-30 a.m.	F.5.c.	77 m.m.	LE CATELET	7	-
10-30 a.m.	LITTLE PRIEL FM.	4.2	LE CATELET	8	-
11-30 a.m.	F.11.a.	4.2	VENDHUILE	5	-
11-30 a.m.	LITTLE PRIEL FM.	4.2	LE CATELET	6	-
12-45 p.m.	TOMBOIS FARM	77 m.m.	VENDHUILE	7	-
5-15 p.m. to 5-30 p.m.	MALASSISE FARM	4.2	LE TERRIERE	11	-

3. GENERAL.

12-45 p.m. 5 men seen in trench about X.30.c.5.4. - this appeared to be an O.P.

One man seemed to be observing while the others dug.

Enemy look-out man seen about X.30.a.9.1.

Many instances of one man pointing out the country to another were seen - this may indicate a relief.

4. HOSTILE AIR ACTIVITY.

9-0 p.m. Hostile plane over our lines.

9-30p.m. 5 or more British planes attacked two German planes - result not seen.

R.A. Headquarters. 2nd Lieutenant, R.H.A.

16th June, 1917. R. O. 3rd Cavalry Divisional Artillery.

SB/26

3rd CAVALRY DIVISIONAL ARTILLERY.

INTELLIGENCE SUMMARY

6 p.m. 15th to 6 p.m. 16th.

1. OUR ARTILLERY

TIME	PLACE SHELLED	NATURE OF SHELL	DIRECTION	NUMBER OF ROUNDS	REMARKS
9-45 a.m.	F.6.a.9.2.	13 pdr.	-	2 7	Datum point
3-0 p.m.	X.29.b.5.5.	4.5 How.	-	5 0	Suspected M. G's.
3-15 p.m.	S.19.d.1.5.	4.5 How.	-	4	Checking lines.
3-20 p.m.	S.14.c.(Quarry)	4.5 How.	-	5	--"--
5-0 p.m.	House at S.27.a.2.6.	13 pdr.	-	1 1	Suspected O Direct hits obtained
5-15 p.m. to 5-40 p.m.	F.6.a.7.4.	13 pdr.	-	2 3	Registratio

2. HOSTILE FIRE.

7-43 a.m.	LITTLE PRIEL FM.	4.2	LECATELET	5	-
8-0 a.m.	F.4.c.	4.2	LE CATELET	8	-
8-20 a.m.	No.12 Copse	4.2	LE CATELET	6	-
8-40 a.m.	"L" Post	5.9	LE PANNERIE	2 0	Intervals o 1 minute.
8-57 a.m.	"M" Post	77 m.m	LA TERRIERE	3	All "duds". Fired at an Officer on our parape

3. GENERAL.

Observation impossible until 8.30a.m.

A loophole can be seen at A.1.a.2.4.

Few coils of wire, and men visible on the crest, in the bend of a trench in X.3.a.4.4.

4.5 p.m. Large clouds of smoke seen rising behind the crest E. of FRANQUE WOOD, extent of smoke 400^{x}. This lasted for about five minutes.

From about X.27.d.2.2. German wire can be seen running towards about the centre of the "T" head of the BIRDCAGE, the wire does not appear much closer than 150^{x} to the BIRDCAGE. No sign of a sap can be seen.

4. HOSTILE AIR ACTIVITY.

A.A. gun which usually fires from the direction of HONNECOURT seems to have moved further South.

3.45 p.m. Two men descended from a balloon behind LA TERRIERE by parachute. One descended fairly straight behind LA TERRIERE and the other was blown farther away and descended behind RANCOURT FARM

The balloon was then hauled down.

This is the first time this balloon has been up for several days and is suspected to be an experiment with dummy men and parachutes.

R.A. Headquarters. Lieutenant, R. H. A.

17th JUNE, 1917. R.O. 3rd Cavalry Divisional Artillery.

SB/27

3rd Cavalry Divisional Artillery.

INTELLIGENCE SUMMARY. 6.0 p.m. 16th to 6.0 p.m. 17th.

1. OUR FIRE.

TIME	PLACE SHELLED	NATURE OF SHELL	DIRECTION	NUMBER OF ROUNDS	REMARKS
6.30 p.m.	S.19.d.5.8.	13 pdr.	-	46	Registration of dug-outs and ladder leading to bridg across Canal.
7.30 p.m.	A.3.a.3.4.	4.5 How.	-	4	Sniping.
9.10 a.m.	S.20.b.8.8.	13 pdr.	-	6	At E.A. which had been brought down.
10.15 a.m.	S.26.c.5.9.	4.5 How.	-	4	-
3.0 p.m. to 4.0 p.m.	X.24.d. X.24d. X.23.d.	13 pdr.	-	30	Registration.
3.30 p.m.	X.30.a.8.6.	4.5 How.	-	7	Registration by balloon.
3.15 p.m.	S.19.b.5.3.	"	-	13	-do-
3.45 p.m. to 6.0 p.m.	X.24.a.9.2. to X.24.c.9.6.	18 pdr.	-	26	Registration.
5.0 p.m.	X.30.a.4.6½.	13 pdr.	-	37	Registration by balloon.

2. HOSTILE FIRE.

TIME	PLACE SHELLED	NATURE OF SHELL	DIRECTION	NUMBER OF ROUNDS	REMARKS
4.0 a.m. to 5.20 a.m.	A.13.a.	4.2	?	50?	-
4.15 a.m.	F.11.d.	4.2 cm	LE CATELET	50	-
10.10 a.m.	CATELET COPSE	4.2 T.H.E.	-do-	8	-
10.15 a.m. to 10.30 a.m.	LITTLE PRIEL FARM	4.2 77 mm	LA TERRIERE LE CATELET	5 7	-
11.0 a.m. to 2.20 p.m.	RONSSOY WOOD	8"	ST. MARTIN (A.13)	50?	-

2. HOSTILE FIRE. (continued)

TIME	PLACE SHELLED	NATURE OF SHELL	DIRECTION	NUMBER OF ROUNDS	REMARKS
12.15 p.m. to 12.35 p.m.	"L" Post	4.2	?	20	-
4.50 p.m.	F.10	5.9	BASKETT WOOD	6	-

3. GENERAL.

5.30 a.m. German seen looking through a telescope at F.3.a.6.4.

7.30 a.m. Six men seen in S.14.b.2.8., disappeared into FRANQUE WOOD.

7.55 a.m. Nine men seen at S.14.b.2.8.

10.0 a.m. Party of men seen working in S.21.b.0.3.

4. HOSTILE AIR ACTIVITY.

7.15 a.m. Three hostile balloons up.

Enemy air activity during the morning more than usual.

9.0 a.m. An air fight took place between a squadron of our battle planes and an unknown number of enemy aeroplanes.

One enemy aeroplane was shot down, bursting into flames. Two men were seen to drop out.

The plane fell in dead ground about S.20.c or b., smoke could be seen rising until about 9.30 a.m.

A probable premature from an A.A. Gun was seen behind the tre trees of VENDHUILE. True bearing 46° from F.4.d.9.8., this agrees with the sound of the report of the gun.

R.A. Headquarters.
18th JUNE, 1917.

Lieutenant, R. H. A.
R.O. 3rd Cavalry Divisional Artillery.

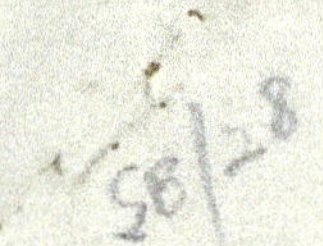

3rd Cavalry Divisional Artillery.

INTELLIGENCE SUMMARY. 6.0 p.m. 17th to 6.0 p.m. 18th.

1. OUR FIRE.

TIME	PLACE SHELLED	NATURE OF SHELL	DIRECTION	NUMBER OF ROUNDS	REMARKS
6.0 p.m. to 8.0 p.m.	X.24.c.	18 pdr.	-	55	Registration by balloon.
12.50 a.m. to 1.40 a.m.	X.30.c.8.4.	13 pdr.	-	61	In support of raid.
12.50 a.m. to 1.40 a.m.	S.25.c.1.0 to A.1.a.2.4.	"	-	40	-do-
12.30 a.m.	X.30.a.5.9. X.30.a.3.9.	4.5 How.	-	29 29	-do-
5.45 a.m.	X.30.c.5.2.	13 pdr.	-	38	Punishment. fire.
9.15 a.m.	OSSUS WOOD	"	-	27	-do-
4.5 p.m.	S.19.d.5.6.	"	-	4	Sniping.
12.15 p.m.	VENDHUILE	4.5 How.	-	6	-
4.30 p.m.	X.23.d.3.5.	13 pdr.	-	20	Suspected O.P direct hits obtained.
5.30 p.m.	Road in S.25.d.	"	-	6	Registration.

2. HOSTILE FIRE.

TIME	PLACE SHELLED	NATURE OF SHELL	DIRECTION	NUMBER OF ROUNDS	REMARKS
4.30 a.m. to 6.20 a.m.	BIRDCAGE	77 mm	?	17	-
5.0 a.m. to 6.0 a.m.	LITTLE PRIEL FARM	77 mm	VENDHUILE	30	-
7.0 a.m. to 7.30 a.m.	TOMBOIS valley	4.2	?	14	-
	No. 12 Copse	4.2	?	9	-
8.0 a.m.	No. 12 Copse	77 mm	?	15	-
8.0 a.m.	LITTLE PRIEL FARM	4.2	LA TERRIERE	20	-
8.0 a.m. to 9.30 a.m.	"L" Post	4.2	OSSUS	30	-
9.0 a.m. to 9.15 a.m.	Communication trench to "G" Post	4.2	BONY	17	-

2. **HOSTILE FIRE.** (continued)

TIME	PLACE SHELLED	NATURE OF SHELL	DIRECTION	NUMBER OF ROUNDS	REMARKS
9.0 a.m.	F.4.c.	77 mm	LE CATELET	8	
9.15 a.m.	No.13 Copse	"	-do-	8	
9.40 a.m.	BIRDCAGE	"	LA TERRIERE	20	
10.10. a.m. to 10.30 a.m.	200x South of No. 12 Copse	77 mm	VENDHUILE	30	
10.20 a.m.	"G" Post	"	LE CATELET	40	

3. **GENERAL.**

During the raid on the night of 17/18th enemy sent up Green spray rockets, apparently calling for artillery support, as shortly afterwards the enemy opened fire. He then put up about 12 red rockets (red) from the vicinity of OSSUS WOOD.

LEMPIRE was intermittently shelled during the day with 5.9 and 4.2.

12 noon German seen observing from trench about X.30.c.4.6. Man seen digging in trench along the Canal bank in S.20.c.

Three men seen digging at S.21.b.1.3.

4. **HOSTILE AIR ACTIVITY.**

11.45 a.m. Enemy aeroplane flew over No. 12 Copse at a height of about 1200 feet, it was heavily but inaccurately fired on by our A.A. Guns.

5.0 p.m. Two enemy aeroplanes over our lines.

R.A. Headquarters.
19th JUNE, 1917.

Lieutenant, R. H. A.
R.O. 3rd Cavalry Divisional Artillery.

SB/39

3rd Cavalry Divisional Artillery.

INTELLIGENCE SUMMARY. 6.0 p.m. 18th to 6.0 p.m. 19th.

1. OUR FIRE.

TIME	PLACE SHELLED	NATURE OF SHELL	DIRECTION	NUMBER OF ROUNDS	REMARKS
4.45 a.m. to	Bush in S.20.a.	13 pdr.	-	9	Men seen.
5.20 a.m.	Line of dug-outs in S.20.a.	"	-	42	-do-
5.50 a.m.	S.19	"	-	46	Punishment fire.
9.30 a.m.	VENDHUILE	4.5 How.	-	12	-do-
10.30 a.m.	KINGSTON QUARRIES	"	-	10	-do-
11.0 a.m.	F.5.a.9.3.	13 pdr.	-	12	Registration.
12.30 p.m.	Chalk pit in S.14.c.	"	-	25	-do-
1.0 p.m.	X.30.d.5.2.	"	-	6	Sniping.
2.30 p.m.	KINGSTON QUARRIES	4.5 How.	-	12	Punishment fire.
2.33 p.m.	OSSUS WOOD	13 pdr.	-	34	-do-
2.50 p.m.	VENDHUILE	"	-	12	-do-
4.15 p.m.	F.6.a.0.3.	"	-	6	Sniping
4.30 p.m. to 5.0 p.m.	Chalk pits (14.c.) Line of dug-outs (S.20.a.)	"	-	18	Registration.
5.0 p.m.	X.30.d.5.2.	"	-	6	Sniping.
5.15 p.m.	LA TERRIERE	"	-	6	Punishment fire.

2. HOSTILE FIRE.

TIME	PLACE SHELLED	NATURE OF SHELL	DIRECTION	NUMBER OF ROUNDS	REMARKS
6.30 a.m. to 8.30 a.m.	LITTLE PRIEL FARM	77 mm	VENDHUILE	30	-
8.20 a.m. to 8.50 a.m.	CATELET COPSE and X.27.d.	"	LA TERRIERE	20	-
8.55 a.m.	F.4.	4.2	?	10	-
9.0 a.m.	F.4.c.	77 mm	?	10	-

2. **HOSTILE FIRE.** (continued)

TIME	PLACE SHELLED	NATURE OF SHELL	DIRECTION	NUMBER OF ROUNDS	REMARKS
9.50 a.m. to 10.30 a.m.	LITTLE PRIEL FARM	13 cm gun	VENDHUILE	20	50% "duds"
10.45 a.m.	X.27.b.	4.2	?	12	-
130 p.m.	F.4.a. & b.	77 mm	?	6	-
2.15 p.m.	CATELET COPSE	4.2	LE CATELET	12	-
2.30 p.m.	"G" Post	77 mm	AUBENCHEUL	15	-
4.0 p.m.	F.4.d.9.8.	"	VENDHUILE	10	-

3. **GENERAL.**

Hostile Artillery active during the morning and an unusual amount of "duds" were fired.

6.30 a.m. 77 mm gun in LA TERRIERE was active firing Northwards.

A stake is visible in front of the new enemy sap opposite the BIRDCAGE, this may possibly be a periscope.

New wire has been put up about 20 yards in front of the German front line at X.30.d.4.5., so far there is only about 10 yards of wire.

A good deal of movement seen in front line trench about X.30.d.4½.0. Two periscopes were put up here and shortly afterwards our trench opposite was shelled with 77 mm.

A good deal of movement in small parties seen, from the line of dug-outs in S.30.a. which were fired on with success.

A few men seen wandering about in VENDHUILE and in the BEAUREVOIR Road. No transport.

9.30 a.m. Puffs of smoke, possibly a trench railway, were seen rising in a bearing of 74° from F.4.d.9.8.

R.A. Headquarters.
20th JUNE, 1917.

Lieutenant, R. H. A.
R.O. 3rd Cavalry Divisional Artillery.

SB/30

2nd Cavalry Divisional Artillery.

Hostile shelling report for week ending Tuesday, JUNE 19th, 1917.

DATE	PLACE SHELLED	NATURE OF SHELL	DIRECTION	NUMBER OF ROUNDS
June 13th.	X.27.b.3.6.	4.2	LE CATELET	7
	"E" Post	4.2	-do-	15
	X.22.c.	4.2	?	12
	CATELET COPSE	77 mm	VENDHUILE	10
	X.29	"	A.17	12
	LITTLE PRIEL FARM	" 4.2	VENDHUILE	41) Inter- 30) mittent.
	F.6.c.	77 mm	LE CATELET	22
	D.10.a. (road)	4.2 or 5.9	-do-	12
	X.21.c.7.6.	4.2	?	90 (approx)
	Junction between "E" & "D" Posts	77 mm	?	15
June [illegible]th.	TOMBOIS FARM	77 mm	LE CATELET	6
	"C" & "D" Posts and LITTLE PRIEL FARM	"	LA TERRIERE } BONY }	15 7
		4.2	AUBENCHEUL } BASKET WOOD }	6 31
	CATELET COPSE	77 mm 4.2	LE CATELET LA TERRIERE	6 3
	X.27.a.1.6. to X.27.b.0.6.	77 mm	LE CATELET	6
	"E" Post	4.2	?	12
	X.29.a. & b.	4.2 or 5.9	VENDHUILE	6
	No. 13 Copse	4.2	LA TERRIERE	87
	F.4.a.9.6.	5.9	LE CATELET	11
	Road from X.28.a. to X.28.b.	77 mm	LA TERRIERE	18
	F.20.a.	4.2	HONNECOURT	29

DATE	PLACE SHELLED	NATURE OF SHELL	DIRECTION	NUMBER OF ROUNDS
June 14th. (continued)	X.20.b.	4.2	?	6
	F.9.	4.2	BASSETT WOOD	50
June 15th.	TOMBOIS FARM	77 mm	VENDHUILE	10
	F.4.a.	"	LE CATELET	11
	F.11.a.	4.2	VENDHUILE	17
	F.5.c.	77 mm	LE CATELET	7
	LITTLE PRIEL FARM	4.2	-do-	14
	F.11.c.	"	VENDHUILE	8
	MALASSISE FARM	"	LA TERRIERE	11
June 16th.	LITTLE PRIEL FARM	4.2	LE CATELET	5
	F.6.c.	"	-do-	6
	No.13 Copse	"	-do-	6
	"L" Post	5.9	LA TERRIERE	60
	"K" Post	77 mm	LA TERRIERE	6
June 17th.	A.10.c.	4.2	?	50?
	F.11.d.	"	LE CATELET	50
	CATELET COPSE	"	-do-	8
	LITTLE PRIEL FARM	4.2 77 mm	LA TERRIERE LE CATELET	6 7
	[illegible] WOOD	8"	ST. MARTIN (A.18)	50?
	"L" Post	4.2	?	30
	F.19.	5.9	[illegible] WOOD	6
June 18th.	BIRDCAGE	77 mm	LA TERRIERE	27
	LITTLE PRIEL FARM	77 mm 4.2	VENDHUILE LA TERRIERE	30 20
	TOMBOIS valley	4.2	?	14
	"L" Post	4.2	OSSUS	30

DATE	PLACE SHELLED	NATURE OF SHELL	DIRECTION	NUMBER OF ROUNDS
June 18th. (continued)	Trench to "[illegible]" Post	4.2	BONY	17
	F.4.c.	77 mm	LE CATELET	8
	No. 13 Copse	"	-do-	8
	200x South of No.13 Copse	"	VENDHUILE	50
	"[illegible]" Post	"	LE CATELET	40
June 19th.	LITTLE PRIEL FARM	77 mm 10 cm gun	VENDHUILE -do-	50 - 20 [illegible]
	CATELET ROAD and X.17.d.	77 mm 4.2	LA TERRIERE LE CATELET	36 12
	F.4.	4.2 77 mm	? VENDHUILE	10 56
	X.[illegible].b.	"	?	6
	"[illegible]" Post	"	AUBENCHEUL	16

R.A. Headquarters.
20th JUNE, 1917.

Lieutenant, R. H. A.
H.Q. 3rd Cavalry Divisional Artillery.

3rd Cavalry Divisional Artillery.

INTELLIGENCE SUMMARY. 6.0 p.m. 19th to 6.0 p.m. 20th.

1. OUR FIRE.

TIME	PLACE SHELLED	NATURE OF SHELL	DIRECTION.	NUMBER OF ROUNDS	REMARKS
6.40 p.m.	S.14.a.2.7.	18 pdr.	-	12	Enemy walking towards Quarry.
8.0 p.m.	VENDHUILE	13 pdr.	-	30	Movement seen.
5.30 a.m. to 7.0 a.m.	X.30.a.) F.6.a.)	13 pdr.	-	110	Punishment fire
8.5 a.m.	X.23.d.3.6.	"	-	25	O.P. several hits obtained.
8.20 a.m.	OSSUS WOOD	"	-	12	Punishment fire
9.30 a.m.	Road about S.13.b.$1\frac{1}{2}$.$8\frac{1}{2}$.	18 pdr.	-	14	Sniping party effectively dispersed.
9.30 a.m.	X.30.a.	13 pdr.	-	15	Registration.
9.45 a.m.	VENDHUILE) OSSUS WOOD) X.30.a.&c.) Sunken road)	13 pdr.	-	26) 40)) 114 36) 18)	Organised punishment fire.
	X.30.a.)	4.5 How.			
10.15 a.m.	X.30.c.	13 pdr.	-	7	Sniping.
11.30 a.m.	VENDHUILE	"	-	24	Punishment fire
12.15 p.m.	Houses in S.29.a.1.9.	"	-	6	Registration.
6.0 p.m.	Trench in X.24.c.	"	-	12	-do-

2. HOSTILE FIRE.

TIME	PLACE SHELLED	NATURE OF SHELL	DIRECTION	NUMBER OF ROUNDS	REMARKS
7.0 a.m. to 7.15 a.m.	Quarry in X.29.d.	4.2	BASKETT WOOD	12	-
7.30 a.m. to 10.0 a.m. 11.30 a.m. to 12 noon 2.30 p.m. to 3.0 p.m.	"G" & "H" Posts and LITTLE PRIEL FARM Quarry in X.29.d.	4.2	LA TERRIERE DE LA LEAU	150	Organised shoot.
7.30 a.m. to 9.15 a.m.	F.3.a.	13 cm H.V. gun	LA PANNERIE	30	50% blind.
7.30 a.m. to 10.0 a.m.	X.29.c. 3 4.	77 mm	LA TERRIERE	50	Intermittent shelling.

3. GENERAL.

Enemy artillery was unusually active during the day, the greater part of the shooting being done with 4.2. During the earlier part of the day he seemed to be registering the BIRDCAGE area.

A man was seen using binoculars from a trench in S.21.b.3.9.

A fire was seen in AUBENCHEUL and at 5.0 p.m. another large fire in VILLERS-OUTREAUX (T.15.a.)

An unusual amount of movement was seen in the HINDENBURG LINE and on the usual roads.

A small red balloon was set fire from enemy observation balloon East of RANCOURT FARM and was carried North by the wind.

4. HOSTILE AIR ACTIVITY.

Hostile observation balloons up during the day as follows:-

(a) 128°)
(b) 108°) street line from F.4.d.9.8.
(c) 41°)

R.A. Headquarters. Lieutenant, R. H. A.

21st JUNE, 1917. R.O. 5th Cavalry Divisional Artillery.

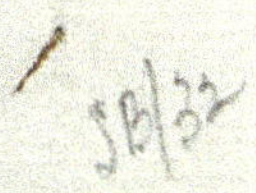

3rd Cavalry Divisional Artillery.

INTELLIGENCE SUMMARY. 6.0 p.m. 20th to 6.0 p.m. 21st.

1. OUR FIRE.

TIME	PLACE SHELLED	NATURE OF SHELL	DIRECTION	NUMBER OF ROUNDS	REMARKS
6.25 p.m. to 7.30 p.m.	Trench in S.21.b.3.9.	18 pdr.	-	6	Sniping at enemy observers.
7.15 a.m.	Cross roads at S.14.a.	"	-	4	Sniping. One man was afterwards carried away on a stretcher.
9.20 a.m.	X.24.c.0.7.	18 pdr.	-	8	Punishment fire.
9.30 a.m.	Trenches in X.30.a & c. OSSUS WOOD	"	-	117	-do-
10.0 a.m.	Trenches in X.30.a & c.	"	-	30	-do-
5.30 p.m.	OSSUS WOOD VENDHUILE	"	-	87	-do-
3.30 p.m.	Trenches in X.30.a & c.	"	-	40	-do-
4.0 p.m.	VENDHUILE	4.5 How.	-	12	-do-

2. HOSTILE FIRE.

TIME	PLACE SHELLED	NATURE OF SHELL	DIRECTION	NUMBER OF ROUNDS	REMARKS
6.0 a.m.	TOMBOIS FARM	77 mm	LA TERRIERE	12	Possible Registration.
8.0 a.m.	TOMBOIS Valley	4.2	VENDHUILE	30	-
10.0 a.m.	LITTLE PRIEL FARM	"	LA TERRIERE	20	-
9.15 a.m.	GREEN LINE	77 mm	-do-	7	-
9.20 a.m.	No.12 Copse	"	VENDHUILE	10	-
3.15 p.m. to 4.0 p.m.	BIRDCAGE and LITTLE PRIEL FARM	4.2	?	30	-
5.30 pm.	Cross roads at X.21.c.4.5.	"	?	6	-
9.10 a.m.	"G" Post	77 mm	LA TERRIERE	40	Possible Registration.

3. GENERAL.

8.15 a.m. Six Germans were seen crawling about in X.30.c.3.6. and continually raising their heads to look at the BIRDCAGE, after about five minutes they proceeded to crawl to X.30.c.5.5. dragging something behind them, probably tape. They also had a mallet with them and presumably were marking out another sap towards the BIRDCAGE or laying tape to guide a raiding party.

4. HOSTILE AIR ACTIVITY.

Hostile balloon up behind LA TERRIERE.

8.15 a.m. Six enemy aeroplanes flew close to our lines following six of our aeroplanes.

H.N. Bennett
Lieutenant, R. H. A.
R.O. 3rd Cavalry Divisional Artillery.

R.A. Headquarters.
22nd JUNE, 1917.

SECRET.

NIGHT FIRING 29th/30th BY 3rd CAVALRY DIVISIONAL ARTY:

TIME	BATTERY	SERIES	TASK	RATE	REMARKS
10-45 p.m. to 10-49 p.m.	D/293 Battery, R. F. A.	I	Roads about KINGSTON QUARRY in S.14.c.	2 rounds per How per minute.	Moving up and down roads and tracks.
11-30 p.m. to 11-54 p.m.	-do-	II	2 Hows. OSSUS WOOD East of X.30.a.1.8. 2 Hows. Tracks round bank S.25.b.1.5. to S.25.b.4.1.	2 rounds per How per minute.	Moving up and down Wood and tracks.
11-50 p.m. to 11-54 p.m.	-do-	III	Road Junctions in S.23.c. & A.2.a.	2 rounds per How per minute.	Moving about between roads.
12-10 a.m. to 12-14 a.m.	-do-	IV	Tracks X.18.c.7.2. to X.24.a.2.6.	2 rounds per How per minute.	Moving about between roads.
1-0 a.m. to 1-4 a.m.	-do-	V	As in II	2 rounds per How per minute.	
1-15 a.m. to 1-19 a.m.	-do-	VI	Banks and Tracks S.25.b. & X.30.a.	2 rounds per How per minute.	
2-5 a.m. to 2-9 a.m.	-do-	VII	North of CANAL S.25.b.8.2.to S.26.a.8.3	2 rounds per How per minute.	
3-0 a.m. to 3-4 a.m.	-do-	VIII	As in I	2 rounds per How per minute.	

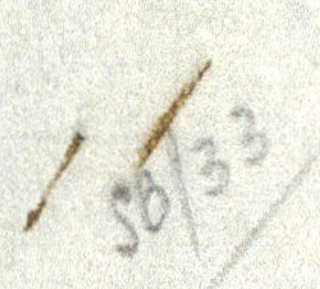

3rd Cavalry Divisional Artillery.

INTELLIGENCE SUMMARY. 6.0 p.m. 21st to 6.0 p.m. 22nd.

1. **OUR FIRE.**

TIME	PLACE SHELLED	NATURE OF SHELL	DIRECTION	NUMBER OF ROUNDS	REMARKS
7.30 p.m. to 7.40 p.m.	FRANQUE WOOD LA TERRIERE	18 pdr.	-	46	Punishment fire
1.10 a.m. to 1.35 [illegible]m.	X.30.a.3.6. to X.30.c.60.65.	18 pdr.	-	150	
	X.24.c.½.8. to X.24.c.0.0.	"	-	90	
	X.30.c.6.5. to X.30.c.5.½.	"	-	78	
	X.30.c.5.½. to F.6.a.5.2½.	"	-	30	In response to S. O. S. for raid on the
	X.18.c.3.½. to X.24.c.½.8.	18 pdr.	-	121	BIRDCAGE.
	X.18.c.5.½. X.24.c.5.½. X.30.a.9.9. X.30.a.75.10.	4.5 How.	-	60	
3.15 p.m.	Emplacements in X.24.c.5.6. & X.24.c.5.9.	18 pdr.	-	6	Registration.
3.30 p.m.	X.28.d.8.2.	"	-	11	-do-
5.10 p.m.	OSSUS WOOD	"	-	18	Punishment fire

2. HOSTILE FIRE.

TIME	PLACE SHELLED	NATURE OF SHELL	DIRECTION	NUMBER OF ROUNDS	REMARKS
7.30 p.m.	"L" Post	4.2	?	20	-
1.10 a.m.	BIRDCAGE	?	?	?	BOMBARDMENT.
8.30 a.m.	X.16.d.	77 mm	LA TERRIERE	15	-
10.15 a.m. to 10.30 a.m.	TOMBOIS FARM	"	VENDHUILE	7	-
1.0 p.m.	X.20.b.5.5.	"	HONNECOURT	3	Burst over No.6 gun of this battery.
5.10 p.m.	X.27.b.	"	?	6	-
5.15 p.m.	X.25	4.2	RICHMOND QUARRY	7	-

3. GENERAL.

A good deal of movement on RANCOURT FARM - LA PIERRE - LE CATELET Road.

A party of 20 enemy were seen for a short time at S.23.b.70.10.

A newly laid air line can be seen running from VENDHUILE on the crest of ~~the~~ Hill 130 in S.28.b.

A party of six men was seen working on this line on JUNE, 19th. It is since then that the 15 cm H.V. gun has been active; this line may possibly be the battery to O.P. line and that the gun itself is in action behind this Hill in one of the unoccupied pits shown on the Hostile Battery Map.

During the raid on the "BIRDCAGE" the enemy put up Green and Red lights, First all Green and then later all Red lights.

R.A. Headquarters.

23rd JUNE, 1917.

Lieutenant, R. H. A.

R.O. 3rd Cavalry Divisional Artillery.

SB/34

3rd Cavalry Divisional Artillery.

INTELLIGENCE SUMMARY. 6.0 p.m. 22nd to 6.0 p.m. 23rd.

1. OUR FIRE.

TIME	PLACE SHELLED	NATURE OF SHELL	DIRECTION	NUMBER OF ROUNDS	REMARKS
7.0 p.m.	OSSUS WOOD	18 pdr.	-	17	Registration.
7.35 a.m.	S.20.b.	"	-	8	Sniping.
7.50 a.m.	LA TERRIERE	18 pdr.	-	12	Punishment fire
10.40 a.m.	FRANQUE WOOD	"	-	12	-do-
12.4 p.m.	X.30.a. and F.6	18 pdr.	-	36	-do-
12.45 p.m.	X.24.a.0.5.	18 pdr.	-	25	Registration.
12.50 p.m.	X.18.c.6.6.	"	-	7	-
1.30 p.m.	S.20.a.0.1.	"	-	3	Sniping.
2.30 p.m.	X.23.d.	18 pdr.	-	84	Checking Registration
6.0 p.m.	X.30.c.5.5.	"	-	12	Sniping.

2. HOSTILE FIRE.

TIME	PLACE SHELLED	NATURE OF SHELL	DIRECTION	NUMBER OF ROUNDS	REMARKS
7.20 a.m.	X.28.c.	77 mm	VENDHUILE	9	-
7.30 a.m.	LITTLE PRIEL FARM	"	BASKETT VALLEY	5	-
7.45 a.m.	GREEN LINE	"	DE LA L'EAU	11	-
7.45 a.m.	PIGEON RAVINE	"	LA TERRIERE	10	-
10.25 a.m. to 10.45 a.m.	X.17	"	HONNECOURT	25	-
12.45 p.m.	PIGEON RAVINE	4.2	-do-	20	-
1.0 p.m.	X.22.d.	"	DE LA L'EAU	4	-

3. **GENERAL.**

Another row of wire has been put up in front of German trench at X.23.d.9.4. to X.23.d.9.5.

A dug-out is being made in the N bank of the sunken road at X.24.c.0.4.

Frequent small parties of enemy were seen all day on the backward slopes in A.1.a., A.10.a. and round VENDHUILE and DE LA L'EAU - and across the two bridges at S.26.b.2.2.

4. **HOSTILE AIR ACTIVITY.**

NIL.

Following balloons up during the day:-

(a) 127°)
(b) 47°) true bearing from F.4.d.9.8.
(c) 12°)

R.A. Headquarters. Lieutenant, R. H. A.

24th JUNE, 1917. R. O. 3rd Cavalry Divisional Artillery.

SB/35.

3rd Cavalry Divisional Artillery.

INTELLIGENCE SUMMARY. 6.0 p.m. 23rd to 6.0 p.m. 24th.

1. OUR FIRE.

TIME	PLACE SHELLED	NATURE OF SHELL	DIRECTION	NUMBER OF ROUNDS	REMARKS
3.15 p.m.	F.6.a.7.3.	13 pdr.	-	8	Registration.
3.30 p.m.	F.6.c.9.0. to F.6.a.7.4.	4.5 How.	-	6	Checking lines.
3.45 p.m.	X.24.c.	13 pdr.	-	30	Punishment fire

2. HOSTILE FIRE.

12.20 p.m.	TOMBOIS FARM	77 mm	VENDHUILE	10	-
2.50 p.m.	PIGEON RAVINE	"	?	25	-
3.15 p.m.	X.22.c.	4.2	?	25	Short range.
3.40 p.m.	X.27.b.	"	LA TERRIERE	10	-

3. GENERAL.

The 4.2 How. shelling X.22.c. appears to be in a new position; approximate direction VENDHUILE, and seemed to be registering this afternoon.

Small working party seen in S.9.d.

11.0 a.m. 33 men seen entering LA PANNERIE S.22.b.8.8.

Fresh work has been done at LA TERRIERE sand pit in S.10.c.

An air line has been built running N.W. from LA TERRIERE (S.10.c.)

4. HOSTILE AIR ACTIVITY.

8.10 a.m. 12 noon. 3.0[illegible].m. to 4.30 p.m.	Enemy aeroplanes crossed over our lines.

Enemy observation balloons up all day.

H M Bennett

R. A. Headquarters. Lieutenant, R. H. A.

25th JUNE, 1917. R.C. 3rd Cavalry Divisional Artillery.

3rd Cavalry Divisional Artillery.

INTELLIGENCE SUMMARY. 6.0 p.m. 24th to 6.0 p.m. 25th.

1. OUR FIRE.

TIME	PLACE SHELLED	NATURE OF SHELL	DIRECTION	NUMBER OF ROUNDS		REMARKS
1.10. a.m. to 2.55 a.m.	X.24.a. & c. S.19.a. & b. S.20.a.	4.5 How.	-		280	Barrage in support of our raid on enemy trenches in X.24.a. & c.
	N. edge of OSSUS WOOD	13 pdr.	-		480	
	Enemy trenches between CANAL and OSSUS WOOD	"	-	186		
				468		
				756	2923	
		18 pdr.	-	332		
		"	-	731		
6.15 a.m.	Party in road S.15.a.2.8.	"	-		6	Party dispersed.

2. HOSTILE FIRE.

TIME	PLACE SHELLED	NATURE OF SHELL	DIRECTION	NUMBER OF ROUNDS	REMARKS
1.45 p.m. to 2.0 p.m.	X.21.a. and X27.c.	4.2	N. of LA TERRIERE	12	-
12 noon to 1.30 p.m.	LEMPIRE	8"	LE CATELET	50 (approx)	
2.15 p.m.	F.10.c.	8"	-do-	5	-

LITTLE PRIEL FARM and Quarry in X.29.d. were lightly shelled with 77 mm and 4.2.

3. GENERAL.

The enemy barrage for our raid last night seemed to be very weak and did not commence until five or ten minutes after Zero hour.

3. GENERAL. (continued)

A new trench has been dug from the support trench at A.1.a.0.8. towards the front line trench at F.6.a.7½.2½., there is no wire in front of it. There is still about seventy yards halfway between them to be dug to connect them up.

The trench PUTNEY - HARGIVAL FARM was much used during the day.

Movement observed in Quarry S.10.c.4.9., HINDENBURG LINE at F.9.d.9.3. and between LA TERRIERE and CANAL WOOD.

4. HOSTILE AIR ACTIVITY.

9.0 p.m. One enemy aeroplane attacked one of our observation balloons N. of EPEHY forcing the observer to descend in a Parachute.

8.0 a.m. Hostile balloons up during the day.

Three enemy aeroplanes driven off by our A.A. Guns.

R. A. Headquarters,
26th JUNE, 1917.

Lieutenant, R. H. A.
R.O. 3rd Cavalry Divisional Artillery.

3rd Cavalry Divisional Artillery.

INTELLIGENCE SUMMARY. 6.0 p.m. 25th to 6.0 p.m. 26th.

1. OUR FIRE.

TIME	PLACE SHELLED	NATURE OF SHELL	DIRECTION	NUMBER OF ROUNDS	REMARKS
8.45 a.m.	VENDHUILE	4.5 How.	-	6	Punishment fire.
9.0 a.m.	MACQUINCOURT FARM	-do-	-	2	-do-
9.50 a.m.	CANAL WOOD	13 pdr.	-	12	-do-
10.0 a.m.	Quarry S.17.d.	4.5 How.	-	2	-do-
10.30 a.m.	Trenches X.30.a.	13 pdr.	-	30	Registration.
11.45 a.m.	OSSUS WOOD	-do-	-	22	Punishment fire.
12.30 p.m.	-do-	-do-	-	30	-do-
12.30 p.m.	S.15.a.15.45	18 pdr.	-	14	Sniping, appears to be a dug-out here.
1.20 p.m.	X.24.a.	13 pdr.	-	6	Punishment fire.
4.0 p.m. to 4.30 p.m.	2nd Div: Area.	-do-	-	22	Registration.
1.50 p.m.	S.25.b.7.3.	4.5 How.	-	4	-do-

2. HOSTILE FIRE.

TIME	PLACE SHELLED	NATURE OF SHELL	DIRECTION	NUMBER OF ROUNDS	REMARKS
8.15 a.m.	Post X.23.b.	4.2	KINGSTON QUARRY	15	-
8.45 a.m.	-do-	4.2	-do-	6	-
9.30 a.m.	X.17.c. & d.	4.2	-do-	5	-
9.50 a.m. to 10.0 a.m.	X.28.a.) X.28.b.)	4.2	HONNECOURT	8	-
10.10 a.m.	CATELET VALLEY	4.2	KINGSTON QUARRY	6	-
10.35 a.m.	F.5.a.	77 mm	LA TERRIERE	10	-
10.30 a.m.	Nos. 2 & 3 Posts	4.2	KINGSTON QUARRY	4	-
12.0 noon to 12.20 p.m.	F.5.a.	77 mm	LE CATELET	15	-
12 noon	LITTLE PRIEL FARM	77 mm	S.26.a. or b.	15	-

3. GENERAL.

The wire in front of FALCON SAP has been considerably strengthened.

Considerable movement seen on the VENDHUILE - LA TERRIERE Road and in BOIS MAILLARD - LA PANNERIE Road.

A wagon load of timber was seen on this road at S.17.c.7.0.

5.40 a.m. Smoke seen rising from behind the houses in A.18.central.

H. Bennett

Lieutenant, R. H. A.

R. O. 3rd Cavalry Divisional Artillery.

R. A. Headquarters.

27th JUNE, 1917.

5B/38.

3rd Cavalry Divisional Artillery.

Hostile shelling report for week ending Tuesday, JUNE, 26th. 1917.

DATE	PLACE SHELLED	NATURE OF SHELL	DIRECTION	NUMBER OF ROUNDS	REMARKS
June 20th.	Quarry in X.29.d.	4.2	BASKETT WOOD	12	-
	"G" & "H" Posts LITTLE PRIEL FARM Quarry in X.29.d.	"	LA TERRIERE DE LA L'EAU	150	Organised Shoot.
	F.5.a.	13 cm H.V. gun	LA PAINERIE	30	50% blind.
	X.29.c & d.	77 mm	LA TERRIERE	50	Intermittent shelling.
June 21st.	TOMBOIS FARM	77 mm	LA TERRIERE	12	Possible Registration
	TOMBOIS VALLEY	4.2	VENDHUILE	30	-
	LITTLE PRIEL FARM BIRDCAGE	"	-do- ?	50	-
	No.12 Copse	77 mm	VENDHUILE	10	-
	Cross roads at X.21.c.4.6.	4.2	?	6	-
	"G" Post	77 mm	LA TERRIERE	40	Possible Registration
June 22nd.	"L" Post	4.2	?	20	-
	BIRDCAGE	?	?	?	Bombardment for raid on BIRDCAGE.
	X.16.d.	77 mm	LA TERRIERE	15	-
	TOMBOIS FARM	"	VENDHUILE	7	-
	X.20.b.5.5.	"	HONNECOURT	3	-
	X.27.b.	"	?	6	-
	X.28	4.2	RICHMOND QUARRY	7	-

DATE	PLACE SHELLED	NATURE OF SHELL	DIRECTION	NUMBER OF ROUNDS	REMARKS
June 23rd.	X.28.c.	77 mm	VENDHUILE	9	-
	LITTLE PRIEL FARM	"	BASKETT WOOD	8	-
	GREEN LINE	"	DE LA L'EAU	11	-
	PIGEON RAVINE	"	LA TERRIERE	10	-
		4.2	HONNECOURT	25	-
	X.17	77 mm	-do-	20	-
	X.22.d.	"	DE LA L'EAU	4	-
June 24th.	TOMBOIS FARM	77 mm	VENDHUILE		
	PIGEON RAVINE	"	?		
	X.22.c.	4.2	?		
	X.27.b.	"	LA TERRIERE		
June 25th.	X.21.a.) X.27.c.)	4.2	N. of LA TERRIERE	12	-
	LEMPIRE	8"	LE CATELET	50	(approx.)
	F.10.a.	8"	-do-	3	-
June 26th.	Post in X.23.b.	4.2	KINGSTON QUARRY		
	X.17.c & d.	"	-do-		
	X.28.a.) X.28.b.)	"	HONNECOURT		
	CATELET VALLEY	"	KINGSTON QUARRY		
	F.5.a.	77 mm	LA TERRIERE		
	Nos.2 & 3 Posts	4.2	KINGSTON QUARRY		
	F.5.a.	77 mm	LE CATELET		
	LITTLE PRIEL FARM	"	S.26.a. or b.		

R.A. Headquarters.

27th JUNE, 1917.

Lieutenant, R. H. A.

R.O. 3rd Cavalry Divisional Artillery.

SB/39.

3rd Cavalry Divisional Artillery.

INTELLIGENCE SUMMARY. 6.0 p.m. 26th to 6.0 p.m. 27th.

1. OUR FIRE.

TIME	PLACE SHELLED	NATURE OF SHELL	DIRECTION	NUMBER OF ROUNDS	REMARKS
7.30 a.m.	OSSUS	13 pdr.	-	8	Punishment fire.
12.20 p.m.	Trench in S.6.a.	"	-	38	-do-
12.45 p.m.	Trench in F.6.a.	"	-	18	-do-
12.45 p.m.	OSSUS	"	-	14	-do-
12.45 p.m.	X.24.a.	18 pdr.	-	25	-do-
2.0 p.m.	S.20.a.	13 pdr.	-	6	Sniping.
3.30 p.m.	S.15.b.1.1.	18 pdr.	-	12	Sniping.
4.40 p.m.	VENDHUILE	"	-	20	Punishment fire.
4.35 p.m.	S.16.a.6.8.	"	-	6	Suspected O.P.
5.0 p.m.	X.23.d. and OSSUS	13 pdr.	-	45	Punishment fire.
5.0 p.m. to 6.0 p.m.	S.20.d. and S.27.c.	"	-	32	-do-
5.30 p.m.	OSSUS	"	-	60	-do-
5.45 p.m.	OSSUS	18 pdr.	-	20	-do-

2. HOSTILE FIRE.

TIME	PLACE SHELLED	NATURE OF SHELL	DIRECTION	NUMBER OF ROUNDS	REMARKS
7.25 a.m.	CATELET COPSE	77 mm	LA TERRIERE	5	-
8.0 a.m.	PIGEON RAVINE	"	FRANQUE WOOD	10	-
9.15 a.m.	Nos.2 & 3 Posts	"	-do-	9	-
10.30 a.m. to 10.55 a.m.	X.17.a.	T.M's	HONNECOURT	30	-
12.45 p.m.	No.18 Copse BIRDCAGE	77 mm	LA TERRIERE	10	-
4.40 p.m.	CATELET COPSE	"	LE CATELET	15	-
5.20 p.m.	F.15	"	LA TERRIERE	20	-
5.45 p.m.	X.28	4.2	LE CATELET	10	-

3. **GENERAL.**

Communication trench from TINO support trench was joined up to TINO trench in the night.

Movement seen in S.20.a. & b.

7.10 a.m. Four men (three Officers and one guide) walked from LA TERRIERE towards VENDHUILE studying a map and the country.

There appears to be a dug-out in the bushes about S.16.b.1.7.

7.30 a.m. While shooting at OSSUS a column of white smoke was sent up about 100 feet. This may have been a bomb or trench mortar dump.

4. **HOSTILE AIR ACTIVITY.**

Hostile balloons up during the day.

6.30 a.m. Five enemy aeroplanes crossed our lines.

8.20 a.m. One enemy aeroplane flew along the front line.

R. A. Headquarters.
20th JUNE, 1917.

Lieutenant, R. H. A.
R. O. 3rd Cavalry Divisional Artillery.

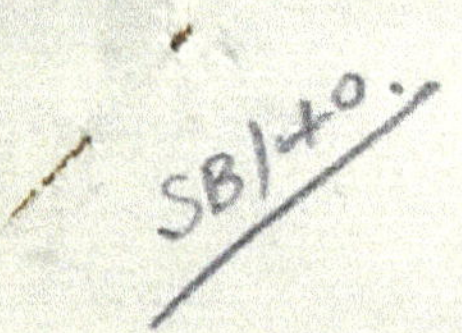

3rd Cavalry Divisional Artillery.

INTELLIGENCE SUMMARY. 6.0 p.m. 27th to 6.0 p.m. 28th.

1. OUR FIRE.

TIME	PLACE SHELLED	NATURE OF SHELL	DIRECTION	NUMBER OF ROUNDS	REMARKS
6.5 p.m.	S.15.b.3.3.	18 pdr.	-	9	At dug-outs.
6.30 p.m.	OSSUS WOOD	18 pdr.	-	33	Punishment fire.
6.40 p.m.	KINGSTON QUARRIES	4.5 How.	-	12	-do-
9.15 p.m.	OSSUS VILLAGE	18 pdr.	-	56	-do-
9.15 p.m.	OSSUS WOOD Dug-outs in S.29.a.3.0.	"	-	60	-do-
[illegible].30 p.m.	Trenches in X.24.a. & c. LA TERRIERE	18 pdr. "	- -	18 12	Punishment fire.
10.30 a.m.	OSSUS VILLAGE	18 pdr.	-	66	-do-
10.50 a.m.	X.30.c.45.45.	"	-	8	Registration for Sniping.
1.10 p.m.	VENDHUILE	4.5 How.	-	2	Punishment fire.

2. HOSTILE FIRE.

TIME	PLACE SHELLED	NATURE OF SHELL	DIRECTION	NUMBER OF ROUNDS	REMARKS
6.0 p.m. to 6.30 p.m.	PIGEON RAVINE	4.2	LA TERRIERE	10	-
7.0 p.m. to 8.25 p.m.	LIMERICK and MEATH Posts	5.9	S.4. or S.5.	6	-
9.0 p.m. to 9.20 p.m.	PIGEON RAVINE	4.2	S.20.d.	14	-
9.15 p.m.	X.27.c.0.0. No.13 Copse	77 mm	VENDHUILE	21	-
8.20 a.m.	TARGELLE RAVINE	4.2	LA TERRIERE	25	-
9.45 a.m.	X.2[illegible]	"	-do-	21	-
10.0 a.m.	X.29.c.	"	FRANQUÉ WOOD	3	-
10.15 a.m.	CATELET GORSE	"	LE CATELET	7	-

2. <u>HOSTILE FIRE.</u> (continued)

TIME	PLACE SHELLED	NATURE OF SHELL	DIRECTION	NUMBER OF ROUNDS	REMARKS
10.30 a.m.	LITTLE PRIEL FARM	77 mm	LA TERRIERE	10	-
10.50 a.m.	-do-	4.2	-do-	8	-
11.10 a.m.	"H" POST and BIRD LANE	77 mm	?	10	-
4.30 p.m. to 5.30 p.m.	X.17.b.	"	?	15	-

3. <u>GENERAL.</u>

A great deal more wire has been put up in frontof FALCON SAP. A considerable number of knife rests can be seen.

More work has been done on the trench in F.6.a. connecting TINO TRENCH to TINO SUPPORT.

Men seen entering and leaving dug-out in S.15.b.3.3.; man seen leading a dog here, he left hurriedly for KINGSTON QUARRIES

Transport on the GOUY - BEAUREVOIR Road was above normal.

Abnormal movement in LA TERRIERE and VENDHUILE.

4. <u>HOSTILE AIR ACTIVITY.</u>

4.30 p.m. Enemy aeroplane flew over our lines at a great height.

5.30 p.m. Enemy aeroplane flew low over our lines but disappeared on the approach of four of our planes.

R. A. Headquarters,

20th. JUNE, 1917.

Lieutenant, R. H. A.

R. O. 3rd Cavalry Divisional Artillery.

SB/41.

3rd Cavalry Divisional Artillery.

INTELLIGENCE SUMMARY. 6.0 p.m. 28th to 6.0 p.m. 29th.

1. OUR FIRE.

TIME	PLACE SHELLED	NATURE OF SHELL	DIRECTION	NUMBER OF ROUNDS	REMARKS
5.5 p.m.	LA TERRIERE	18 pdr.	-	48	Punishment fire.
9.5 a.m.	F.3.a.7.3.	13 pdr.	-	7	-do-
10.0 a.m. to 10.15 a.m.	S.15.c.	18 pdr.	-	8	Sniping at enemy party causing casualties.
11.10 a.m.	A.1.a.2.8.	13 pdr.	-	24	Punishment fire.
11.15 a.m.	OSSUS	13 pdr. H.E.	-	27	-do-
11.20 a.m.	VENDHUILE	4.5 How.	-	12	Sniping.
2.5 p.m.	KINGSTON QUARRIES	18 pdr.	-	10	Punishment fire.
4.40 p.m.	Trenches X.24.d.	13 pdr. H.E.	-	18	-do-
5.30 p.m.	VENDHUILE	4.5 How.	-	2	Sniping.

2. HOSTILE FIRE.

TIME	PLACE SHELLED	NATURE OF SHELL	DIRECTION	NUMBER OF ROUNDS	REMARKS
5.45 p.m. to 6.30 p.m.	Nos.3. & 4 Posts Quarry -	4.2	BANTOUZELLE	50	Observed by enemy aeroplane.
8.10 a.m. to 8.25 a.m.	X.17.d.	77 mm	?	12	-
8.40 a.m. to 9.30 a.m.	LITTLE PRIEL FARM and BIRDCAGE	4.2 77 mm	LE CATELET	12 9	- -
9.0 a.m.	F4.3. and F.3.c.	77 mm	VENDHUILE	15	-
11.20 a.m.	LITTLE PRIEL FARM	4.2	?	15	-
11.30 a.m.	X.20	4.2	FRANQUEVILLE	9	-
12 noon	F.5.c.	4.2	LE CATELET	20	-
1.45 p.m.	Out-post line	77 mm	FRANCQUE WOOD	20	-
3.15 p.m.	"T" Post X.20.c.	77 mm 4.2	? FRANCQUE WOOD	22 10	75% blind. -
4.25 p.m.	X.28.b.	"	LE CATELET	4	-

3. GENERAL.

6.30 a.m. A large working party of about one hundred men was seen West of the Farm at T.20.b.9.9.

6.45 a.m. Two men were seen patrolling a telephone wire which ran through the Quarry at S.20.d.7.7.

More work has been done on the trenches in F.6.a. connecting TINO TRENCH to TINO SUPPORT.

4. HOSTILE AIR ACTIVITY.

3.0 p.m. to 5.0 p.m. One enemy aeroplane made two attempts to attack one of our observation balloons in rear of VILLERS FAUCON.

R.A. Headquarters.
30th JUNE, 1917.

Lieutenant, R. H. A.
R. O. 3rd Cavalry Divisional Artillery.

SB/42.

3rd Cavalry Division 1 Artillery.

INTELLIGENCE SUMMARY. 6.0 p.m. 29th to 6.0 p.m. 30th.

1. OUR FIRE.

TIME	PLACE SHELLED	NATURE OF SHELL	DIRECTION	NUMBER OF ROUNDS	REMARKS
6.5 p.m.	LA TERRIERE	18 pdr.	-	12	Punishment fire.
10.45 pm. to 3.0 a.m.	-	13 pdr. 18 pdr. 4.5 How.	-	1792) 762) 256)	Organised Shoot. Harassing fire for German relief.
6.45 a.m.	HONNECOURT	18 pdr.	-	24	Punishment fire.
6.45 a.m.	Trenches in X.23.d.	18 pdr.	-	12	-do-
7.0 a.m.	CANAL WOOD	4.5 How.	-	12	-do-
1.30 p.m.	New S.O.S. Lines in F.6.a.	13 pdr.	-	9	-
2.0 p.m.	New S.O.S. Lines X.30.a.& c.	"	-	8	-
6.0 p.m.	CANAL WOOD	"	-	36	-

2. HOSTILE FIRE.

3.30 a.m. to 3.45 a.m. Enemy gun and trench mortar barrage on the Sector N. of CANAL WOOD, this was reported to have been an enemy raid.

During this barrage three red lights were sent up.

No hostile shelling on this front.

3. GENERAL.

During last night's shoot an explosion was heard in VENDHUILE.

Visibility poor all day.

R.A. Headquarters.

1st JULY, 1917.

Lieutenant, R. H. A.

R.O. 3rd Cavalry Divisional Artillery.

Instructions regarding War Diaries and Intelligence Summaries are contained in F. S. Regs., Part II. and the Staff Manual respectively. Title pages will be prepared in manuscript.

WAR DIARY
or
INTELLIGENCE SUMMARY. 4th Bde RHA.

(*Erase heading not required.*)

Army Form C. 2118.

Vol 18

Place	Date	Hour	Summary of Events and Information	Remarks and references to Appendices
LANEUVILLE	JULY 1st		British attack North of the Somme commenced. 3rd Cavalry Division concentrated in new billetting area ready to move at ½ an hour's notice. C, G, K Batteries with their respective Brigades.	
–	2nd		Capt E.C. FLEMING joined the Bde and took command of "G" Battery vice Major L.W. Joyce at home sick.	
	3rd		Heavy fighting continuing.	
	4th		The 3rd Cavalry Division received orders to proceed to new billetting area South of ABBEVILLE	
HALLENCOURT			Div. HQ and RHA HQ at HALLENCOURT. "C" at ALLERY 'G' close to PONT REMY 'K' at SOREL	
	5th		At HALLENCOURT	
	6th } 7th }		Orders received to be ready to move at 1½ hours notice	

T2134. Wt. W708—776. 500000. 4/15. Sir J. C. & S.

Instructions regarding War Diaries and Intelligence Summaries are contained in F. S. Regs., Part II. and the Staff Manual respectively. Title pages will be prepared in manuscript.

WAR DIARY
or
INTELLIGENCE SUMMARY.
(Erase heading not required.)

Army Form C. 2118.

Place	Date	Hour	Summary of Events and Information	Remarks and references to Appendices
HALLENCOURT	JULY 8th		3rd Cavalry Division received orders to return to its former billetting area in the valley of the SOMME in and around CORBIE with its HQrs at DAOURS RHA HQ also to DAOURS via AIRAINES SOWES and AMIENS	
DAOURS	JULY 9th		C Battery at VAUX sur SOMME, G Battery at BONNAY, K at CORBIE. The Division remained in a state of readiness in this area until the end of the month at first at ½ an hours notice and later at 4 hours notice.	
	JULY 14th		After an infantry attack by XIII + XV Corps 2 squadrons from regiments of the 2nd INDIAN CAV DIV. were ordered forward and for a few hours operated as Cavalry; the situation did not develop sufficiently in our favour and the 3rd Cavalry Div. never moved from its billets	
	JULY 15th to 31st		HQ R.H.A. and the three Batteries remained in same billets	

R. W. Leathes [?] Lt. Col.
Comdg 4th Bde R.H.A.

T2134. Wt. W708—776. 500000. 4/15. Sir J. C. & S.

Instructions regarding War Diaries and Intelligence Summaries are contained in F. S. Regs., Part II. and the Staff Manual respectively. Title pages will be prepared in manuscript.

WAR DIARY
or
INTELLIGENCE SUMMARY.
(Erase heading not required.)

Vol 19

Army Form C. 2118.

HQ 4th Bde R.H.A.

Place	Date	Hour	Summary of Events and Information	Remarks and references to Appendices
DAOURS	Aug 1st		3rd Cavalry Division marched back to area around LE QUESNOY west of AMIENS	
LE QUESNOY			HQ RHA. to LE QUESNOY also Ammunition Column. Batteries with their Bdes.	
	Aug 2nd		Marched to GAPENNES at 7am. via LONGPRÉ, VAUCHELLES les DOMART, GORENFLOS	
GAPENNES			ONEUX	
	Aug 3rd		Billetted in Chateau at GAPENNES	
LIGESCOURT	Aug 4th		Received orders to march to LIGESCOURT. Marched at 9am. via NOYELLES en CHAUSSÉE thence along Roman road to WADICOURT. Got into billets at LIGESCOURT at 12.30pm.	
	Aug 5th		Marched back to old billets at CRÉQUY via DOMPIERRE, GUIGNY HESDIN + FRESSIN started at 9am. arrived at 3.30 pm.	
			During all marching Batteries were with their Bdes.	
CRÉQUY	Aug 6th to 31st		Ammunition Col. returned to its old billets in COUPELLE-VIEILLE	
			Remained in billets at CRÉQUY	
			"C" Battery at WAMBERCOURT, G at GRIGNY near HESDIN, K at RENTY	
	Aug 24th		Lt Col A.R. WAINEWRIGHT R.H.A. arrived to command R.H.A. 3rd Cavalry Div. vice Lt Col P. WHEATLEY promoted Brigadier General and posted to 17th Division.	

A R Wainewright Lt Col.
Cmdg 4th Bde R.H.A.

T2134. Wt. W708—776. 500000. 4/15. Sir J. C. & S.

Instructions regarding War Diaries and Intelligence Summaries are contained in F. S. Regs., Part II. and the Staff Manual respectively. Title pages will be prepared in manuscript.

WAR DIARY
or
INTELLIGENCE SUMMARY.
(Erase heading not required.)

Army Form C. 2118.

Vol 20

HQ 4th Bde R.H.A.

Place	Date	Hour	Summary of Events and Information	Remarks and references to Appendices
CRÉQUY	Sept 1st–9th		Resting in billets at CRÉQUY	
	10th		Marched from CRÉQUY at 8 am. Went into billets for the night at DOMPIERRE on the	
DOMPIERRE			AUTHIE River. Amm. Col. ditto.	
	11th		Marched to CONTÉVILLE via LE BOISLE GUESCHART + MAISON PONTHIEU started 10.30 am arr. 4.15	
CONTÉVILLE			got into billets for night	
	12th		Received orders overnight to march to BELLOY-s-SOMME. Started 11am arrived 4 pm.	
BELLOY	13th		Remained in billets at BELLOY. Lt H.A. BAKER joined from 9th Division on 14th inst.	
DAOURS	14th		Marched to DAOURS via St SAUVEUR ARGOEUVRES AMIENS citadelle CAMON	
	15th		Received orders to move forward at 10am. and remain ready at half an hours	
LANEUVILLE			notice off saddled near the road from DAOURS to LANEUVILLE. Remained there all	
			day. At 6.30 received orders to bivouac in the same place for the night	
	16th		Still bivouacked near LANEUVILLE at ½ an hours notice, remained there all day.	
			At 1 am. received orders to march back to DAOURS at 8 am. next day.	
DAOURS	17th		Returned to DAOURS and bivouacked.	
	17th–21st		Remained at DAOURS	
CROUY	22nd		Marched back to CROUY s SOMME where we billeted for the night.	

T2134. Wt. W708—776. 500000. 4/15. Sir J. C. & S.

Instructions regarding War Diaries and Intelligence Summaries are contained in F. S. Regs., Part II. and the Staff Manual respectively. Title pages will be prepared in manuscript.

WAR DIARY
or
INTELLIGENCE SUMMARY.
(Erase heading not required.)

HQ 4th Bde R.H.A.

Army Form C. 2118.

Place	Date	Hour	Summary of Events and Information	Remarks and references to Appendices
FROHEN le GRAND	23rd		Marched next day at 10.30 am to FROHEN le GRAND on the AUTHIE stayed there for the night in billets. Received orders at 11 pm. to move at 7 am. and	
"	24th		march to MOURIEZ west of the main HESDIN - ABBEVILLE road.	
"	25th } 30 }		Remained in billets at MOURIEZ. Ammunition Column at SAULCHOY.	

6/10/16.

A. Wainwright Lt Col
4 Brigade R.H.A.

T2134. Wt. W708—776. 500000. 4/15. Sir J. C. & S.

Instructions regarding War Diaries and Intelligence Summaries are contained in F. S. Regs., Part II. and the Staff Manual respectively. Title pages will be prepared in manuscript.

WAR DIARY
or
INTELLIGENCE SUMMARY.
(Erase heading not required.)

Army Form C. 2118.

4th Bde RHA. 3rd Cav: Divn:

Vol 21

Place	Date	Hour	Summary of Events and Information	Remarks and references to Appendices
MOURIEZ	Oct 1st to 18th		In billets at MOURIEZ. Ammunition Column at SAULCHOY	
BOIS JEAN	19th		HQ R.H.A. moved back to BOIS JEAN, Hdqrs 3 Cav. Div having moved to WAILLY	
	20th		Received orders at 2·30 a.m. for Hdqrs, Batteries and Ammunition Column less SAA section to march early next morning. SAA Section of Column remained at SAULCHOY under 2nd Lt D.R. LAMBERT	
	21st		Brigade marched to LE PONCHEL area on the AUTHIE river	
LE PONCHEL + WILLENCOURT			Batteries moved independently and went into billets for the night, C and K at LE PONCHEL HQrs and G Batty at WILLENCOURT, Ammunition Column at VITZ. Came under the orders of 1st Cavalry Division on reaching billets.	
	22nd		Brigade ordered to march to St OUEN remaining there for the night	
	23rd		marching next day to wagon lines close to and just SW of ENGLEBELMER	
	24th		to join V Corps and went into action at AVELUY wood under orders of 63 Division in the early morning, being temporarily attached to the 18th Division for shooting.	
	25th to 29th		Spent in improving positions and registration. Weather very wet and light poor except on rare occasions. Batteries registered trenches in the	

T2134. Wt. W708—776. 500000. 4/15. Sir J. C. & S.

Instructions regarding War Diaries and Intelligence Summaries are contained in F. S. Regs., Part II. and the Staff Manual respectively. Title pages will be prepared in manuscript.

WAR DIARY
or
INTELLIGENCE SUMMARY.
(*Erase heading not required.*)

Army Form C. 2118.

Place	Date	Hour	Summary of Events and Information	Remarks and references to Appendices
MESNIL	29th		neighbourhood of St PIERRE DIVION and along the River Road	
	30th		Fine day and very good light. Batteries continued their registration. Between 12.30 and 2 pm. 'C' Battery gun position and ground around HQ dugouts shelled by 5.9" inch about 50 shell, no damage done and a high proportion of the shell detonated badly. This was repeated about midnight the Germans keeping up a slow rate of fire for about an hour and a half.	
	31st		Quiet day very little shelling by the enemy. Usual intermittent bombardment ~~[illegible]~~ carried on by us.	
			[signature] Lt Col R.H.A. Commanding IVth Bde R.H.A.	

T2134. Wt. W708—776. 500000. 4/15. Sir J. C. & S.

Instructions regarding War Diaries and Intelligence Summaries are contained in F. S. Regs., Part II. and the Staff Manual respectively. Title pages will be prepared in manuscript.

WAR DIARY
or
INTELLIGENCE SUMMARY.
(Erase heading not required.)

Army Form C. 2118.

HQ 4th Bde RHA.

Vol 22

Place	Date	Hour	Summary of Events and Information	Remarks and references to Appendices
MESNIL	Nov 1st		Quiet day	
	" 2nd 3rd		Nothing of importance to report. Weather still wet and very windy	
	4th		Orders received that Z. day had been indefinitely postponed.	
	5th		Very high South West wind. Usual intermittent bombardment by our artillery	
	6th, 7 8th		Three very wet days	
	9th		Fine day for first time for several days. Batteries continued their registration. Great aeroplane activity. Several German aeroplanes over and our Anti Air Craft Guns having plenty of practise	
	10th		Fine and very clear day again very marked aeroplane activity on both sides	
	11th 12th		Fine weather continues country drying up very fast.	
	13th		At 5.45 am our infantry attacked on both sides of the Ancre. C G and K. Batteries assisted in covering the advance of the 39th Division Infantry firing on barrage lines under orders of 18th Divisional Artillery on right bank until Zero + 1 hour when the 4th Bde. RHA came under orders of 63rd Divisional Artillery ~~for~~ ~~purposes~~ ~~of~~ in case of an advance. At 6.45 am. all three Batteries pulled	

T2134. Wt. W708—776. 500000. 4/15. Sir J. C. & S.

Instructions regarding War Diaries and Intelligence Summaries are contained in F. S. Regs., Part II. and the Staff Manual respectively. Title pages will be prepared in manuscript.

WAR DIARY
or
INTELLIGENCE SUMMARY.
(Erase heading not required.)

HQ 4th Bde R.H.A.

Army Form C. 2118.

Place	Date	Hour	Summary of Events and Information	Remarks and references to Appendices
MESNIL	13th	7.am	out of their gunpits and limbered up going to places of assembly in AVELUY WOOD	
		9.45am.	Received orders to move forward and if possible to get into action with one Battery in a position near our old front line by HAMEL. K Battery ordered to	
		10.20am	move and came into action close behind HAMEL at 10.20 am. with 4 guns	
		12.30	G Battery ordered to move forward and take up a position alongside K Battery. This order was cancelled a few minutes later and C and G Batteries ordered to go into position at their old gun positions and be ready to fire a protective barrage along the line of the BEAUCOURT Road to BEAUCOURT sur ANCRE from BEAUMONT HAMEL. Reports from the Infantry very conflicting. It seemed probable that the right Brigade of 63rd Division had got their objective and were on the YELLOW Line in front of BEAUCOURT. This proved to be correct. The attack on the left had not been so successful and it was doubtful if the GREEN line had been taken, there were still small bodies of germans holding out in their own old front line trenches and in shell holes behind. On the right of the River ANCRE we had captured and held the HANSA LINE with very slight losses.	

T2134. Wt. W708—776. 500000. 4/15. Sir J. C. & S.

Instructions regarding War Diaries and Intelligence Summaries are contained in F. S. Regs., Part II. and the Staff Manual respectively. Title pages will be prepared in manuscript.

WAR DIARY
or
INTELLIGENCE SUMMARY.
(Erase heading not required.)

H.Q. 4th Bde R.H.A.

Army Form C. 2118.

Place	Date	Hour	Summary of Events and Information	Remarks and references to Appendices
MESNIL	14th		K. Battery remained in action in the same place and registered the PUISIEUX Trench and BOIS d'HOLLANDE. At about 1am 1 man killed 2 wounded of G. Battery at gun position	
		3.15pm	Received orders to reconnoitre about Q.12 for a more forward Battery position this was done and it was found to be impossible to get guns past No-Mans Land owing to state of the ground from shell fire	
		6pm	Received news that Capt E.C. FLEMING commanding G Battery and three men had been wounded and 1 man killed by three shells at their Battery position.	
	15th	12 noon	Received orders to move C Battery into action alongside K Battery. At the same time the two remaining guns of "K" joined the Battery in action. At dusk G Battery moved forward a section into action in front of HAMEL and just behind our old front line trench.	
	16th		C Battery registered on PUISIEUX TRENCH and points behind. Remainder of G. Battery went into action in the forward position at dark	
	17th		All three Batteries continued registering from their forward positions points about BOIS de HOLLANDE, RIVER TRENCH, ARTILLERY ALLEY and the PUISIEUX ROAD ~~...~~ 1000 to 1500 yards North of BEAUCOURT sur ANCRE.	

Instructions regarding War Diaries and Intelligence Summaries are contained in F. S. Regs., Part II. and the Staff Manual respectively. Title pages will be prepared in manuscript.

WAR DIARY
or
INTELLIGENCE SUMMARY.
(Erase heading not required.)

HQ 4th Bde RHA.

Army Form C. 2118.

Place	Date	Hour	Summary of Events and Information	Remarks and references to Appendices
MESNIL	17th		West end of MESNIL and vicinity of our HQ dugouts repeatedly crumped during the evening.	
	18th	6.10am	Attack by the II and V Corps on both sides of River ANCRE at 6.10 am.	
		11am	C & K Batteries ordered to form Barrage for an attack on the PUISIEUX Trench. News very conflicting after this, apparently we held part of the trench with a few men, and our barrage was ordered to be well over this trench. It was reported that attack on South of the river had been successful and that we were in the outskirts of GRANDCOURT. C & K Batteries continued a slow rate of fire until ~~the of~~ evening at the rate of about 6 salvoes per hour.	
	19th	2.56	Attack organised to take place at 2.56 objectives being MUCK TRENCH & LEAVE AVENUE. All 3 Batteries ordered to form a Barrage for this attack commencing at the rate of 2 rounds per gun per minute for the first 20 minutes continuing afterwards at 1 round per gun per minute until further orders. At 4.30 Batteries ordered to go to a slower rate of fire and later to fire salvoes on all approaches	

T2134. Wt. W708—776. 500000. 4/15. Sir J. C. & S.

WAR DIARY
or
INTELLIGENCE SUMMARY. HQ 4th Bde R.H.A.
(Erase heading not required.)

Army Form C. 2118.

Instructions regarding War Diaries and Intelligence Summaries are contained in F. S. Regs., Part II. and the Staff Manual respectively. Title pages will be prepared in manuscript.

Place	Date	Hour	Summary of Events and Information	Remarks and references to Appendices
MESNIL	19th		at approximately 6 to 8 salvos per hour. This was continued throughout the night until 8am. next morning.	
	20th		At 10.30 received orders to withdraw all Batteries from the line this evening and return to bivouacs for the night. "C Battery withdrew at 5 pm. "K" at 5.30 pm and G Battery at 6 pm. A large quantity of ammunition had to be withdrawn and dumped at the wagon lines. This necessitated considerable work on the part of the Ammunition Column and the Battery horses.	
	21st		The Brigade marched to MARIEUX and billeted there for the night via ACHEUX and LOUVENCOURT	
	22nd		Continued the march to BERTEAUCOURT and billeted there via BEAUQUESNE CANAPLES and HALLOY les PERNOIS. Column stayed at PERNOIS	
	23rd		Marched at 9.30 to St RIQUIER, Column to ONEUX, via DOMART and GORENFLOS.	
	24th		Batteries Ammunition Column and HQ RHA. marched independently back to their respective winter billeting villages. HQ to BOISJEAN	

T2134. Wt. W708—776. 500000. 4/15. Sir J. C. & S.

Instructions regarding War Diaries and Intelligence Summaries are contained in F. S. Regs., Part II. and the Staff Manual respectively. Title pages will be prepared in manuscript.

WAR DIARY
or
INTELLIGENCE SUMMARY.
(Erase heading not required.)

Army Form C. 2118.

4th Brigade R.H.A.

Vol 23

Place	Date	Hour	Summary of Events and Information	Remarks and references to Appendices
BOIS JEAN.	Dec	1st–19th	Still in winter billets with 3rd Cavalry Division.	
		19th	Major K.G. Young D.S.O. to 4th Brigade R.H.A from Guards Divisional artillery, and assumed command of "G" Battery.	
		15th	One section of Divisional ammunition Column marched to EMBRY to join "K" Battery.	
		16th	"K" Battery with section A.C. marched to VERCHIN.	
		"	"C" Battery marched to RENTY from ROUSSENT	
		17th	"K" Battery continued the march to VALHUON via MONCHY-CAYEUX and the next day on to AUBIGNY for temporary attachment to the 3rd Canadian Division in the line. Wagon lines at MAROEUIL.	
		17th	"C" Battery continued march to AIRE coming under orders of the 1st Army on that date as depot Battery at the 1st Army Artillery School.	
		23rd	"G" Battery marched from LESPINOY and took over "C" Battery's billets at ROUSSENT.	
			Following Remounts joined during December.	

T2134. Wt. W708—776. 500000. 4/15. Sir J. C. & S.

Instructions regarding War Diaries and Intelligence Summaries are contained in F. S. Regs., Part II. and the Staff Manual respectively. Title pages will be prepared in manuscript.

WAR DIARY
or
INTELLIGENCE SUMMARY.
(Erase heading not required.)

HQ 4th Bde R.H.A.

Army Form C. 2118.

Place	Date	Hour	Summary of Events and Information	Remarks and references to Appendices
BOIS JEAN	24th		C Battery to ROUSSENT. "G" to LESPINOY "K" to EMBRY Ammunition Column to BUIRE le SEC.	
	25th to 30th		In similar billets with 3rd Cavalry Division	
			[illegible] 2nd Lt Adjt for O.C. 4th Bde R.H.A.	

T2134. Wt. W708—776. 500000. 4/15. Sir J. C. & S.

Vol 24

HEADQUARTERS

3rd CAVALRY DIVISION.

Herewith War Diary of 4th Brigade, R.H.A. for January, 1917, with the exception of "G" Battery, R.H.A. which has been sent direct to A.G's Office, Base.

H.R. Bennett
for 2/Lt RHA + aAdj

9-2-1917.

Lieutenant Colonel, R.H.A.
Commanding 4th Brigade, R. H. A.

Army Form C. 2118.

WAR DIARY
or
~~INTELLIGENCE SUMMARY.~~
(Erase heading not required.)

Instructions regarding War Diaries and Intelligence Summaries are contained in F. S. Regs., Part II. and the Staff Manual respectively. Title pages will be prepared in manuscript.

JANUARY 1917

Place	Date	Hour	Summary of Events and Information	Remarks and references to Appendices
January	1st	31st	Brigade Staff & 'G' Battery in rest billets at BOIS JEAN and ROUSSENT respectively – 'C' Battery at the R.A School of Instruction 1st Army AIRE and 'K' Battery in the line at NEUVILLE-ST-VAST with wagon lines at MAROEUIL attached to 2nd Canadian Division.	
"	7th		Lieut J.M. HILLYARD rejoined from leave and joined 'K' Battery in the line for instruction	
			'K' Battery changed the Battery position to GRENAY with wagon lines at BOYEFFLES	
"	8th		2Lieut G.N. GASKELL left the Brigade and was posted to 130th Heavy Battery IXth Corps, reporting to H.Q. at BAILLEUL.	
"	15th		Captain R.F.T. FOLJAMBE left the Brigade to take over command of 135th Field Battery 4th Division.	
			Gunner Greenwood joined the Brigade Staff from 'C' Battery as a signaller vide Gunner Best to 'C' Battery.	
"	22nd		'K' Battery transferred from 2nd to 1st Canadian Division but the battery position remained the same.	

2353 Wt. W2544/1454 700,000 5/15 D. D. & L. A.D.S.S./Forms/C. 2118.

Instructions regarding War Diaries and Intelligence Summaries are contained in F. S. Regs., Part II. and the Staff Manual respectively. Title pages will be prepared in manuscript.

Army Form C. 2118.

WAR DIARY
or
~~INTELLIGENCE SUMMARY.~~

(Erase heading not required.)

JANUARY 1918

Place	Date	Hour	Summary of Events and Information	Remarks and references to Appendices
January	26th		Lieut H.E. CHAPMAN 'C' Battery RHA attached to 'G' Battery as acting captain pending letter of promotion.	
–	28th		2/Lieut L.R. GALSWORTHY left the Brigade and was posted to the 17th Divisional ~~Art~~ Artillery reporting at MORLANCOURT [3 miles S of ALBERT]	
– 28th –	30th		'G' Battery relieved 'K' Battery in the line on January 30th. 'G' Battery marched from ROUSSENT on 28th inst billeting the night of 28th/29th at HERNICOURT N.N.W of ST POL – the march was continued on the 29th inst to BARLIN SW of NOEUX-LES-MINES where billets were alloted by 1st Canadian Division. The relief was conducted under arrangements by 1st Canadian Division. On January 30th 'K' Battery having been relieved marched to billets at BARLIN. On	
–	31st		the 31st instant the march was continued to HERNICOURT.	
			<u>Reinforcements received</u>.	
–	11th		4 Other Ranks	
–	18th		2 - Other Ranks – 1 Light Draft.	
–	26th		7 - Other Ranks	

2353 Wt. W2544/1454 700,000 5/15 D. D. & L. A.D.S.S./Forms/C. 2118.

Instructions regarding War Diaries and Intelligence Summaries are contained in F. S. Regs., Part II. and the Staff Manual respectively. Title pages will be prepared in manuscript.

WAR DIARY
or
INTELLIGENCE SUMMARY.

(Erase heading not required.)

Army Form C. 2118.

JANUARY 1917

Place	Date	Hour	Summary of Events and Information	Remarks and references to Appendices
			During the month the weather was abnormally cold with heavy fall of snow – 'K' Battery making a toboggan run and holding sports.	
			A.D. Manning Lt Col	

2353 Wt. W2544/1454 700,000 5/15 D. D. & L. A.D.S.S./Forms/C. 2118.

Instructions regarding War Diaries and Intelligence Summaries are contained in F. S. Regs., Part II. and the Staff Manual respectively. Title pages will be prepared in manuscript.

WAR DIARY
or
~~INTELLIGENCE SUMMARY.~~
(Erase heading not required.)

Army Form C. 2118.

4th Brigade R.H.A.
February 1917

Vol 25

Place	Date	Hour	Summary of Events and Information	Remarks and references to Appendices
	Feb			
VERCHOCQ	1st		Bde Hqrs moved to Chateau VERCHOCQ, "K" Battery moved to RENTY	
			"C" Battery acting as depot Battery at 1st Army Artillery School AIRE	
			"G" Battery acting as sniping Battery to 1st Army.	
	3rd		Lt H.G Morrison posted to "C" Battery vice Chapman promoted temporary Captain and posted to "G" Battery	
	6th		2/Lt M.E.S Thompson rejoined "K" Battery from R.H.A school	
			Lt DASHWOOD joined "K" Battery on posting to R.H.A from A/301 How. Battery	
	7th		2/Lt M.E.S. Thompson posted to 4th Bde R.H.A. Amtn Column	
	8th		Lt R Patrick R.F.A. posted to "C" Battery ~~vice Chapman~~ from "G" Battery vice Boylan	
	9th		2/Lt T. Stevens was posted to "C" Battery joining from sick leave from England.	
	16th		Brig. Genl Portal comdg 7th Cav. Bde inspected "K" Battery	
	17th		Lieut E.T. Boylan left "C" Battery R.H.A. and took over duties of Adjutant to 4th Bde R.H.A	
	23rd		Lieuts Morrison and Dashwood went to R.H.A. School Cav Corps.	
	27th		D.D.R. Cav. Corps (Col ~~[illegible]~~ HARDY). inspected horses for casting in "K" Battery and Amtn. Column and cast 50 horses in Amtn Column	

2353 Wt. W2544/1454 700,000 5/15 D. D. & L. A.D.S.S./Forms/C. 2118.

Army Form C. 2118.

Instructions regarding War Diaries and Intelligence Summaries are contained in F. S. Regs., Part II. and the Staff Manual respectively. Title pages will be prepared in manuscript.

WAR DIARY
or
~~INTELLIGENCE~~ ~~SUMMARY.~~
(Erase heading not required.)

Place	Date	Hour	Summary of Events and Information	Remarks and references to Appendices
	FEB			
VERCHOCQ			Reinforcements received	
	10th		"K" Bty RHA 2 chargers	
			Extract fr London Gazette 22.1.17	
			No 56796. Cpl. Lascel F. } Awarded Military Medal for Bravery in the Field. { Both men belong to "C" Battery R.H.A.	
			No 12504 Gr Mahody W }	
			Throughout the month the weather was very cold with hard frosts and some snow outdoor work was made almost impossible owing to this.	
			10/3/17 [illegible] Lt. RHA.	

2353 Wt. W2544/1454 700,000 5/15 D. D. & L. A.D.S.S./Forms/C. 2118.

Instructions regarding War Diaries and Intelligence Summaries are contained in F. S. Regs., Part II. and the Staff Manual respectively. Title pages will be prepared in manuscript.

WAR DIARY
or
~~INTELLIGENCE SUMMARY.~~
(Erase heading not required.)

4th Bde R.H.A.
MARCH 1917.
Vol 26

Army Form C. 2118.

Place	Date	Hour	Summary of Events and Information	Remarks and references to Appendices
VERCHOCQ	MAR. 1st	–	Headquarters at rest Billet VERCHOCQ C Battery at AIRE, G Battery with 1st Army	
			K Battery at RENTY Ammunition Column at RUMILLY.	
	2nd		'G' Battery returned to rest Billet at EMBRY.	
			'C' Battery returned to rest Billet at LESPINOY.	
	12th		Practice in taking ZONE Calls, with aeroplane of 35th Squadron R.F.C. and three Batteries at EMBRY. Successful practice.	
	14th		Inspection of horses and gunparks of Hqrs. RHA C, G, and K Batteries RHA and Ammunition Column in their own billets by Brig. Genl. J. Seligman D.S.O. G.O.C. R.H.A Cavalry Corps.	
MERLIMONT	20th		Hqrs R.H.A moved to MERLIMONT to prepare ranges for practice of three batteries. 3000 rounds being allowed to R.H.A of Cavalry Corps for Practice Purposes.	
	21st – 22nd		Two ranges marked out one north of the MERLIMONT-MERLIMONT PLAGE road the other south of this road and north of BERCK.	
			Targets represented by calico screens on the sea range of sand hills.	
	23rd.		'C' Battery R.H.A arrived MERLIMONT with firing Battery only.	

2353 Wt. W2544/1454 700,000 5/15 D. D. & L. A.D.S.S./Forms/C. 2118.

Instructions regarding War Diaries and Intelligence Summaries are contained in F. S. Regs., Part II. and the Staff Manual respectively. Title pages will be prepared in manuscript.

WAR DIARY
or
~~INTELLIGENCE SUMMARY~~.
(Erase heading not required.)

Army Form C. 2118. 2

Place	Date	Hour	Summary of Events and Information	Remarks and references to Appendices
	MAR			
MERLIMONT	24th		"C" Battery R.H.A fired on the range from 10 am to 12 midday. firing 140 rounds shrapnel at ranges about 2700 to 3200 yards.	
	25th		"C" Battery R.H.A fired experimental series with HE filled with T+P fuze Shells burst in air successfully.	
	26th		C Battery returned to LESPINOY, "K" Battery R.H.A arrived MERLIMONT	
	27th		"K" Battery R.H.A fired in afternoon. 131 Shrapnel 39 HE with 100 fuze.	
	29th		"K" Battery R.H.A returned to RENTY "G" Battery R.H.A arrived MERLIMONT	
	30th 31st		G Battery R.H.A fired 303 Sh. 101 H.E.	
	31st		Limbered G.S. wagon complete with 4 horses joined H.Q. R.H.A to carry wireless set + operators.	
	22nd		2/Lt. M.H. Cooper R.H.A joined from Base posted to Amtn Column.	
	26th		Capt. C. Milner C.F. joined Amtn Column.	
			Reinforcements Received by Amtn Col.	
	[illegible]		Personnel. 20 on 12th 18 on 22nd Horses. Nil.	
			A D Wainwright [illegible]	

2353 Wt. W2544/1454 700,000 5/15 D. D. & L. A.D.S.S./Forms/C. 2118.

I

Army Form C. 2118.

Instructions regarding War Diaries and Intelligence Summaries are contained in F. S. Regs., Part II. and the Staff Manual respectively. Title pages will be prepared in manuscript.

WAR DIARY
or
~~INTELLIGENCE SUMMARY.~~
(Erase heading not required.)

APRIL 1917 — IV Brigade R.H.A. 3rd Cav

Vol 27

Place	Date	Hour	Summary of Events and Information	Remarks and references to Appendices
In the Field	APRIL 1st	–	Headquarters R.H.A and G Battery R.H.A. marched from MERLIMONT to VERCHOCQ and EMBRY respectively on conclusion of Practice.	
			C Battery R.H.A at LESPINOY and K Battery at RENTY in Rest Billets	
			Ammunition Column at RUMILLY.	
	2nd		Orders were received from 3rd Cav. Div. to evacuate stores and form dump as division was about to move from its winter area.	
			Heavy Snow fall	
	5th		3rd Cavalry Division moved from its winter area to take part in Offensive operations of 3rd Army East of ARRAS.	
			Headquarters R.H.A., K Battery and Ammunition Column marched from VERCHOCQ 8.30am	
			A deep snow drift was met with which necessitated reversing and taking another road	
			K Battery fell out of Column at OFFIN where they came under orders of 7th Cav Bde	
			Headquarters R.H.A. to MARESQUEL. Amm Column to BEAURAIN CHATEAU	
			C Battery from LESPINOY to CONTES. G Battery from EMBRY to BOUBERS. under their own Cavalry Brigades.	

2353 Wt. W2544/1454 700,000 5/15 D. D. & L. A.D.S.S./Forms/C. 2118.

Instructions regarding War Diaries and Intelligence Summaries are contained in F. S. Regs., Part II. and the Staff Manual respectively. Title pages will be prepared in manuscript.

APRIL 1917.

WAR DIARY or ~~INTELLIGENCE SUMMARY~~.

(*Erase heading not required.*)

IV Brigade R H A.

Army Form C. 2118.

II

Place	Date	Hour	Summary of Events and Information	Remarks and references to Appendices
	6th		Division did not move	
	7th		3rd Cav. Divn marched to FREVENT area Hqrs R.H.A and Amtn Column marched with divisional troops and were billetted at CONCHY sur CANCHE The three batteries marched under orders of their Cavalry Brigades	
	8th		3rd Cav. Divn moved up to its forward Area of Concentration at GOUY-en-ARTOIS Billets bad & very concentrated	
	9th		The day on which 3rd Army commenced their offensive, a wet day with high wind and frequent snow showers.	
		AM 10.30.	Division moved out of GOUY, 8th Bde leading at 10.30am Batteries with their Cav Bdes in following order: G with 8th the leading Brigade "C" following with 6th Bde Hqrs R.H.A. with Divisional Troops, K Battery with 7th Bde S.A.A. carts of Divl Amtn Column in rear of A1 Echelon, Heavy Section Amtn Column left at GOUY under orders of Cavalry Corps. C.R.H.A. (Lt. Col. Wainwright) and Adjutant (Lt. Baylay) were with G.O.C 8th Cav Bde. Amtn Dump had been formed by Cav Corps in ARRAS.	
		P.M. 1.30	Head of 8th Bde and Divisional Report Centre halted on ST POL - ARRAS road about 1 1/2 miles from western outskirts of ARRAS.	

2353 Wt. W2544/1454 700,000 5/15 D. D. & L. A.D.S.S./Forms/C. 2118.

Instructions regarding War Diaries and Intelligence Summaries are contained in F. S. Regs., Part II. and the Staff Manual respectively. Title pages will be prepared in manuscript.

APRIL 1917

WAR DIARY
or
~~INTELLIGENCE SUMMARY~~.
(Erase heading not required.)

IV Brigade R.H.A. Army Form C. 2118. III

Place	Date	Hour	Summary of Events and Information	Remarks and references to Appendices
	9th	P.M. 2.45	Orders received that Division would move forward along Cavalry Track to point H.31b. (ref 1/40000 51B)	
		4. PM.	Head of 8th Bde reached this point about 4 pm and halted, remainder of division in column of route along Cavalry Track, through streets of ARRAS and along ARRAS–ST POL road. Enemy could be seen moving in and out of trenches in H34 and N4 (ref 1/40000 51B).	
		PM 5.30	G Battery moved into action about 300x N of TILLOY LEZ MAFFLAINES in H31 ref (1/40,000 51B) to shell enemy ~~[illegible]~~ mentioned above at request of Brig. Genl. BERKELEY-VINCENT who commanded attacking Infantry Brigade. About 80 rounds fired apparently with good effect.	
		PM 6.30	About 6.30 PM orders received for Division to bivouac on Cavalry Track.	
		PM 11.30	All division less H.Qrs moved west of ARRAS. Hqrs R.H.A remained with Divnl Hqrs in ARRAS. G Battery reached former point of concentration on ARRAS–ST POL road about 5.0 AM on 10th.	
	10th	10. AM	Orders received that Division would move forward again to H.31b. C.R.H.A reconnoitred main ARRAS–CAMBRAI road to H32d with a view to its use by R.H.A Batteries, Cavalry track being ~~[illegible]~~ very heavy going.	

2353 Wt. W2544/1454 700,000 5/15 D. D. & L. A.D.S.S./Forms/C. 2118.

APRIL 1917.

WAR DIARY
or
~~INTELLIGENCE SUMMARY.~~
(Erase heading not required.)

IV Bde RHA

Army Form C. 2118.

IV

Instructions regarding War Diaries and Intelligence Summaries are contained in F. S. Regs., Part II. and the Staff Manual respectively. Title pages will be prepared in manuscript.

Place	Date	Hour	Summary of Events and Information	Remarks and references to Appendices
	10th	1.30PM	8th and 6th Cavalry Brigades ~~was~~ accompanied by G and C Batteries R.H.A. moved forward to line H28 - H34 (Ref 1/40000 51B).	
		2.30PM	G. Battery went into action about H34D with orders to shell MONCHY-LE-PREUX owing to reports that this village was in our hands fire was not opened on it.	
			G Battery fired with good effect on enemy moving near BOIS DU SART and on BOIRY-NOTRE-DAME - PELVES road.	
		6 PM.	Advanced Squadron 10th Hussars tried to gallop PELVES ridge about 6pm but were met by heavy machine gun fire. G Battery received no orders to open covering fire to support this attack.	
		4PM.	C Battery went into action about ~~4~~ 5 PM at H34C but did not fire.	
			K Battery in reserve ~~[illegible]~~ with 7th Cav Bde about H31B.	
			Hqrs R.H.A with Divnl Hqrs at H31B.	
		7.30PM	8th and 6th Cav Brigades withdrawn west of Brown Line H34 - H28 & bivouaced west of FEUCHY CHAPEL road.	
			Casualties G Battery 1 O.R. wounded	
			Weather very cold with frequent snow storms.	

2353 Wt. W2544/1454 700,000 5/15 D. D. & L. A.D.S.S./Forms/C. 2118.

Army Form C. 2118.

V

Instructions regarding War Diaries and Intelligence Summaries are contained in F. S. Regs., Part II. and the Staff Manual respectively. Title pages will be prepared in manuscript.

WAR DIARY
or
~~INTELLIGENCE SUMMARY.~~
(Erase heading not required.)

APRIL 1917.

IV Bde R.H.A.

Place	Date	Hour	Summary of Events and Information	Remarks and references to Appendices
	11th	5.30AM	Orders to "stand to". R.H.A were disposed as follows. Hqrs RHA at point H 31 b with Divisional Headquarters. C Battery about H 34 with 6th Cav Bde. G Battery about H 27 c with 8th Cav Bde. K Battery about G 36 with 7th Cav Bde.	
		8.30am	About 8.30am Advanced Squadrons of 8th Cav Bde moved forward to ORANGE HILL. News received that MONCHY LE PREUX had fallen.	
			8th Bde moved forward with a view to occupying N & S line through LONE COPSE. G Battery ordered into a position of readiness under cover of MONCHY.	
			And advanced by sections across open between ORANGE HILL and MONCHY as shelling was heavy.	
		10.30am	O.C. G Battery received message from F.O.O. 3/4 Bond that Cavalry were held up on East edge of MONCHY by M.G. fire.	
			Under orders from O.C. 8th Cav Bde (Lt Col Tweedmouth). G Battery retired behind ORANGE HILL less 1 gun whose team had been knocked out by shell fire.	
			While this was in progress. 6th Cav Bde to the south had captured the Sun Pan	
		11 AM	road LA BERGERE – MONCHY and 2 sections of C Battery moved into action at N 6 c 5.1.	

2353 Wt. W2544/1454 700,000 5/15 D. D. & L. A.D.S.S./Forms/C. 2118.

Instructions regarding War Diaries and Intelligence Summaries are contained in F. S. Regs., Part II. and the Staff Manual respectively. Title pages will be prepared in manuscript.

APRIL. 1917.

WAR DIARY
or
~~INTELLIGENCE SUMMARY.~~
(Erase heading not required.)

IV Bde R.H.A.

Army Form C. 2118.

VI.

Place	Date	Hour	Summary of Events and Information	Remarks and references to Appendices
	11TH		The line on their front ran roughly as follows O1d60 - LA BERGERE - N12d - 18a - 17d - 17a - 16d.	
			Fire of the four guns of C Battery was directed by Lieut. PATRICK on Enemy infantry digging in front of BOIS DU SART and BOIS DE VERT. Rounds fired about 60.	
		1.30pm	Orders received from G.O.C. 6th Cav Bde to retire C Battery behind ORANGE HILL. This was done without Casualties though Battery came under fire from machine guns and 5.9" guns.	
			Casualties up to date "C" Battery { O.R. Killed 3, O.R. Wounded 18 } Horses killed or wounded 27.	
		AM. 11.50pm	Orders were received that R.H.A. was to be divisionalized, the task being to prevent Enemy digging in on a line running N and S from W of B du SART to ARRAS - CAMBRAI road.	
			Orders to all B.C's to meet C.R.H.A at pt. 17 in H33d.	
			These orders took some time to reach Brigades; it was not till they got about 1pm that B.C's got their orders.	
			C Battery was to remain in N11b and engage working parties from HILL 100 to ARRAS - CAMBRAI road.	

2353 Wt. W2544/1454 700,000 5/15 D. D. & L. A.D.S.S./Forms/C. 2118.

Instructions regarding War Diaries and Intelligence Summaries are contained in F. S. Regs., Part II. and the Staff Manual respectively. Title pages will be prepared in manuscript.

APRIL. 1917.

WAR DIARY
or
~~INTELLIGENCE SUMMARY.~~
(Erase heading not required.)

IV Bde R.H.A.

Army Form C. 2118.

VII

Place	Date	Hour	Summary of Events and Information	Remarks and references to Appendices
	11th		G and K Batteries to come into action about H 34 d and to engage working parties about B. des AUBEPINES. R.H.A Bde Hqrs to be at N 5 c 1.8. As wires were being laid to Batteries it was discovered that C Battery had been ~~ordered~~ ordered to retire from N 11 b by G.O.C 6th Cav. Bde. O.C. 'C' Battery was then ordered to bring his Battery into action at N 4 d 5.5. which movement was completed about 2 pm.	
		3 pm	G.O.C 3rd Cav Div. met C.R.H.A and gave him verbal orders to establish a protective barrage with all Batteries East of MONCHY as the village was held on Eastern Edge by Cavalry only.	
			Batteries were ordered to barrage on a N+S line through F of FONTAINE LES CHIENS (Ref 1/40,000 51 B) rate of fire Battery fire 20 secs. subsequently reduced to 1 salvo every 5 minutes, and later to 1 salvo every 10 mins. The barrage was established about 3.30 pm and report was sent to Divisional Headquarters to this effect giving also dispositions. While visibility was good K and G Batteries engaged various targets of masses of enemy and transport. About 5 pm a heavy blizzard commenced rendering observation impossible and the barrage was continued from the map.	

2353 Wt. W2544/1454 700,000 5/15 D. D. & L. A.D.S.S./Forms/C. 2118.

Instructions regarding War Diaries and Intelligence Summaries are contained in F. S. Regs., Part II. and the Staff Manual respectively. Title pages will be prepared in manuscript.

APRIL 1917.

WAR DIARY
or
INTELLIGENCE SUMMARY.
(Erase heading not required.)

IV Bde R.H.A.

Army Form C. 2118.

VIII

Place	Date	Hour	Summary of Events and Information	Remarks and references to Appendices
	11TH	7pm	Orders were received that 3rd Cav Div would be relieved by Infantry and were to withdraw as soon as relieved and Bivouac on Race Course W. of ARRAS. IV Bde R.H.A to withdraw at 7pm.	
			The casualties up to date had been.	
			C. Battery Killed 3 O.R. wounded 15 O.R. Horses 27 Killed and wounded	
			G. Battery Killed 3 O.R. wounded {1 officer (Lieut MILNE slightly) {13 O.R. Horses 20	
			K Battery Killed 1 O.R (R.Q.M.S WILLMENT). wounded 6 O R Horses 13	
			Ammn expended C Bty 450 rounds. G Bty 400 " K Bty 500 "	
		7.30pm	Adjutant rode back to RACECOURSE to meet Bivouac for the Batteries withdrew in heavy snow storm about 8 pm. G Battery bringing their gun from MONCHY.	

2353 Wt. W2544/1454 700,000 5/15 D. D. & L. A.D.S.S./Forms/C. 2118.

Instructions regarding War Diaries and Intelligence Summaries are contained in F. S. Regs., Part II. and the Staff Manual respectively. Title pages will be prepared in manuscript.

APRIL 1917

WAR DIARY
or
~~INTELLIGENCE SUMMARY~~.
(Erase heading not required.)

IV Bde R.H.A.

Army Form C. 2118.

IX

Place	Date	Hour	Summary of Events and Information	Remarks and references to Appendices
	11th	8.30pm	C.R.H.A went to Divisional Headquarters. On arrival there orders were received that bivouac area was altered to ground S of ARRAS ST POL road about L 17 D. By this time Batteries were withdrawing very slowly on account of congestion of traffic along CAMBRAI-ARRAS road. C.R.H.A having discovered position of Amm Column and Wagon Echelons instructed Military Police at Cross roads in ARRAS to divert Batteries from RACE COURSE. [illegible] Batteries reached their areas	
	12th	5am	about 5.0 am & bivouaced with their Cavalry Bdes about L 17 D. A very cold night. Men and horses completely done up.	
		8am	C.R.H.A received orders at Divnl Headquarters that Division would move back to GOUY-EN-ARTOIS. Batteries were with their Brigades but some did not receive this order till about noon. C. Battery marched to FOSSEUX, Hqrs R.H.A. G & K Batteries and Amm Column to original billets at GOUY.	
	13th 14th 15th		Remained at GOUY. Remounts joined as under C Battery 5, K Battery 19 very heavy horses, G " 5, Amm Column 18	

2353 Wt. W2544/1454 700,000 5/15 D. D. & L. A.D.S.S./Forms/C. 2118.

Instructions regarding War Diaries and Intelligence Summaries are contained in F. S. Regs., Part II. and the Staff Manual respectively. Title pages will be prepared in manuscript.

APRIL 1917.

WAR DIARY
or
~~INTELLIGENCE SUMMARY.~~
(Erase heading not required.)

IV Bde R.H.A.

Army Form C. 2118.

X

Place	Date	Hour	Summary of Events and Information	Remarks and references to Appendices
	16th		3rd Cav Div moved westwards to area about FROHEN-LE-GRAND Hqrs R.H.A to WAVANS Amtn Column to BEAUVOIR-RIVIERE Batteries with their Cav. Bdes as under ~~[illegible]~~ G Battery to MEZEROLLES, C Battery to BOUFFLERS, K Battery to NOEUX. LT. O.M.C CREAGH from G Battery posted to C/108 Bde RFA.	
	17th 18th		Remained in FROHEN-LE-GRAND area.	
	19th		Division moved into billeting area further west. Hqrs RHA to Farm 1 mile N. of CRECY on ~~[illegible]~~ CRECY-LIEGESCOURT road (Ref ABBEVILLE 1/100,000) C Battery to ROUSSENT, under 6th Cav. Bde. G Battery to LESPINOY. K Battery to MOURIEZ, Amtn Column to VIRONCHAUX.	
	25th		Reinforcements received 42 Drivers 20 Gunners from HAVRE.	
	30th		LIEUT H.P.M. MILNE posted to 4th Division.	
	29th		2Lieut S.P. WHITELEY RHA posted to G Battery from 4th Division	
	30th		CAPT. ADAMSON RAMC joined Hqs R.H.A.	
			No records of messages sent and received during the operations are attached as they all became unreadable owing to the snow and wet.	

A. Manning [?] Lt Col
4 Bde R.H.A.

2353 Wt. W2544/1454 700,000 5/15 D. D. & L. A.D.S.S./Forms/C. 2118.

Instructions regarding War Diaries and Intelligence Summaries are contained in F. S. Regs., Part II. and the Staff Manual respectively. Title pages will be prepared in manuscript.

Army Form C. 2118.

I

WAR DIARY
or
~~INTELLIGENCE SUMMARY.~~
(Erase heading not required.)

MAY 1917 — I Brigade R.H.A.

Vol 28

Place	Date	Hour	Summary of Events and Information	Remarks and references to Appendices
In the Field	1st		3rd Cav. Division in Rest Billets. R.H.A distributed as under. Hqrs R.H.A at farm 1 mile N of CRECY-EN-PONTHIEU on CRECY-LIEGESCOURT road (Ref ABBEVILLE 1/100,000) C. Battery with 6th Cav. Bde at ROUSSENT, G Battery with 8th Cav Bde at MARESQUEL, K Battery with 7th Cav Bde at MOURIEZ Amm Column at VIRONCHAUX.	
			C.R.H.A and Adjt. attended Divisional Staff ride on Intercommunication	
	4th		C RHA and Adjt attended " " " " Administration	
	1st		Capt J.H. DAVYS RAMC left H.Qrs R.H.A. to be attached to Amn Park 3rd Cav Div	
	10th		C.R.H.A. inspected horses sent from Cavalry to complete Batteries. Standard was fair but K.RHA had the worst. Remounts were good standard.	
	11th		C.R.A. went down to see 42nd Division N of St QUENTIN. Cavalry Corps taking over line from III Corps. Artillery Arrangements see Appendix I attached	See Appendix I.
	13th		3rd Cavalry division left its Back Billets to march to St QUENTIN area. H.Q. RHA marched to WAVANS Batteries marched with their Cavalry Brigades	

2353 Wt. W2544/1454 700,000 5/15 D. D. & L. A.D.S.S./Forms/C. 2118.

Instructions regarding War Diaries and Intelligence Summaries are contained in F. S. Regs., Part II. and the Staff Manual respectively. Title pages will be prepared in manuscript.

MAY 1917.

WAR DIARY
or
~~INTELLIGENCE SUMMARY.~~
(Erase heading not required.)

IV Bde R.H.A.

Army Form C. 2118.

Place	Date	Hour	Summary of Events and Information	Remarks and references to Appendices
	MAY			
	14th	–	H.Q. marched with Divisional Troops to TALMAS.	
	15th		H.Q. marched independently to join 3rd Cav. Bde at SUZANNE.	
			Batteries marched with their Cav. Bdes.	
	16th		H.Q. marched to ROISEL thence to 42nd Div Arty H.Q. in quarry at K11b2.9.	Ref 1/20000 Sheet 62c NE.
			Preliminary orders issued as to relief of 42nd Div Arty by 2nd Cav Div Arty.	See Appendix II
			C & K Batteries R.H.A. marched to HABONNIERES. G Battery remained with its Cav. Bde	
	17th		Reconnoitring by Battery Commanders.	
	18th		" " " "	
	19th		Relief of 42nd Div Arty commenced 1 section per battery.	See Appendix III
	20th		" " " " " continued	
	21st		" " " " completed	
	22nd		Lt. Col. Wainwright took over command of Artillery of 2nd Cav Division from Brig Gen Lowrie C.R.A. 42nd Division.	
			Distribution of Artillery as in Appendix IV.	See Appendix IV
	23rd		Registration carried out by batteries.	

2353 Wt. W2544/1454 700,000 5/15 D. D. & L. A.D.S.S./Forms/C. 2118.

Instructions regarding War Diaries and Intelligence Summaries are contained in F. S. Regs., Part II. and the Staff Manual respectively. Title pages will be prepared in manuscript.

MAY 1917.

WAR DIARY
or
~~INTELLIGENCE SUMMARY.~~
(Erase heading not required.)

IV Bde R.H.A.

Army Form C. 2118.

111.

Place	Date	Hour	Summary of Events and Information	Remarks and references to Appendices
	24th		Registration continued.	
	25th		3rd Cav Division took over left sector of front previously held by part of 2nd Cav Divn.	
			H.Q. R.H.A. moved to EPEHY taking over Northern group from O.C. 296th Bde RFA.	
			Distribution table and Intelligence Summaries attached	Appendices V & VI
			Front generally quiet. Work carried out on Battery positions and OP's. Registration done assisted by Balloon.	

A.L. Wainwright Lt Col

2353 Wt. W2544/1454 700,000 5/15 D. D. & L. A.D.S.S./Forms/C. 2118.

S E C R E T   APPENDIX I.

CAVALRY CORPS ARTILLERY OPERATION ORDER No.4.

* *

12th May, 1917.

1. The following will be the arrangements for the Artillery support of the 5th and 2nd Cavalry Divisions while they are holding the line to be shortly taken over from the III Corps

A. 5th Cavalry Division DIVISIONAL ARTILLERY GROUP. (to cover 5th Cavalry Division front).

COMMANDER. Lieut. Col. W. STIRLING, D.S.O. R.H.A.

17th Brigade, R.H.A.
R.C.H.A. Brigade.
16th Brigade, R.H.A. less 1 battery.
1 Brigade 59th Divisional Artillery.

B. 2nd Cavalry Division DIVISIONAL ARTILLERY GROUP. (to cover 2nd Cavalry Division front).

COMMANDER. Lieut. Col. A.R. WAINEWRIGHT, R.H.A.

3rd Brigade, R.H.A.
4th Brigade, R.H.A., less 1 battery.
1 Battery 4.5" Howitzers from 42nd Division.
1 Brigade 59th Divisional Artillery.

Sub Groups will be formed at discretion of Cavalry Divisional Artillery Group Commanders.

2. Lieut. Col. A.R. WAINEWRIGHT, R.H.A. should get into touch as soon as possible with G.O.C. 2nd Cavalry Division a programme of whose movements in the near future is attached.

3. Similarly, Lieut. Col. A. MELLOR should get into touch with Lieut. Col. A.R. WAINEWRIGHT; and Lieut. Col. H. ROCHFORT BOYD with Lieut. Col. W. STIRLING as soon as possible. The necessary details of the movements of the above officers are attached.

4. Detailed orders for reliefs will be issued by IIIrd Corps, under whose orders all the above artillery will work until Cavalry Corps takes over.

Sgd. H.S. SELIGMAN, Brigadier General.

G. O. C. R. H. A. Cavalry Corps.

S E C R E T.   APPENDIX II.

2nd CAVALRY DIVISIONAL ARTILLERY ORDER No.1.

16th May, 1917.

1. 2nd Cavalry Divisional Artillery will be disposed as follows:-

SOUTHERN GROUP.

GROUP COMMANDER - Lieutenant Colonel A. MELLOR, R.H.A.

3rd Brigade, R. H. A.

4th Brigade, R. H. A. (less "G" Battery, R.H.A.)

1 Battery 4.5" Howitzers from 42nd Division.

NORTHERN GROUP.

GROUP COMMANDER - Lieutenant Colonel SHAW-STEWART, R.F.A.

296th Brigade, R. F. A.

2. 2nd Cavalry Divisional Artillery will releive 42nd Divisional Artillery on night of 19th/20th, 20th/21st, 21st/22nd.

C.R.A. 2nd Cavalry Division will take over from B.G.R.A. 42nd Division on completion of relief, time and date to be notified later.

3. Copy of 42nd Divisional Artillery Order attached, this has been approved by G.O.C. 2nd Cavalry Division.

4. Copy of 2nd Cavalry Division for relief of Infantry also attached.

5. Detailed orders will follow.

Sgd. E.T. BOYLAN, Lieutenant, R. H. A.

A/Brigade Major 2nd Cavalry Divisional Arty;

S E C R E T. C.R.A./15/B.M. **APPENDIX III.**

O.C. 3rd Brigade, R.H.A.
O.C. 296th Brigade, R.F.A.
C.R.A. 42nd Division)
2nd Cavalry Division) for information.

Reference 42nd Divisional Artillery Order No.10 and 2nd Cavalry Division Order No.20.

1. The reliefs of 210th Brigade, R.F.A. and 211th Brigade, R.F.A. by R.H.A. 2nd Cavalry Division and 296th Brigade, R.F.A. respectively will be carried out by one section on first nights of relief and remainder of Batteries on second night of relief.

"K" Battery, R.H.A. moving into action on night 19th/20th and 20th/21st under orders of O.C. 3rd Brigade, R.H.A.

D/296 Battery, R.F.A. remains in action and comes under the orders of O.C. 3rd Brigade, R.H.A. on completion of relief.

2. All releifs will take place ~~and~~ after 9-30 p.m. under arrangements between Group Commanders.

3. Group Commanders and Battery Commanders will hand over command on completion of reliefs, at an hour arranged between Group Commanders, a report to be rendered to this office as soon as possible after.

4. C.R.A. 2nd Cavalry Division takes over command from G.O.C. R.A. 42nd Division at 10 a.m. on 22nd May.

5. The following dumps will be maintained at gun positions :-

300 rounds per 13 and 18 pounder Gun.
250 rounds per 4.5" Howitzer.

13 pounder Batteries will dump 252 rounds per gun on first night if sufficient cover is available. If not at least 176 rounds per gun will be dumped, either under cover or in wagons in close vicinity. Dumps will be made up to 300 rounds per gun before 3 a.m. on 23rd inst.

6. 296th Brigade, R.F.A. will take over existing dumps at gun positions of 211th Brigade, R.F.A.

13 pounder Batteries will take over and give a receipt for any 18 pounder ammunition handed over to them by 210th Brigade, R.F.A. the amount of this will be reported to this office and arrangements will be made for its collection by 296th Brigade, R.F.A.

7. The supply of ammunition will be under control of Group Commanders from the A. R. P. (Ammunition refilling point). The A.R.P. will be under Divisional control.

18 pdr. and 4.5" Ammunition Refilling Point is at E.29.b.1.3. an officer of 59th Division will be in charge from 12 noon 21st inst. 59th Division is responsible for all Ammunition and Ammunition Returns

13 pdr. A.R.P. will be at VILLERS FAUCON and will be taken over by an officer from 3rd Brigade, R.H.A. on a date to be notified later.

8. Telephone wires, map boards, Registers, Panoramas etc. will be taken over by Batteries and in the case of empty positions by Groups.

9. Existing arrangements for S.O.S. Barrages, Zones, Night lines, Night firing etc. will remain in force until further orders, and all Group Commanders and Battery Commanders should ask for full particular in these matters when taking over.

10. Existing arrangements for S.O.S. Signals, Liaison with Infantry and Cavalry and manning of O.P's will continue in force until further orders

11. A list of all area stores taken over by releiving units will be forwarded to this office as soon as possible after completion of releif.

12. Supplies will be drawn from dump at ROISEL Station, time to be notified later.

13. These orders have been approved by C.R.A. 42nd Division who does not hand over command until 10 a.m. on 22nd May.

R.A. Headquarters. Sgd. E. T. BOYLAN, Lieutenant, R.H.A.

20th May, 1917. A/Brigade Major 2nd Cavalry Divisional Arty;

APPENDIX 1V.

2nd CAVALRY DIVISIONAL ARTILLERY.

Disposition of Batteries.

Reference 1/20,000 - Sheets 57c,S.E.,57b,S.W.,62c,N.E., and 62b,N.W.

U N I T	P O S I T I O N	R E M A R K S
Hdqrs: 3rd Bde: R.H.A.	F.13.c.24	
"[illegible]" Battery, R. H. A.	F.14.c.9.8.	
"J" Battery, R. H. A.	F.26.b.7.2½.	
"E" Battery, R. H. A.	F.20.c.9.8.	
D/210 Battery, R.F.A.	F.14.d.8½.8.	
Hdqrs: 296 Bde: R.F.A.	F.1-d.9.8.	
"K" Battery, R. H. A.	F.8.c.5.4.	
B/296 Battery, R.F.A.	X.20.b.4.0.	
C/296 Battery, R.F.A.	F.8.a.3.4.	
D/296 Battery, R.F.A.	F.7.b.6.7.	
"C" Battery, R. H. A.	F.21.d.9.0.	

R.A. Headquarters. Sgd. E.T. BOYLAN, Lieutenant, R.H.A.

22nd MAY, 1917. A/Brigade Major 2nd Cavalry Divisional Arty:

2nd Cavalry Divisional Artillery.

INTELLIGENCE SUMMARY. 6.0 p.m. 20th to 6.0 p.m. 21st.

1. **OUR ARTILLERY.**

TIME	PLACE SHELLED	NATURE OF SHELL	DIRECTION	NUMBER OF ROUNDS	REMARKS
12 mid-night to 6.0 a.m.	A.2.c.9.0. A.2.c.9..9	18 pdr.	-	40	In salvoes
	A.2.c.o.o. A.2.c.5.9.	"	-	48	"
	Cross roads in VENDHUILE	4.5 How.	-	40	-
12.30 p.m.	Trench in F.6.c.25	18 pdr	-	9	Enemy movement.

2. **HOSTILE ARTILLERY.**

8.0 a.m.	PETIT PRIEL FARM	5.9	-	13	-
8.30 a.m.	TOMBOIS FARM	5.9	-	10	-
	F.5.b.& F.11.a.	4.2	-	6	-
5.30 p.m.	F.18.c.	5.9	-	6	-

3. **MISCELLANEOUS.**

Visibility poor.

Trench being dug yesterday from FARM to MALAKOFF FARM.

Smoke visible from trees in AUBERCHAUX-BOIS and 10 seconds later the report of a 4.2. heard which seemed to coincide with the above.

Windmill in T.20.b. seen to be working.

R.A. Headquarters.

22nd MAY, 1917.

Lieutenant, R. H. A.

A/S.O. for Reconnaisance, 2nd Cav: Div: Arty

2nd Cavalry Divisional Artillery.

INTELLIGENCE SUMMARY.

A. OUR ARTILLERY.

12.1 p.m. 20th — 18 pdrs obtained direct hits on tree in S.9.a.4.9. where men had been seen - suspected O.P.

1.47 p.m. 20th — 18 pdrs fired 5 rounds on trench in F6.a.3.2. - movement was observed.

2.30 p.m. 20th — 4.5 Hows. fired 12 rounds on a G.S. wagon on a road in S.27.c.5.9.

30 p.m. to 5.0 p.m. — 18 pdrs. fired on X.30.a.7.3. to X.30.a.8.9. in co-operation with aeroplane.

Registration and night firing carried out as ordered.

12 mid-night to 6.0 a.m. 21st. — 18 pdrs. fired 40 rds. in salvoes on road in A.2.c.9.0. to A.2.c.9.9.

18 pdrs. fired 48 rds. in salvoes on road in A.2.c.0.0. to A.2.c.5.9.

4.5 Hows. fired 40 rds. on cross roads in VENDHUILE.

B. HOSTILE ARTILLERY.

12.25 p.m. 20th	Sunken road S.28.a.3.4.	7 rds.	5.9	Direction unknown
3.10 p.m. 20th	At L.5.d.7.3.	5 rds.	4.2	" "
3.55 p.m. to 4.15 p.m.	Trenches and sunken road in F.29.b.	-	77 mm	" "
8.0 p.m.	PETIT PRIEL FARM	13 rds.	5.9	" "
8.30 a.m. 21st.	TOMBOIS FARM	10 H.E.	5.9	" "

2nd Cavalry Divisional Artillery.

INTELLIGENCE SUMMARY. 6.0 p.m. 22nd to 6.0 p.m. 23rd.

1. OUR ARTILLERY.

TIME	PLACE SHELLED	NATURE OF SHELL	DIRECTION	NUMBER OF ROUNDS	REMARKS
2.30 a.m.	KNOLL	13 pdr.	-	30	Punishment fire.
10.30 a.m.	"	13 pdr.	-	12	"
11.30 a.m.	Suspected T.M. at A.13.b.8.1.	"	-	8	Good effect.
11.30 a.m.	A.8.c.3.2.	"	-	12	Punishment fire.
12 noon.	O.P tree at cross roads A.20.c.	4.5 How.	-	40	Direct hit.
2.30 p.m.	Wood at A.20.b. & d.	13 pdr.	-	54	Punishment fire.
3.30 p.m.	O.P tree at cross roads A.20.c.	4.5 How.	-	30	Tree much knocked about.
5.0 p.m.	A.8.c.3.2.	13 pdr.	-	12	Punishment fire.

Remainder of the day spent in registration and calibration.

The tree at cross roads in A.20.c is a suspected O.P.

2. HOSTILE FIRE.

TIME	PLACE SHELLED	NATURE OF SHELL	DIRECTION	NUMBER OF ROUNDS	REMARKS
2.30 p.m.	"F" Post	77 mm	-	15	-
10.30 a.m.	"	"	-	10	-
10.0 a.m. to 11.0 a.m.	EPEHY and St.EMELIE	4.2	-	8	-
11.30 a.m.	Birdcage	5.9.	-	6	-
2.25 p.m.	F.23.d.	77 mm	-	16	-

3. **HOSTILE AEROPLANE ACTIVITY.**

Hostile aeroplane active during the day.

1.50 p.m. Hostile aeroplane observed flying over battery position in F.8.

2.20 to 3.25 p.m. Two Hostile aeroplanes over our front driven off by A.A. Guns.

12 noon to 2.0 p.m. Enemy planes over RONSSOY and district. At one time five were seen.

4. **MISCELLANEOUS.**

Several columns of smoke observed East of LA TERRIERE about 4.30 p.m.

Little movement observed.

R.A. Headquarters. Lieutenant, R. H. A.

24-5-1917. A/S.O. for Reconnaisance, 2nd Cav: Div; Arty:

2nd Cavalry Divisional Artillery.

INTELLIGENCE SUMMARY. 6.0 a.m. 23rd to 6.0 a.m. 24th.

1. **OUR ARTILLERY.**

TIME	PLACE SHELLED	NATURE OF SHELL	DIRECTION	NUMBER OF ROUNDS	REMARKS
7.15 p.m. to 8.30 p.m.	Cross roads S.27.c. VENDHUILE	4.5 How.	-	6.	Party of Germans, one shell fell in party, causing casualties.
10.55 p.m.	Barrage Lines	13 pdr. 18 pdr. 4.5 How.	-	-	In answer to S.O.S. Signal.
10.0 p.m. to 11.0 p.m.	S.26.d.1.7. S.27.c.5.2.	"	-	12	Punishment fire
10.15 a.m.	LA TERRIERE	18 pdr.	-	10	-do-
9.45 a.m.	S.27.c.5.9.	4.5 How.	-	12	-do-
4.45 p.m. to 6.0 p.m.	Copse A.14.b. Cross roads at A.14.d.9.1.	"	-	20	Balloon observation

2. **HOSTILE FIRE.**

TIME	PLACE SHELLED	NATURE OF SHELL	DIRECTION	NUMBER OF ROUNDS	REMARKS
5.0 a.m.	F.15.a.5.9.	5.9	-	10	-
9.0 a.m. to 10.0 a.m.	A.13.b.	4.2.	BONY	6	-
10.25 a.m.	A.13.b.	"	-do-	6	-
11.15 a.m.	F.5 central	5"9	-	15	-
1.30 p.m..	"B" Post.	77 mm	-	30	-
2.15 p.m.	F.24.a.	"	-	40	-
3.0 p.m. to 4.0 p.m.	"C" Post	4.2	-	20	-

3. **HOSTILE AEROPLANE ACTIVITY.**

Hostile plane flew low over RONSSOY.

Hostile balloons up all day.

4. MISCELLANEOUS.

7.30 a.m. Men seen entering Wood in S.8.c. and d. - men seen leaving it again at 4.0 p.m.

Much enemy movement was observed during the day between trenches due West of LA TERRIERE and houses about S.10.c.4.1.

Five wagons seen on road GOUY - BEAUREVOIR going East.

R.A. Headquarters. Lieutenant, R. H. A.

25-5-1917. A/S.O. for Reconnaisance, 2nd Cav: Div:Ar

3rd Cavalry Divisional Artillery.

INTELLIGENCE SUMMARY. 6.0 p.m. 24th to 6.0 p.m. 25th.

1. OUR ARTILLERY.

TIME	PLACE SHELLED	NATURE OF SHELL	DIRECTION	NUMBER OF ROUNDS	REMARKS.
7.0 p.m.	T.M. in X.30.a.7.2.	18 pdr.	-	18 H.E.	T.M. silenced.
7.30 p.m.	OSSUS	18 pdr.	-	20	With balloon Observation.
9.15 a.m.	DE LA LEAU	4.5 How.	-	8	Punishment fire
9.30 a.m.	MACQUINCOURT FARM	"	-	12	With balloon observation
12 noon	Working party in S.10.c.1.9.	18 pdr.	-	14	-
3.30 p.a.	Quarry S.14.d.	4.5 How.	-	7.	Punishment fire.
3.30 p.m.	Enemy dug-outs in S.9.c.2.3.	18 pdr.	-	38	-
5.45 p.m.	On road - X.30.c.5.5. to X.30.a.7.4.	13 pdr.	-	6	Balloon observation.

2. HOSTILE ARTILLERY.

TIME	PLACE SHELLED	NATURE OF SHELL	DIRECTION	NUMBER OF ROUNDS	REMARKS.
7.10 a.m.	LEMPIRE	5.9	-	6	-
10.30 a.m.	EPEHY	"	-	10	-
12.25 p.m.	Road from F.3.b.7.6. to F.3.b.2.3.	77 mm	-	10	Party of our men walking down road at time.
1.30 p.m.	RONSSOY	4.2	-	8	-

X.22.c. shelled frequently during the day, with 4.2.

3. **HOSTILE AEROPLANE ACTIVITY.**

Hostile Aeroplanes very active during the afternoon two fights took place.

At 5.30 p.m. a German plane dived at one of ours Wireless planes at a height of about 400 feet - hostile plane fired several rounds then returned over his own lines.

At 6.0 p.m. six hostile aeroplanes over our front line.

4. **MISCELLANEOUS.**

Several hostile balloons up during the day.

Two Germans seen entering a house in E.27.c.1.9. the house was fired at and hit.

Enemy seen crossing a field in S.27.b. they were fired on without success.

Very little enemy movement, mostly in ones and twos and well out of range.

R.A. Headquarters. Lieutenant, R. H. A.

26th MAY, 1917. A/S.O. for Reconnaisance, 2nd Cav: Div:Arty

3rd Cavalry Divisional Artillery.

INTELLIGENCE SUMMARY. 6.0 p.m. 25th to 6.0 p.m. 26th.

1. OUR ARTILLERY.

TIME	PLACE SHELLED	NATURE OF SHELL	DIRECTION	NUMBER OF ROUNDS	REMARKS
6.0 p.m. to 8.0 p.m.	-	13 pdr.	-	17	Registering night lines.
6.45 p.m.	T.M. in OSSUS WOOD	18 pdr.	-	23 H.E. 15 Shrap.	Trench Mortar silenced.
8.15 a.m.	VENDHUILE	4.5 How.	-	4	Punishment fire.
9.0 a.m.	Quarry S.14.d.	"	-	30	Observation by No. 14 balloon with good results.
3.30 p.m.	CANAL WOOD	13 pdr.	-	25	With balloon observation.
4.30 p.m.	S.14.a.7.6.	18 pdr.	-	62	Calibration purposes.
5.30 p.m.	S.14.a.5.9.	"	-	8	Registration.
7.0 a.m.	TOMBOIS FARM	77 mm) 5.9)	-	-	-
7.0 a.m.	F.16.a.	77 mm	BASKETT WOOD	20	-
7.40 a.m.	F.10.d.	"	-do-	20	-
9.30 a.m. to 11.10 a.m.	F.28.c.	5.9	-	14	-
9.45 a.m.	TOMBOIS FARM	4.2	-	30	-
11.50 a.m. to 12.15 p.m.	F.16.a.	77 mm	BASKETT WOOD	25	-
12.30 p.m. to 2.30 p.m.	F.15.b.) F.15.a.)	4.2	LE CATELET	100	In section salvoes.
3.45 p.m. to 4.0 p.m.	F.15.b.) F.16.a.)	4.2	-do-	60	-do-
4.30 p.m.	LITTLE PRIEL FARM	4.2	-	25	-

3. **HOSTILE AEROPLANE ACTIVITY.**

Hostile A.A. Guns fired tracer shells at one of our Patrol machines, trajectory of shell quite noticeable.

3.40 p.m. One of our planes brought down about X.8.d. central. Hostile planes active during the evening, hostile balloons up during the day.

4. **MISCELLANEOUS.**

The street in S.27.c.3.9. has been fired at frequently by the Howitzers, few of the enemy are seen in this street now and they always run hard.

10.0a.m. Transport seen on GOUY - BEAUREVOIR road moving East.

5.30 p.m. Two Germans seen in S.15.a. walking East, they appeared to be patrolling telephone wires, they disappeared into LA TERRIERE at S.15.b.9.6.

R.A. Headquarters.
27th MAY, 1917.

Lieutenant, R. H. A.
R.O. 3rd Cavalry Divisional Artillery.

3rd Cavalry Divisional Artillery.

INTELLIGENCE SUMMARY. 6.0 p.m. 26th to 6.0 p.m. 27th.

1. OUR ARTILLERY.

TIME	PLACE SHELLED	NATURE OF SHELL	DIRECTION	NUMBER OF ROUNDS	REMARKS
7.0 p.m.	X.18.c.3.2. X.24.a.5.0.	18 pdr.	-	39	With balloon observation.
11.30 a.m.	-	13 pdr.	-	44	Registration.
2.0 p.m.	Quarry in S.14.a.3.8.	18 pdr.	-	16	Movement seen in Quarry.
3.45 p.m. to 5.0 p.m.	-	13 pdr.	-	76	Registration.
4.0 p.m.	VENDHUILE	18 pdr.	-	20	Punishment fire.

2. HOSTILE ARTILLERY.

TIME	PLACE SHELLED	NATURE OF SHELL	DIRECTION	NUMBER OF ROUNDS	REMARKS
6.0 a.m. to 6.30 a.m.	X.23.	4.2	-	10	-
9.15 a.m. to 9.40 a.m.	Road in - F.10.c.2.2.	77 mm	LE CATELET	25	-
11.30 a.m.	F.16.c.4.4.	4.2	-	8	-
4.0 p.m.	X.22.	77 mm	-	20	-

3. HOSTILE AIR ACTIVITY.

One hostile plane seen only.

Our aeroplanes were not fired on by A.A. Guns until this evening and then only slightly.

No hostile balloons up.

4. **MISCELLANEOUS.**

7.50 a.m. Working party seen in X.24.a. - the party was fired on and took to cover.

10.0 a.m. A.A. Gun@ was seen about M.35.a. and moved away again about 11.30 a.m.

10.55 a.m. Cart seen moving along road from M.35.c. in direction of BOIS MAILLARD.

12.40 p.m. Men seen pushing a barrow in S.20.a.

A salve was fired and the party hastily took cover.

1.20 p.m. A flock of 15 pigeon was seen flying over one of our battery positions in F.8.a.3.4.

R.A. Headquarters.

28th MAY, 1917.

Lieutenant, R. H.A.

R.O. 3rd Cavalry Divisional Artillery.

3rd Cavalry Divisional Artillery.

INTELLIGENCE SUMMARY. 6.0 p.m. 27th to 6.0 p.m. 28th.

1. OUR ARTILLERY.

TIME	PLACE SHELLED	NATURE OF SHELL	DIRECTION	NUMBER OF ROUNDS	REMARKS
7.0 p.m.	HONNECOURT WOOD	4.5 How.	-	8	With balloon observation.
6.30 p.m.	Bridge in A.3.a.9.2.	"	-	-	With balloon observation 2 hits recorde
2.30 p.m.	CANAL WOOD Quarry in S.14.c.5.4.	13 pdr.	-	26	-

2. HOSTILE ARTILLERY.

TIME	PLACE SHELLED	NATURE OF SHELL	DIRECTION	NUMBER OF ROUNDS	REMARKS
9.30 a.m.	X.23.c. and X.29.a.	4.2	BONY	6	From a very long range.
10.30 a.m.	Road in X.17.c.0.1	"	-	6	-
1.35 p.m. to 2.30 p.m.	LITTLE PRIEL FARM	77 mm	-	16	Probable registration of zero line.
2.0 p.m. to 2.30 p.m.	X.23.d. X.23.b.	77 mm	-	20	-
4.45 p.m.	X.28.d.	"	-	8	Seven "duds"

3. HOSTILE AIR ACTIVITY.

11.15 a.m. Six enemy aeroplanes flew over CANAL and OSSUS WOOD and proceeded in a South Easterly direction.

4. MISCELLANEOUS.

5.40 a.m. Three motor lorries were observed going East along the BOIS MAILLARD - LAPAVY road.

8.30 a.m. A horseman seen moving in easterly direction in S.24.

9.25 a.m. to 11.45 a.m. 5.0 p.m. Enemy shelled our working parties in X.32.d.central with 4.2 and 77 mm., both these guns appear to be in the direction of BASKETT WOOD.

12.40. p.m. Large fire observed at AUBENCHEUL which was apparently extinguished about 1.0 p.m.

4.50 p.m. About 30 Germans seen in the HINDENBURG LINE near LA TERRIERE, a suspected relief.

It was observed that the Periscope Tree near FARM has been removed.

There is a suspected A.A. Gun in the wood at S.8.d.

Party in sunken road at S.27.a.6.1. was fired at causing casualties.

R.A. Headquarters.
28th MAY, 1917.

Lieutenant, R. H. A.
R.O. for Reconnaisance, 3rd Cav: Div: Arty:

3rd Cavalry Divisional Artillery.

INTELLIGENCE SUMMARY. 6.0 p.m. 28th to 6.0 p.m. 29th.

1. OUR ARTILLERY.

TIME	PLACE SHELLED	NATURE OF SHELL	DIRECTION	NUMBER OF ROUNDS	REMARKS
11.15 p.m.	X.30.a.6.8.	13 pdr.	-	8	Punishment
12.30 p.m.	X.30.a.8.8.	"	-	10	fire
6.45 p.m.	VENDHUILE	4.5 How	-	6	-do-
12.50 p.m.	"	"	-	7	-do-
6.0 p.m.	X.30.a.8.8.	18 pdr.	-	40	-do-

Battery registered sveral targets with balloon observation.

2. HOSTILE ARTILLERY.

10.30 a.m.	X.29.c.	4.2	-	18	-
11.0 a.m.	F.5.c.2.2.	"	-	10	-
11.20 a.m.	F.6.c.2.2.	"	-	12	-
1.45 p.m.	F.4.b.8.2.	"	-	10	-
12.50 p.m.	LITTLE PRIEL FARM X.22.d.6.8.	77 mm 4.2	-	40	-

3. HOSTILE AIR ACTIVITY.

Two aeroplanes crossed over our lines at 5.0 p.m. and one at 6.30 p.m.

Hostile balloons up during the afternoon.

4. MISCELLANEOUS.

M.G. reported at junction of trench with sunken road at F.6.c.3½.9.

Eight wagons seen on the main road from RANCOURT FARM.

Unusual amount of transport seen on the road between GOUY and BEAUREVOIR.

R.A. Headquarters.
30th MAY,1917.

Lieutenant, R. H. A.
R.O. 3rd Cavalry Divisional Artillery.

3rd Cavalry Divisional Artillery.

INTELLIGENCE SUMMARY. 6.0 p.m. 29th to 6.0 p.m. 30th.

1. OUR ARTILLERY.

TIME	PLACE SHELLED	NATURE OF SHELL	DIRECTION	NUMBER OF ROUNDS	REMARKS
3.15 p.m.	S.O.S. Line	13 pdr.	-	15	-
5.15 p.m.	S.19.c.1.5.	4.5 How.	-	8	Balloon observation.
5.30 p.m.	X.18.c.5.0.	"	-	10	-do-

2. HOSTILE ARTILLERY.

TIME	PLACE SHELLED	NATURE OF SHELL	DIRECTION	NUMBER OF ROUNDS	REMARKS
7.30 p.m.	F.8.c. TEMPLEUX	8"	A.18.c.9.9.	20	Information from kite balloon.
9.0 p.m. to 11.0 p.m.	LEMPIRE and EPEHY	77 mm	VENDHUILE	15	-
9.30 p.m.	RONSSOY and LEMPIRE	5.9	BELLICOURT	6	-
4.20 p.m.	F.15.c.	5.9	VENDHUILE	12	-
12.15 p.m. to 2.0 p.m.	Road in F.28.a.3.5.	77 mm 4.2	-	25	-
5.0 p.m.	RONSSOY and BASSEE BOULOGNE	5.9	BELLICOURT	60	-

3. GENERAL.

About 7.30 p.m. "K" Battery, R. H. A. (F.8.c.8.4.) were shelled with 5.9 - about eight rounds were fired . The shelling then ceased and a Hostile aeroplane flew close over position and appeared to be taking photographs.

The enemy appeared to be ranging by balloon observation.

Observation balloon No. 14 reports these shell are 8" and not 5.9 from the direction of A.18.c.9.9.

4. MISCELLANEOUS.

.10 a.m. Four rounds were fired at a party of men in S.13.a. with good effect.

1.47 p.m. A party of twenty five Germans seen on the road in A.4.a.3.4.- forward gun fired at this party causing casualties with the first round, this was clearly seen.

1.15 p.m. Cavalry seen on the LORMISSET - BEAUREVOIR road about B.15.a.0.5.

A party of Germans seen in S.14.a. central and fired on with good results.

Hostile balloons up in the early morning and the late afternoon.

R.A. HEADQUARTERS. Lieutenant, R. H. A.

31st MAY, 1917. R.O. 3rd Cavalry Divisional Artillery.

3rd Cavalry Divisional Artillery.

INTELLIGENCE SUMMARY. 6.0 p.m. 30th to 6.0 p.m. 31st.

1. OUR ARTILLERY.

TIME	PLACE SHELLED	NATURE OF SHELL	DIRECTION	NUMBER OF ROUNDS	REMARKS
7.30 p.m.	LA TERRIERE	18 pdr.	-	20	Punishment fire.
5.0 p.m.	S.27.c.5.9.	4.5 How.	-	12	-do-
10.30 p.m.	S.26.a.3.3.	"	-	12	-do-
10.45 p.m.	VENDHUILE	18 pdr.	-	35	-do-
9.0 a.m. to 9.45 a.m.	S.14.a.7.6.	18 pdr.	-	40	Calibration purposes.
10.45 a.m.	Quarry S.14.a.9.8.	18 pdr.	-	17	Punishment fire.
2.0 p.m.	S.26.b.5.7.) S.27.c.5.9.) A.4.a.5.4.)	4.5 How.	-	40	Registration of forward gun
5.0 p.m.	CANAL WOOD	13 pdr.	-	38	Registration.
5.0 p.m.	S.26a.5.3.	4.5 How.	-	6	-

2. HOSTILE ARTILLERY.

TIME	PLACE SHELLED	NATURE OF SHELL	DIRECTION	NUMBER OF ROUNDS	REMARKS
8.0 p.m.	LEMPIRE.	4.2 5.9	VENDHUILE	20	-
8.30 p.m.	EPEHY	77 mm	-do-	8	-
8.45 p.m.	LITTLE PRIEL FARM	77 mm	-do-	15	10 "duds"
10.30 a.m.	F.21.a.6.0.	77 mm	-	10	-
10.45 a.m. to 11.15 a.m.	X.17.c.2.8.	5.9.	-	8	-
1.45 p.m.	X,29.a.	5.9	BONY	9	-
1.45 p.m. to 2.0 p.m.	X.21.d.	77 mm	OSSUS	10	-
3.0 p.m. to 3.30 p.m.	F.5.c.8.7.	77 mm	-	10	-
5.30 p.m.	X.29.a.	77 mm	OSSUS	50	-

3. GENERAL.

5.15 a.m. Five men working in trench X.30.d.5.6.

Engine seen in AUBENGUBIL travelling N.W.

9.15 a.m. Two men seen coming out of Quarry in S.20.d.8.6., they stopped, one man appeared to be pointing out various objects, they then went into an earthwork at S.20.b.9.8. returning to the Quarry again.

A new trench appears to be in course of construction at F.6.a.8.2.

Working party seen in S.22.b.

3.0 p.m. Party seen carrying planks into VENDHUILE.

A tripod supporting a white flagseen at S.14.a.4.9. and a white flag also at S.15.c.8.1.

4. HOSTILE AIR ACTIVITY.

Normal.

R.A. Headquarters.
1st JUNE, 1917.

Lieutenant, R. H. A.
R.O. 3rd Cavalry Divisional Artillery.

Instructions regarding War Diaries and Intelligence Summaries are contained in F. S. Regs., Part II. and the Staff Manual respectively. Title pages will be prepared in manuscript.

WAR DIARY or ~~INTELLIGENCE SUMMARY.~~

(*Erase heading not required.*)

June 1917. H.Q. 4th Bde R.H.A.

Army Form C. 2118. 1

Place	Date	Hour	Summary of Events and Information	Remarks and references to Appendices
	1st		IV Bde R.H.A in action East of ROISEL covering 3rd Cavalry Division for distribution see APPENIX I.	
	2nd 3rd		Relief of C Battery R.H.A by G/Battery R.H.A G Battery going to new position at W 30 B 5.3 see appendix II.	
	4th		One Section of G Battery R.H.A moved forward to F2B.	
	8th		Inspection of Gun Positions by Major Genl. BUDWORTH M.G.R.A. IV Army	
	10th		One Section of K/RHA moved forward to ENFER WOOD in F9d	
			One Section of C/R.H.A. relieved 1 Section K/RHA at F8c 5.4 see Appendix III	
	11th		C/296 Battery went out of line to train. For distribution see Appendix IV.	
	12th		One gun of C Battery R.H.A placed in a forward position to cut wire for an operation	
	13th		One gun of G/RHA and B/296 placed in forward positions for wire cutting.	
	14th		Wire cut, but observation very difficult	
	14th		All wire cutting guns withdrawn proposed operation indefinitely postponed	
	17th		Warning order issued to Batteries regarding an Operation to be undertaken from BIRDCAGE. Appendix V.	

2353 Wt. W2544/1454 700,000 5/15 D. D. & L. A.D.S.S./Forms/C. 2118.

Instructions regarding War Diaries and Intelligence Summaries are contained in F. S. Regs., Part II. and the Staff Manual respectively. Title pages will be prepared in manuscript.

WAR DIARY
or
~~INTELLIGENCE SUMMARY.~~
(Erase heading not required.)

Army Form C. 2118.

June 1917. 4th Bde R.H.A.

Place	Date	Hour	Summary of Events and Information	Remarks and references to Appendices
	17th		Two Patrols going out one to capture man seen working about X23c centre the other to capture or kill party working on FALCON SAP near BIRDCAGE. Artillery not to fire unless asked for. No support was asked for. Patrol to X23c centre found trench empty. Patrol to Sap unable to capture any of the enemy.	
	18th		K Battery R.H.A. and C/296 Battery R.F.A. came into action at F8 centre and old position at F8a34 respectively to register for operation near BIRDCAGE. This operation indefinitely postponed.	
	19th		Plans for raid between CANAL & OSSUS WOODS discussed.	
	20th		Warning order issued giving probable barrages for this raid. Appendix VI for moves of K/RHA and C/296 see also Appendix VI.	
	21st		Enemy reported laying a tape to BIRDCAGE also registration by enemy.	
	22nd		S.O.S. Signal sent up from BIRDCAGE about 1.10 am. Batteries opened on their S.O.S. lines. No news till 1.25 then report from Regimental H.Q. that all communications cut. But apparently all was well. Batteries slackened rate of fire. Batteries stopped firing about 1.45 am. Report from Regimental H.Q. 2.10 all O.K. Wire received 7 am stating attempted enemy raid on BIRDCAGE about 1.10 am stopped by our fire. 9 enemy dead 3 prisoners captured.	

2353 Wt. W2544/1454 700,000 5/15 D. D. & L. A.D.S.S./Forms/C. 2118.

Instructions regarding War Diaries and Intelligence Summaries are contained in F. S. Regs., Part II. and the Staff Manual respectively. Title pages will be prepared in manuscript.

WAR DIARY

or

~~INTELLIGENCE SUMMARY.~~

(Erase heading not required.)

June 1917 — 4th Bde RHA

Army Form C. 2118.

Place	Date	Hour	Summary of Events and Information	Remarks and references to Appendices
	23rd		Orders issued for raid by ROYALS on night 25th July see Appendix VII	
	24th		Registration for above complete by 6 pm.	
	25th	9pm-midnight	Occasional rounds fired to prevent the enemy suspecting that anything unusual was preparing.	
	26th	1.10am	Zero hour guns opened punctually.	
		1.14am	1st message from Major Young D.S.O RHA acting as liaison officer to O/c Operation. "Barrage opened apparently alright have heard one Bangalore torpedo explode no German barrage at present."	
		1.25am	Message from Major Young "Machine gun firing from CANAL WOOD may impede retreat of raiders"	
		1.27am	4 guns of B/296 ordered to fire on CANAL WOOD instead of two reported firing on this line 1.30 am. Major Young reports machine gun stopped firing.	
		1.26am	Green Rocket signal for withdrawal reported.	
		1.35	Report received right party failed torpedo failing to explode. B Party not yet returned	
		1.40	Batteries ordered to fire 3 rds p.g. p. min. for last 5 mins	

2353 Wt. W2544/1454 700,000 5/15 D. D. & L. A.D.S.S./Forms/C. 2118.

Instructions regarding War Diaries and Intelligence Summaries are contained in F. S. Regs., Part II. and the Staff Manual respectively. Title pages will be prepared in manuscript.

June 1917.

WAR DIARY

or

~~INTELLIGENCE SUMMARY.~~

(Erase heading not required.)

4th Bde RHA.

Army Form C. 2118.

Place	Date	Hour	Summary of Events and Information	Remarks and references to Appendices
	26th	am 1.45	Liaison Officer reports all raiders in except some wounded please continue Barrage at slow rate to cover collecting parties.	
			Batteries ordered to fire 1 round per gun per min until further orders on German front line.	
		am 1.55	Liaison Officer reports all quiet. Barrage ordered to die down in 3 mins	
		am 2.15	All quiet.	
		2.52	Batteries ordered to stand down. ~~[illegible]~~	
			Barrage reported very accurate.	
	27th		Relief of 3rd Cav Div by 2nd Cav Div.	
	28th			
	29th		Night shoot to cause casualties to German relief arranged by Cav Corps RA. Instructions issued SEE APPENDIX ~~IX~~ VIII	
			For further information re targets engaged &c see Intelligence Summaries attached.	

2353 Wt. W2544/1454 700,000 5/15 D. D. & L. A.D.S.S./Forms/C. 2118.

Army Form C. 2118.

Instructions regarding War Diaries and Intelligence Summaries are contained in F. S. Regs., Part II. and the Staff Manual respectively. Title pages will be prepared in manuscript.

WAR DIARY
or
~~INTELLIGENCE SUMMARY.~~
(Erase heading not required.)

June 1917. 4th Bat RHA.

Place	Date	Hour	Summary of Events and Information	Remarks and references to Appendices
			2Lieut E.L.V. POPE Joined G Battery R.H.A on 23/6/17 from "AA" Battery R.H.A.	
			No 52801 Sgt J.F. SHEPPARD from "C" Bty. RHA to be 2Lieut posted to 35th Div Arty ~~[struck out]~~. 4/6/17.	
			2Lieut Edge Austin Coleman to England with fractured collar bone 7/6/17.	
			A. Wainwright Lt	

2353 Wt. W2544/1454 700,000 5/15 D. D. & L. A.D.S.S./Forms/C. 2118.

APPENDIX I.

3rd CAVALRY DIVISIONAL ARTILLERY.

Disposition of Batteries.

Reference 1/20,000 - Sheets 57c,S.E.,57",S.W.,62c,N.E.,and 62b,N.W..

UNIT	POSITION	REMARKS.
R.A. Divisional Hdqrs.	F.1.d.9.8.	
"K" Battery, R. H. A.	F.8.c.5.4.	
B/296 Battery, R.F.A.	X.20.b.4.0.	
C/296 Battery, R.F.A.	F.8.a.3.4.	
D/296 Battery, R.F.A.	F.7.b.6.7.	
"C" Battery, R. H. A.	F.21.d.9.0.	

Sgd. E.T. BOYLAN, Lieutenant, R. H. A.

Adjutant 3rd Cavalry Divisional Artillery.

APPENDIX II.

S E C R E T. C.R.AM/857.
* * * * * *

O.C. "C" Battery, R.H.A.

O.C. "G" Battery, R.H.A.
Headquarters 'D' Sector.)
6th Cavalry Brigade.) For information.
3rd Cavalry Division.)
Cavalry Corps R.A.)

WARNING ORDER.

The following moves of Artillery Units of 3rd Cavalry Division will take place on dates as under -

1. On night 2nd/3rd June "G" Battery, R.H.A. from COURCELLES to a position in action about W.30.b.

2. "C" Battery, R.H.A. will pull out of action on night of 3rd/4th June or 4th/5th June, the exact date depending on registrative carried out by "G" Battery, R.H.A.

3. Detailed orders will follow.

R.A. Headquarters. Sgd. E.T. BOYLAN, Lieutenant, R.H.A.
30th May, 1917. for C. R. A. 3rd Cavalry Division.

APPENDIX III.

C.R.A./ 903/1.

O.C. "C" Battery, R.H.A.
O.C. "G" Battery, R.H.A.
O.C. "K" Battery, R.H.A.
O.C. B/296 Battery, R.F.A.
O.C. C/296 Battery, R.F.A.
O.C. D/296 Battery, R.F.A.
Cavalry Corps R.A.)
3rd Cavalry Division.) For information.
Headquarters 'D' Sector.)
8th Cavalry Brigade)

Reference my C.R.A./903, para. 3.

This should now read -

' on night 11th/12th 1 Section "C" Battery, R.H.A. will releive 1 Section "K" Battery, R.H.A. at F.8.c.8.4.

' on night 12th/13th remaining Section "C" Battery, R.H.A. will releive remaining Section of "K" Battery, R.H.A. at F.8.c.8.4.

E. F. Boyle

R.A. Headquarters. Lieutenant, R. H. A.

10th June, 1917. Adjutant 3rd Cavalry Divisional Arty:

C.R.A./903/1

C/296 Battery, R.F.A.
O.C. 296th BRIGADE, R.F.A. } for information.
3rd Cavalry Division.

In continuation of my C.R.A./903

1. C/296 Battery, R.F.A. will go out of action on night 11/12th and will move to its present wagon line, where it will come under the orders of O.C. 296 Brigade, for training.

2. Limbers will be kept filled and the Battery be prepared to reoccupy its present position at shortnotice.

R.A. Headquarters. Lieutenant, R. H. A.

10th JUNE, 1917. Adjutant, 3rd Cavalry Divisional Arty:

C.R.A./903.

S E C R E T.
= = = = = =

O.C. "G" Battery, R.H.A.
O.C. "C" Battery, R.H.A.
O.C. "K" Battery, R.H.A.
O.C. B/293 Battery, R.F.A.
O.C. C/293 Battery, R.F.A.
O.C. D/293 Battery, R.F.A.
Cavalry Corps, R.A.)
3rd Cavalry Division.) For information.
Headquarters 'D' Sector.)
6th Cavalry Brigade.)
****

With reference to Cavalry Corps, R.A., R.2 of 8th instant and 3rd Cavalry Division Order No.2 dated 7th instant.

The following moves will take place -

1. On the night of 10th/11th June 1 Section of "K" Battery, R.H.A. will move to a position previously occupied by a Section of "C" Battery, R.H.A. in ENFER WOOD.
On night 10th/11th 1 Section of "C" Battery, R.H.A. will move into position vacated by above Section of "K" Battery, R.H.A. at F.8.c.8.4.

2. On night 11th/12th June C/293 Battery, R.F.A. will move out of action.

3. On night 12th/13th 2 Sections of "C" Battery, R.H.A. will relieve 2 Sections of "K" Battery, R.H.A. at F.8.c.8.4.
The exact date of this relief is subject to alteration under certain circumstances "K" R.H.A. will not be releived until a later date.

4. The forward Section of "K" Battery, R.H.A. in ENFER WOOD will have two Officers with it.
For the purposes of O.P. duties and Liaison this Section and the detached Section of "C" Battery, R.H.A. at F.2.b.9.2. will be regarded as a Battery.
They will be connected laterally line to be laid by Signals.

5. The day zones for these two sections will be as follows:-

X.30.c.5.5. Southwards to F.6.c.5.2.

6. The S.O.S. Lines will be as follows:-

Section "G" R.H.A. - X.30.c.5.4. to X.30.c.5.0.
Section "K" R.H.A. - X.30.c.5.0. to F.6.a.5.8.
sweeping fire.

7. 170 rounds per gun will be dumped at "K" R.H.A. forward Section position on night 10th/11th, this dump will be made up to 500 rounds per gun on night 11th/12th, of which 50% will be H.E.

"C" Battery, R.H.A. will take over existing dumps at "K" Battery position on relief.

8. Liaison duties for D 1 Sub-Sector will be found as follows -

June 10th - C/293 Battery, R.F.A.
" 11th - "K" Battery, R.H.A.
" 12th - Detached Section "C" R.H.A.
" 13th - "C" Battery, R.H.A.
" 14th - Detached Section "K" R.H.A.
" 15th - "C" Battery, R.H.A.
" 16th - Detached Section "C" R.H.A.

and so on.

Night O.P. will be manned by D/293 Battery, R.F.A. nightly from night of 11th inclusive.

9. The detached sections of "C" and "K" Batteries R.H.A. will take over the O.P. now occupied by C/293 Battery, R.F.A. at F.4.b.9.2. Each section will run a wire to this point and will make arrangements to man the O.P. in turn.

All wires of C/293 Battery, R.F.A. will be left intact.

R.A. Headquarters, Lieutenant, R.H.A.

8th June, 1917. Adjutant 3rd Cavalry Divisional Arty:

APPENDIX IV.

SECRET C.R.A./843/6.

O.C. "C" Battery, R.H.A.
O.C. "G" Battery, R.H.A.
O.C. "K" Battery, R.H.A.
O.C. B/296 Battery, R.F.A.
O.C. D/296 Battery, R.F.A.
Headquarters 'D' Sector.)
3rd Cavalry Division.)
Cavalry Corps R.A.)
35th Divisional Artillery.)
2nd Cavalry Divisional Arty:)

Herewith Location Statement and amended Table A.IV of Defence Scheme 3rd Cavalry Divisional Artillery.

This cancels previous editions.

R.A. Headquarters. Sgd. R.T. BOYLAN, Lieutenant, R.H.A.

12th June, 1917. Adjutant 3rd Cavalry Divisional Artillery.

APPENDIX IV

TABLE A.I.

Reference 1/20,000 - Sheets [illegible].,S.E., 57b,S.W., 62c,N.E., and 62b,N.W.

UNIT		POSITION	O. P.	MAXIMUM ARC	ZONE	WAGON LINE.
Headquarters		F.1.d.9.8.	F.2.a.7.0. Night O.P.	-	-	K.~~17~~14.a.4.0.
"G" Battery, R. H. A.	(4 Guns)	W.30.b.5.3.	F.3.a.7.2.	42°-102°	S.20.d.0.0. to Quarry in S.14.d. inclusive	K.15.b.
"C" Battery, R. H. A.	(6 Guns)	F.8.c.8.4.	F.5.c.1.0.	110°-20°	S.20.d.0.0. to S.26.b.0.0.	K.15.b.
B/296 Battery, R. F. A.	(4 Guns) (2 Guns)	X.20.b.4.0. X.20.b.4.4.	X.22.c.5½.3.	123°-62°	Cross roads S.9.a.3.3. to Quarry in S.14.d. inclusive.	K.13.a.
D/296 Battery, R. F. A.	(2 Hows) (2 Hows)	F.7.b.6.7. F.9.a.1.7.	X.22.d.8.2.	103°-30° 106°-32°	Whole of Group Front.	K.13.a.
Detached Section "K" R. H. A.	(2 Guns)	F.9.d.3.4.	F.4.d.9½.8	43°-83°	X.30.c.5.0. to F.6.a.3.2.	K.15.b.
Detached Section "G" R. H. A.	(2 Guns)	F.2.a.8.7.	F.3.a.8.8.	no limit	X.30.c.5.4. to X.30.c.5.0.	K.15.b.
C/296 Battery,R.F.A.		In reserve ...	...	... ...	... ...	K.13.a.
Ammunition Column 4th Brigade, R. H. A.		...	...	... ...	... ...	K.14.a.4.0.
Ammunition Column 296th Brigade, R. F. A.		...	...	... ...	... ...	E.29.d.1.1.
A. R. P.	...	... ...	... ...	... ...	... ...	E.29.b.3.3.

TABLE A.IV.

(A) SUPPORT FOR 2nd CAVALRY DIVISION BY ARTILLERY of 3rd CAVALRY DIVISION.

Code Call - "ASSIST BOB"

UNIT.		
Detached Section "G" Battery, R.H.A.	2 13 pdrs	- A.2.a.5.0. - A.2.a.8.8.
Detached Section "K" Battery, R.H.A.	2 13 pdrs	- A.2.a.9.8. - A.2.b.1.9.
"C" Battery, R.H.A.	6 13 pdrs	- A.2.d.0.0. - A.8.b.4.3. - A.8.b.5.1.
D/296 Battery, R.F.A.	2 Hows. 2 Hows.	- S. and S.E. exits of VENDHUILE. In valley in A.2.a. and A.1.d.

(B) SUPPORT FOR 3rd CAVALRY DIVISION BY ARTILLERY OF 2nd CAVALRY DIVISION.

Code Call - "ASSIST JOHN"

No. of Guns	
6 Guns	Search and sweep VENDHUILE.
6 Guns	From A.1.b.2.5. - S.25.d.1.9.
2 Hows.	From X.30.a.8.9. - X.30.a.6.6.
1 How.	A.1.b.6.8.
1 How.	S.26.c.2.2.

Army Form C. 2118.

Instructions regarding War Diaries and Intelligence Summaries are contained in F. S. Regs., Part II. and the Staff Manual respectively. Title pages will be prepared in manuscript.

WAR DIARY
or
~~INTELLIGENCE SUMMARY.~~
(Erase heading not required.)

JULY 1917 — H.Q. IV Bde R.H.A.

Vol 30

Place	Date	Hour	Summary of Events and Information	Remarks and references to Appendices
	1st		The IV Bde was disposed in action near EPEHY as in distribution list for end of June.	
	2nd		Orders for Relief of 4th Bde R.H.A and 296th Bde R.F.A by 159th Bde R.F.A. SEE APPENDIX I.	
	3rd		Registration for raid ~~on~~ near GILLEMONT FARM carried by "C" Battery R.H.A. and detached Section "K" R.H.A. Part of 296th Bde R.F.A relieved and 1 Section C Battery R.H.A.	
	4th		Raid ~~[illegible]~~ carried out by 2nd Cav Div near GILLEMONT Farm successful. Relief of 296th Bde R.F.A continued.	
	5th	1.30a.m.	S.O.S. from GILLEMONT FARM. There was reported on our front and guns opened fire. was stopped at 1.45 a.m. Relief of 296th Bde R.F.A ~~[illegible]~~ C Battery R.H.A. and 1 Section C Battery R.H.A completed.	
	6 7		Handed over to incoming group and also to 35 Divl Arty.	
	8		Handed over to Major Purney R.F.A commanding 159 Bde R.F.A	

2353 Wt. W2544/1454 700,000 5/15 D. D. & L. A.D.S.S./Forms/C. 2118.

Army Form C. 2118.

WAR DIARY
or
~~INTELLIGENCE SUMMARY.~~
(*Erase heading not required.*)

Instructions regarding War Diaries and Intelligence Summaries are contained in F. S. Regs., Part II. and the Staff Manual respectively. Title pages will be prepared in manuscript.

July 1917. IV Bde R.H.A.

Place	Date	Hour	Summary of Events and Information	Remarks and references to Appendices
	8th		2 Sections of C Battery R.H.A. and 1 Section K R.H.A. pulled out of action about 10.0 pm.	Ref 1/100000 Sheet 17 11. 5a.
	9th		At wagon lines at MARQUAIX.	
	10th			
	11th		IV Bde R.H.A. marched to BRAY-sur-SOMME. Orders received from Cav. Corps that IV Bde R.H.A. must be drawn up 200 yds S. of SARTON by 10 am, and would not move into SARTON until H.M. The King had passed.	
	12th		Marched to point given above at 4.0 am. H.M. the KING did not pass down the Brigade as expected. Brigade marched into SARTON 11.0 am.	
	13th		Brigade marched to ETREE WAMIN.	
	14th		IV Bde R.H.A. less K Battery R.H.A. marched to GAUCHIN and HERNICOURT K Battery marched to rejoin 7th Cav Bde at FERMONT CAPELLE.	
	15th		Units marched independently as follows H.Q. R.H.A. to rejoin 3rd Cav Div at PERNES	

Instructions regarding War Diaries and Intelligence Summaries are contained in F. S. Regs., Part II. and the Staff Manual respectively. Title pages will be prepared in manuscript.

WAR DIARY
or
~~INTELLIGENCE SUMMARY.~~
(Erase heading not required.)

Army Form C. 2118.

July 1917 — IV Bde R.H.A.

Place	Date	Hour	Summary of Events and Information	Remarks and references to Appendices
	15th		C Battery R.H.A. to rejoin 6th Cav. Bde at AUCHEL.	
			G " " " 8th " " at SACHIN.	
			Ammn Column to rejoin S.A.A. Portion ~~[illegible]~~ at MAREST	
	16th		H.Q. R.H.A. marched to LA PIERRIERE close to Div H.Q. at BUSNES.	
			Batteries marched with their Bdes.	
			Are now Cantoned as follows on 18th	
	18th		"C" R.H.A. at LE CORBIE.	
			G " at PECQUER.	
			K " at LE BAS HAMEL.	
			Ammn Column at ST FLORIS.	
			Lieut Hillyard left G Battery to join 17th Divnl Artillery	
			A. M. Mainwaring Lt Col, 4 Bde RHA	

2353 Wt. W2544/1454 700,000 5/15 D. D. & L. A.D.S.S./Forms/C. 2118.

APPENDIX I.

S E C R E T.

Copy No. 14.

NORTHERN GROUP 2nd CAVALRY DIVISIONAL ARTILLERY

OPERATION ORDER No.5.

Reference 1/20,000 Map, Sheets 62.c.N.E., 62.b.S.W., 57.c.S.E., 57.b.S.W.

1. The Artillery of Northern Group 2nd Cavalry Divisional Artillery will be relieved by 159th Brigade, Royal Field Artillery as in attached Table of Reliefs.

2. On relief Batteries of 296th Brigade, R.F.A. will take over from Batteries of 159th Brigade, R.F.A.
Batteries of 4th Brigade, R.H.A. will move to their Wagon Lines and will be prepared to move out of the area on 11th instant.

3. Battery Commanders will hand over command on night 4th/5th instant with the exception of "G" Battery, R.H.A., Detached Section "G" Battery, R.H.A. and Detached Section "K" Battery, R.H.A.

4. Lieutenant Colonel A.R. WAINEWRIGHT, R.H.A. will hand over command at 11 p.m. on night 8th/9th instant.

5. No relief will commence before 10 p.m. but to be carried out as soon as possible after this hour.
Completion of relief each night to be reported to this office by Code word "RUM RECEIVED".

6. No telephone wires will be taken up without authority from these Headquarters.

7. Relieving Units will take over the Wagon Lines of the Units they relieve.

8. All tents and trench covers at Wagon Lines will be taken away by Units but no Trench covers at Battery Positions will be moved.
Mutual arrangements will be made between Units concerned as to handing over semi-permanent structures at Wagon Lines such as Kitchens etc.

9. Detachment 59th Divisional Ammunition Column will remain at its present position until further orders.

10. Headquarters 296th Brigade, R.F.A. will hand over all structures to Headquarters 159th Brigade, R.F.A. on relief. But will take tents away.

11.

11. Mounted guides will be at Battery Positions at time of relief to guide teams for relieving Units to Wagon Lines.

12. All 18 pounder and 4.5" Howitzer Ammunition dumped at guns will be handed over. Units will move with full wagons.
18 pounder Batteries of 159th Brigade, R.F.A. relieving R.H.A. Batteries should dump 176 rounds per gun on first night of relief this being made up to 300 rounds per gun on second night.

13. Wireless Station with 4.5" Howitzer Batteries will be relieved on night 4th/5th June.

14. Acknowledge.

E. T. Boylan.

R.A. Headquarters. Lieutenant, R. H. A.

2nd July, 1917. Adjutant Northern Group 2nd Cavalry Divisional Arty:

Copy No.1 "C" Battery, R.H.A.
No.2 "G" Battery, R.H.A.
3 & 4 "K" Battery, R.H.A.
No.5 B/296 Battery, R.F.A.
No.6 C/296 Battery, R.F.A.
No.7 D/296 Battery, R.F.A.
No.8 Headqrs: 296 Brigade, R.F.A.
No.9 Southern Group 2nd Cav: Div: Arty:
No.10 159th Brigade, R.F.A.
No.11 Headqrs: 'D' Sector.
No.12 2nd Cavalry Division.
No.13 Cavalry Corps R.A.
No.14 War Diary.
No.15 " "
No.16 File.

RELIEF TABLE.

NIGHT	UNIT RELIEVED	PRESENT POSITION	DESTINATION OF RELIEF	RELIEVING UNIT	GOES TO	REMARKS
	1 Section - "C" Battery, R.H.A.	F.8.c.5.3.	Wagon Lines	1 Section - A/159, R.F.A.	F.8.c.5.3.	
3rd/4th	1 Section - A/296, R.F.A. ø	F.15.c.3.4.	X.7.b.99.19	-	-	ø Under orders of S. Group, 2nd Cav: Div: Arty:
JULY	1 Section - B/296, R.F.A.	X.20.b.4.0.	X.7.d.97.17.	1 Section - B/159, R.F.A.	X.20.b.4.0.	
	1 Section - C/296, R.F.A.	Wagon Lines	X.7.b.85.99.	1 Section * C/159, R.F.A.	F.8.a.3.4.	* An officer of C/296 to hand over.
	1 Section - D/296, R.F.A.	F.7.b.6.7.	X.8.b.95.72.	1 Section - D/159, R.F.A.	F.7.b.6.7.	
	1 Section - "C" Battery, R.H.A.	F.8.c.5.3.	Wagon Lines	1 Section - A/159, R.F.A.	F.8.c.5.3.	
4th/5th	1 Section - A/296, R.F.A. ø	F.15.c.3.4.	X.7.b.99.19	-	-	ø Under orders of Southern Group, 2nd Cavalry Divl: Artillery.
JULY	1 Section - A/296, R.F.A. ø	F.15.c.3.4.	Wagon Lines	-	-	
	1 Section - B/296, R.F.A.	X.20.b.4.0.	X.7.d.97.17.	1 Section - B/159, R.F.A.	X.20.b.4.0.	
	1 Section - C/296, R.F.A.	Wagon Lines	X.7.b.85.99.	1 Section - * C/159, R.F.A.	F.8.a.3.4.	* An officer of C/296 to hand over.
	1 Section - D/296, R.F.A.	F.9.a.1.7.	X.8.b.95.72.	1 Section - D/296, R.F.A.	F.9.a.2.8.	

RELIEF TABLE.

NIGHT	UNIT RELIEVED	PRESENT POSITION	DESTINATION OF RELIEF	RELIEVING UNIT	GOES TO	REMARKS
5th/6th JULY	1 Section - "C" Battery, R.H.A.	F.8.c.5.3.	Wagon Lines	1 Section - A/159, R.F.A.	F.8.c.5.3.	
	1 Section - A/296, R.F.A. ∅	Wagon Lines	X.7.b.99.19	-	-	∅ Under orders of Southern Group.
	1 Section - B/296, R.F.A.	X.20.b.4.0.	X.7.d.97.17.	1 Section - B/159, R.F.A.	X.20.b.4.0.	
	1 Section - C/296, R.F.A.	Wagon Line	X.7.b.85.99.	-	-	
	1 Section - "C" Battery, R.H.A.	F.2.b.1.6.	Wagon Lines	1 Section - C/159, R.F.A.	F.2.b.1.6.	
8th/9th JULY	1 Section - "K" Battery, R.H.A.	ENFER WOOD	Wagon Lines	-	-	
	2 Sections - "G" Battery, R.H.A.	W.30.b.5.3.	Wagon Lines	-	-	
	Headquarters 4th Brigade, R.H.A.	F.1.d.9.8.	Wagon Lines	Headquarters 159 Brigade, R.F.A.		

SB/44

3rd Cavalry Divisional Artillery.

INTELLIGENCE SUMMARY. 6.0 p.m. 30th to 6.0 p.m. 1st.

1. OUR FIRE.

TIME	PLACE SHELLED	NATURE OF SHELL	DIRECTION	NUMBER OF ROUNDS	REMARKS
6.5 p.m.	OSSUS	13 pdr.	-	23	Punishment fire.
9.45 a.m.	F.6.a.45.65.	"	-	6	Sniping.
10.45 a.m.	KINGSTON QUARRY	18 pdr.	-	10	Punishment fire.
12.25 p.m.	F.6.a.45.65.	13 pdr.	-	2	Sniping.
2.30 p.m.	X.30.a.	"	-	15	Registration.
4.20 p.m. to 4.45 p.m.	X.29 / X.30	18 pdr.	-	23	Registration.

2. HOSTILE FIRE.

TIME	PLACE SHELLED	NATURE OF SHELL	DIRECTION	NUMBER OF ROUNDS	REMARKS
2.35 p.m. to 3.0 p.m.	X.17	4.2	LA TERRIERE	30	-
5.15 p.m.	LITTLE PRIEL FARM and BIRDCAGE	5.9	LA PANNERIE	4 2	-

3. GENERAL.

6.0 a.m. Three men seen in TINO trench at F.6.a.45.65. One man kept jumping out of the trench and appeared to be laying a telephone wire.

10.5 a.m. Four men were seen crawling about 100 yards in front of TINO trench at X.30.c.50.45. They were apparently laying a tape, this was patrolled by an Officer later this afternoon but no trace could be found of the tape.

Exceptionally quiet day on this front.

R.A. Headquarters.

2nd JULY, 1917.

Lieutenant, R. H. A.

R.O. 3rd Cavalry Divisional Artillery.

3rd Cavalry Divisional Artillery.

INTELLIGENCE SUMMARY. 6.0 p.m. 1st. to 6.0 p.m. 2nd.

1. OUR FIRE.

TIME	PLACE SHELLED	NATURE OF SHELL	DIRECTION	NUMBER OF ROUNDS	REMARKS
11.15 p.m. to 3.50 a.m.	OSSUS WOOD	4.5 How.	-	44)	Organised shoot, harassing fire for suspected enemy raid.
	Trenches in X.30.a. & c.	18 pdr.	-	40)	
8.30 a.m.	Trenches in X.24.c.)	18 pdr.	-	12	Punishment fire.
10.15 a.m.	X.30.c.5.0.4	13 pdr.	-	7	Sniping.
11.30 a.m.	FRANQUE WOOD	18 pdr.	-	5	Hostile M.G. firing at our aeroplane.
12 noon to 1.30 p.m.	VENDHUILE	4.5 How.	-	3	Sniping.
5.0 p.m.	A.7.b.	13 pdr.	-	25	Registration.
5.45 p.m.	Dug-outs in - S.20.a.3.0.)	"	-	30	-

2. HOSTILE FIRE.

TIME	PLACE SHELLED	NATURE OF SHELL	DIRECTION	NUMBER OF ROUNDS	REMARKS
8.0 a.m.	CATELET COPSE	77 mm	?	7	-
8.0 a.m.	X.16.a.	77 mm H.E.	?	10	-
10.30 a.m.	OSSUS No.2	4.2	LA TERRIERE	5	-
10.30 a.m. to 10.35 a.m.	OSSUS No.3	77 mm	HONNECOURT	6	-
5.30 p.m.	LEMPIRE TOMBOIS FARM)	15 cm	LE CATELET	30	-
5.45 p.m.	X.16.d.	77 mm	LA TERRIERE	10	-

3. GENERAL.

Transport and men observed on the GOUY - BEAUREVOIR Road all day.

Enemy appear to have done a good deal of work in the support trench in A.1.a.2.8.

Men seen entering dug-out at S.15.a.3.3., more work done on these dug-outs.

A small trench has been dug just behind XI WILLOWS in F.5.d. this appears to be a German L.P.

Nine camouflage sticks, which appear to be posts for an air line, run from the enemy trench in X.30c.5.5. to a point on the LITTLE PRIEL - VENDHUILE Road about 200 yards E.of the large Quarry in X.29.d. It was along this line of posts that two Germans were seen crawling yesterday morning.

4. HOSTILE AIR ACTIVITY.

Enemy aeroplane flew over our lines at intervals during the morning.

An enemy aeroplane was brought down by our A.A. guns at W.26.

R. A. Headquarters.
3rd JULY, 1917.

Lieutenant, R. H. A.
R. O. 3rd Cavalry Divisional Artillery.

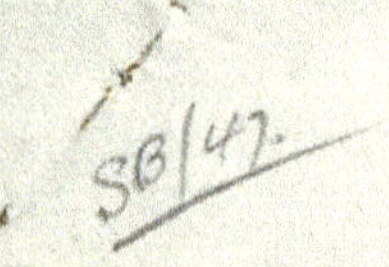

3rd Cavalry Divisional Artillery.

INTELLIGENCE SUMMARY. 6.0 p.m. 2nd to 6.0 p.m. 3rd.

1. OUR FIRE.

TIME	PLACE SHELLED	NATURE OF SHELL	DIRECTION	NUMBER OF ROUNDS	REMARKS
7.30 a.m.	OSSUS WOOD	13 pdr.	-	18	Punishment fire.
10.0 a.m.	X.29.b.9.9.	"	-	12	-do-
11.0 a.m.	OSSUS WOOD	"	-	36	-do-
12.15 p.m.	KINGSTON QUARRY	18 pdr.	-	10	-do-
12.40 p.m.	F.6.a.7.3½.	13 pdr.	-	10	Sniping.
5.0 p.m.	Ladder in S.19.a.4.4. Dug-outs	"	-	35	Registration.

2. HOSTILE FIRE.

TIME	PLACE SHELLED	NATURE OF SHELL	DIRECTION	NUMBER OF ROUNDS	REMARKS
7.40 a.m.	X.22	77 mm	LA TERRIERE	6	-
8.0 a.m.	CATELET VALLEY	4.2	LE CATELET	9	8 blind.
8.15 a.m.	LITTLE PRIEL FARM	77 mm	VENDHUILE	12	-
9.30 a.m. to 12.30 p.m.	LITTLE PRIEL FARM and BIRD LANE	5.9	LE CATELET	30	-
10.0 a.m. and 12 noon	CATELET COPSE	"	N. of LE CATELET	9 8	- -
10.30 a.m. to 10.45 a.m.	X.17.d. and road in X.15.a & d.	"	RANCOURT FARM	15	-
11.35 a.m.	Quarry in X.29.d.4.0.	77 mm	?	6	-
12.45 p.m. to 1.30 p.m.	X.22.a. & c.	"	LA TERRIERE	20	6 blind.
2.0 p.m. to 2.15 p.m.	"L" Post and PIGEON RAVINE	"	OSSUS	20	-
3.15 p.m. to 3.45 p.m.	X.20 and X21	"	-do-	30	-

3. GENERAL.

Visibility bad during the morning.

12.15 p.m. Movement seen in trench at F.6.a.7.3., direct hits obtained.

1.0 p.m. Smoke of a gun probably 5.9, which was shooting in the direction of EPEHY was observed at S.16.a.1.1. The heavies fired at this gun at 3.15 p.m.

4.0 p.m. to 5.0 p.m. Considerable movement in VILLERS-OUTREAUX and AUBENCHEUL. Suspected O.P. in house at S.15.c.9.1.

4. HOSTILE AIR ACTIVITY.

9.30 a.m. to 10.30 a.m. Enemy aeroplane flew up and down our front line several times.

R. A. Headquarters.
4th JULY, 1917.

Lieutenant, R. H. A.
R. O. 3rd Cavalry Divisional Artillery.

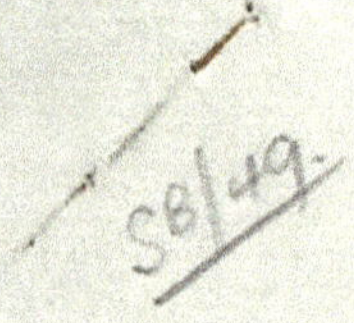

3rd Cavalry Divisional Artillery.

INTELLIGENCE SUMMARY. 6.0 p.m. 3rd to 6.0 p.m. 4th.

1. OUR FIRE.

TIME	PLACE SHELLED	NATURE OF SHELL	DIRECTION	NUMBER OF ROUNDS	REMARKS
12.30 a.m. to 12.52 a.m.	Trenches in A.17.d.	13 pdr.	-	550	Barrage for raid near GILLEMONT.
3.15 a.m. to 7.30 a.m.	Trenches in X.30.a.	"	-	60	Punishment fire.
6.00 a.m. to 11.30 a.m.	Road and Banks S.25.b.	4.5 How.	-	100	-do-
9.30 a.m. to 11.30 a.m.	X.30.c.5.1. OSSUS WOOD Trenches in X.30.a. & c.	13 pdr.	-	170	-do-
9.50 a.m.	KINGSTON QUARRY	18 pdr.	-	10	-do-
10.0 a.m.	X.30.c.9.3.	13 pdr.	-	8	Sniping at Germans on crest.
10.50 a.m.	F.6.c.8.8.	"	-	10	Suspected O.P.
11.0 a.m.	Trench X.24.a.2.3. to X.24.c.05.70.	18 pdr	-	17	Punishment fire.
11.15 a.m.	Cross roads S.14.a.7.6.	"	-	18	Registration.
11.40 a.m.	F.6.c.8.8.	13 pdr.	-	7	Suspected O.P.
5.30 p.m.	F.6.c.7.9.	"	-	12	At M.G. position.
3.15 p.m.	FALCON SAP	"	-	15	Registration.

2. HOSTILE FIRE.

TIME	PLACE SHELLED	NATURE OF SHELL	DIRECTION	NUMBER OF ROUNDS	REMARKS
3.15 a.m. to 7.30 a.m.	LITTLE PRIEL FARM and BIRDCAGE	77 mm 4.2 T.M.	LE CATELET VENDHUILE About S.25.c.3.7.	60	-
9.30 a.m. to 11.30 a.m.	Quarry in X.29.d.1.7. BIRDCAGE LITTLE PRIEL FM. CATELET COPSE	77 mm 4.2 T.M.	LE CATELET VENDHUILE	100	-

2. **HOSTILE FIRE.** (continued)

TIME	PLACE SHELLED	NATURE OF SHELL	DIRECTION	NUMBER OF ROUNDS	REMARKS
9.50 a.m.	No.1 Post	77 mm	-	8	-
11.45 a.m.	X.22.c.	4.2	VENDHUILE	9	-
1.30 p.m.	X.20.d.	"	-do-	4	-
2.50 p.m. to 3.30 p.m.	BIRDCAGE Quarry in X.29.d.1.7.	"	-do-	15	-
	LITTLE PRIEL FM.	"	BANKETT VALLEY	6	-

3. **GENERAL.**

9.30 a.m. to 11.30 a.m. The quarry in X.29.d.1.7. and the BIRDCAGE were shelled this morning at short range. At 10.30 a.m. he lengthened his range and searched near the LITTLE PRIEL - VENDHUILE Road for about 200^x. He then switched to No Man's Land in X.30.central between the BIRDCAGE and his front line, and appeared to put a round in his own trenches. He again lenghtened his range and put six rounds on the BIRDCAGE wire and the last few rounds into the BIRDCAGE itself, this How. seems to be close up and from the sound in the direction of VENDHUILE.
He again registered at 2.50 p.m.

11.50 a.m. During the registration of F.6.a.9.2. two Germans bolted from the trench on the N.W. side of the road in to the bank on the S. side.
An artillery O.P. is suspected in the enemy trench at F.6.c.9.8. This was fired on while the BIRDCAGE was being shelled, with the result that the firing ceased.
A dent can be seen in the parapet at F.6.c.9.2. where a M.G. is suspected to fire from at night.

Fresh work has been done in the trenches at A.1.a.2.5.
New wire has been put up at F.6.a.4.6. Three Germans were seen at F.6.a.4.6., one of them jumped out of the trench and put something up.
There is probably a gap in the wire at X.24.a.0.6.

10.0 a.m. to 10.15 a.m. While one of our Batteries were shooting at OSSUS WOOD, he apparently hit an S.A.A. dump as reports of S.A.A. going off could be heard for about five minutes.

The light was bad during the early part of the day but improved later, getting worse again about 4.30 p.m.

R. A. Headquarters.
5th JULY, 1917.

Lieutenant, R. H. A.
R. O. 3rd Cavalry Divisional Artillery.

SB/51

3rd Cavalry Divisional Artillery.

INTELLIGENCE SUMMARY. 6.0 p.m. 4th to 6.0 p.m. 5th.

1. OUR FIRE.

TIME	PLACE SHELLED	NATURE OF SHELL	DIRECTION	NUMBER OF ROUNDS	REMARKS.
1.45 a.m.	S. O. S. Lines	4.5 How.	-	41)	
	-do-	18 pdr.	-	35)	False S. O. S.
	-do-	13 pdr.	-	50)	
9.0 a.m.	OSSUS WOOD	"	-	80	Punishment fire.
9.10 a.m.	Zero Lines	18 pdr.	-	17	Registration.
11.0 a.m.	-do-	"	-	10	-do-
3.0 p.m.	Road in S.27.d.	13 pdr.	-	15	Sniping at enemy party.
5.0 p.m.	OSSUS WOOD	"	-	40	Punishment fire.
5.45 p.m.	Trench in X.30.a. & c.)	"	-	20	-do-
6.0 p.m.	S.26.b.40.60.) S.27.c.50.80.) X.24.d.)	4.5 How.	-	30) 8) 4)	Registration.

2. HOSTILE FIRE.

TIME	PLACE SHELLED	NATURE OF SHELL	DIRECTION	NUMBER OF ROUNDS	REMARKS.
3.50 a.m. to 9.30 a.m.	LIMERICK Post	77 mm	FRANQUET WOOD	15	-
9.0 a.m.	CATELET COPSE No.13 COPSE	"	VENDHUILE	20	-
9.0 a.m. to 9.45 a.m.	LITTLE PRIEL FM.	4.2	-do-	20	-
9.30 a.m.	-do-	?	LA TERRIERE	12	-
5.0 p.m.	CATELET COPSE) "H" Post)	77 mm	VENDHUILE	20	-
5.45 p.m.	Trenches in) X.28.a. and) X.22.c.)	"	-do-	?	Heavy fire for two minutes.

3. <u>GENERAL.</u>

Work, being done in KING SUPPORT in A.1.b., where four large mounds can be seen.

11.0 a.m. Three parties, each of about six Germans, walked down the road in S.27.d.

4.0 p.m. Four men walked down the track in S.14.d.

11.0 a.m. The smoke of a train was observed moving Southwards along a line in S.30.

3.0 p.m. A motor lorry going slowly Southwards was seen in S.23. and S.29.

A possible Sniper's post can be observed at X.29.a.85.90.

R. A. Headquarters.
8th JULY, 1917.

Lieutenant, R. H. A.
R. O. 3rd Cavalry Divisional Artillery.

3rd Cavalry Divisional Artillery.

INTELLIGENCE SUMMARY. 6.0 p.m. 5th to 6.0 p.m. 6th.

1. OUR FIRE.

TIME	PLACE SHELLED	NATURE OF SHELL	DIRECTION	NUMBER OF ROUNDS	REMARKS
11.30 a.m.	S.21.c.00.00.	4.5 How.	-	19	Registration.
12.5 p.m. to 1.0 p.m.	F.6.a.40.38.	18 pdr.	-	28	-do-
1.5 p.m.	OSSUS WOOD (S.20.a.)	13 pdr.	-	48	Punishment fire.
1.30 p.m.	X.23.b.9.2. and CANAL WOOD	"	-	50	-do-
2.15 p.m. to 3.50 p.m.	Houses in PUTNEY	"	-	60	Registration.
3.0 p.m. to 3.33 p.m.	S. O. S. Lines	18 pdr.	-	24	Registration.
4.3 p.m. to 4.35 p.m.	-do-	"	-	15	
5.45 p.m.	FRANQUE WOOD in S.14.b.85.05.	"	-	15	Punishment fire, E.A.A. guns shooting at our aero-planes.

2. HOSTILE FIRE.

TIME	PLACE SHELLED	NATURE OF SHELL	DIRECTION	NUMBER OF ROUNDS	REMARKS
5.45 a.m.	X.17.d.	77 mm	FRANQUE WOOD	10	-
10.30 a.m. to 12.5 p.m.	Battery position in X.20.b.45.50.	4.2	?	25	Chiefly air bursts.
12.30 p.m. to 1.15 p.m.	-do-	4.2 5.9	?	300	About.
2.0 p.m.	-do-	77 mm	FRANQUE WOOD	40	-

2. **HOSTILE FIRE.** (continued)

TIME	PLACE SHELLED	NATURE OF SHELL	DIRECTION	NUMBER OF ROUNDS	REMARKS
12.55p.m. to 1.30 p.m.	X.28.b.)) X.28.c.)	4.2 4.2	15° left of S.21.c.00.00. from O.P. X.22.d.60.10.	32	Short range.
1.5 p.m.	CATELET COPSE	5.9	?	4	-
1.45 p.m. to 2.10.p.m.	LITTLE PRIEL FM.	4.2	LA TERRIERE	25	-

3. **GENERAL.**

10.30 a.m. to 12.5 p.m. — The Battery position in X.20.b.45.50. was shelled with 4.2, 5.9 and later on 77mm., the shelling was chiefly with 4.2 For the first part og the shoot an enemy aeroplane was observing, getting most of the bursts in air. At 12.30p.m. the shelling started again with fire for effect, Six guns 4.2 and two 5.9 seemed to be doing the shelling. No damage was done,

9.0 a.m. — Four Germans seen walking in and out of the trench in X.23.d. and X.24.a., carrying sand-bags, work ceased on being fired at.

4. **HOSTILE AIR ACTIVITY.**

6.0 a.m. to 4.0 p.m. enemy aeroplane active, and enemy A.A. guns firing from the direction of FRANQUE WOOD.

R.A. Headquarters. Lieutenant, R. H. A.

7th JULY, 1917. R.O. 3rd Cavalry Divisional Artillery.

3rd Cavalry Divisional Artillery.

INTELLIGENCE SUMMARY. 6.0 p.m. 6th to 6.0 p.m. 7th.

1. OUR FIRE.

TIME	PLACE SHELLED	NATURE OF SHELL	DIRECTION	NUMBER OF ROUNDS	REMARKS
10.0 a.m.	Dug-outs in S.20.a.	13 pdr.	-	24	Sniping.
12.25 p.m.	S.21.c.00.00.	4.5 How.	-	15	Registration.
12.45 p.m.	S.27.a.00.60.	"	-	10	-do-
1.0 p.m.	Aeroplane in S.20.a.	13 pdr.	-	30	-
2.20 p.m.	South end of FRANQUE WOOD	18pdr.	-	4	Punishment fire, E.A.A. active.
3.30 p.m.	S.20.a.	"	-	40	-

2. HOSTILE FIRE.

TIME	PLACE SHELLED	NATURE OF SHELL	DIRECTION	NUMBER OF ROUNDS	REMARKS
1.20 p.m.	X.23.c.	77 mm	?	10	-
1.20 p.m. to 1.45 p.m.	No.1 Post	"	FRANQUE WOOD	8	-
1.56 p.m.	X.23.b. & d.	"	?	8	-
2.0 p.m.	"K" Post	"	LA TERRIERE	10	-

3. GENERAL.

One of our aeroplanes (F.E.14) brought down, apparently by machine gun fire, at about S.14.c. or d. the occupants appeared to be injured, they were taken away by several Germans.

1.50 p.m. Parties of men seen loading wagons in B.1.d. and B.13.a.

1.55 p.m. Dense white smoke rising behind the railway embankment in A.5.d.75.45.

A good deal of movement on the GOUY - BEAUREVOIR Road, screens have been erected on either side of this road.

R. A. Headquarters. Lieutenant, R. H. A.

8th July, 1917. R. O. 3rd Cavalry Divisional Artillery.

Instructions regarding War Diaries and Intelligence Summaries are contained in F. S. Regs., Part II. and the Staff Manual respectively. Title pages will be prepared in manuscript.

WAR DIARY
or
INTELLIGENCE SUMMARY. HQ IV Bde R.H.A.

(Erase heading not required.)

AUGUST 1917

Army Form C. 2118.

Vol 31

Place	Date	Hour	Summary of Events and Information	Remarks and references to Appendices
			Ref 1/100000 HAZEBROUCK Sheet 5a.	
In the field	1st		Brigade was billeted in I Army Area, Batteries being with their Cav Bdes, as follows. H.Q. R.H.A at LA PIERRIERE C Battery R.H.A at LE CORBIE, G Battery R.H.A at PECQUER K Battery R.H.A at BAS HAMEL, Amtn Column at ~~[illegible]~~ ST FLORIS	
	12th		G Battery moved to HAM-EN-ARTOIS, Amtn Column to LE SART.	
	25th		3rd Cavalry Division held Horse Show at BUSNES to select competitors for Cavalry Corps Horse Show.	
			Gun team class won by K Battery R.H.A. G Battery Second. Wagon team class - - Bay team from Amtn Column. Chestnut team from Amtn Column second, G Battery third.	
	31st		C and G Batteries marched to ST. OMER on their way to V Army area for purpose of training gunless Brigades.	
			The month was spent in training so far as conditions of the country permitted. C Battery practiced Canal crossing on two occasions on latter of which Corps Commander was present.	

2353 Wt. W2544/1454 700,000 5/15 D. D. & L. A.D.S.S./Forms/C. 2118.

Army Form C. 2118.

WAR DIARY
or
INTELLIGENCE SUMMARY.
(Erase heading not required.)

Instructions regarding War Diaries and Intelligence Summaries are contained in F. S. Regs., Part II. and the Staff Manual respectively. Title pages will be prepared in manuscript.

AUGUST 1917 H. Q. IV Bde R.H.A.

Place	Date	Hour	Summary of Events and Information	Remarks and references to Appendices
	–		Weather was generally wet throughout the month & as much assistance as possible was given to the French farmers with their harvest.	
			A.M. [illegible] Lt Col	

2353 Wt. W2544/1454 700,000 5/15 D. D. & L. A.D.S.S./Forms/C. 2118.

CONFIDENTIAL

Army Form C. 2118.

WAR DIARY
or
~~INTELLIGENCE SUMMARY.~~
(Erase heading not required.)

Instructions regarding War Diaries and Intelligence Summaries are contained in F. S. Regs., Part II. and the Staff Manual respectively. Title pages will be prepared in manuscript.

SEPT 1917

H.Q. IV Bde R.H.A.

(1)

Vol 32

Place	Date	Hour	Summary of Events and Information	Remarks and references to Appendices
			ref 1/100000. HAZEBROUCK Sheet 5A	
LAPIERRIERE -	1st.		H.Q. R.H.A at LA PIERREIERE 2 miles NNW of BUSNES. Amtn Column at ~~[illegible]~~ ~~[illegible]~~ LESART. 2 miles W. of MERVILLE. K Battery R.H.A at BASHAMEL 2 miles W of HAVERSKERQUE. all a Bois in billets K. Battery R.H.A under 7th Cav. Bde. C and G Batteries R.H.A marched to NIEURLET from ~~[illegible]~~ ST OMER for the purpose of training gunless brigades of V Army K Battery R.H.A won 3rd prize for Best gun Team and Amtn Column won 2nd " " " Wagon - at Cav. Corps. Horse Show held near ST. POL.	
	2nd.		K Battery moved with 7th Cav Bde to PERNES area, - billeted at MAREST.	
LAMIQUELLERIE	6th		H.Q. R.H.A moved to LA MIQUELLERIE near BUSNES. C Battery R.H.A. moved to HERZEELE Area and bivouacked 2 miles N.W of the town G Battery R.H.A. moved to DROGLANDT and bivouacked.	
	11th		C Battery R.H.A moved to Bivouac N.E of HOFLANDE near River YSER.	

(A7092) Wt. W12839/M1293 750,000. 1/17. D. D. & L., Ltd. Forms/C.2118/14.

Instructions regarding War Diaries and Intelligence Summaries are contained in F. S. Regs., Part II. and the Staff Manual respectively. Title pages will be prepared in manuscript.

WAR DIARY
or
~~INTELLIGENCE SUMMARY~~.
(Erase heading not required.)

Army Form C. 2118.

Sept. 1917 — H.Q. IV Bde R.H.A.

(2)

Place	Date	Hour	Summary of Events and Information	Remarks and references to Appendices
	16th		One section of K Battery R.H.A under LT. FERGUSON proceeded to IV Army School near AMIENS to be lent for practice, returned on 21st	
	28th		G. Battery R.H.A marched to BROXEELE and bivouacked.	
GENERAL.–			The weather throughout the month was on the average fine & dry. The C.R.H.A took part in several divisional staff rides, and attended drill orders of K Battery on 2 occasions. C and G Batteries lent guns and horses to F.A. Brigades resting in their area, for the purpose of instruction	

A. Wainwright Lt Col

(A7092). Wt. W12839/M1293. 750,000. 1/17. D. D. & L., Ltd. Forms/C.2118/14.

Instructions regarding War Diaries and Intelligence Summaries are contained in F. S. Regs., Part II. and the Staff Manual respectively. Title pages will be prepared in manuscript.

WAR DIARY
or
~~INTELLIGENCE SUMMARY.~~ H.Q. IV Bde R.H.A.

OCTOBER 1917. *(Erase heading not required.)*

Army Form C. 2118.

(1)

Ref 1/100000 HAZEBROUCK. 5A

Vol 33

Place	Date	Hour	Summary of Events and Information	Remarks and references to Appendices
	1st		The IV Bde R.H.A was distributed as follows. H.Q at LA MIQUELLERIE near BUSNES. "K" Battery R.H.A at ~~[illegible]~~ MAREST near PERNES. "C" and "G" Batteries R.H.A with V Army at HOFLANDE on the Belgian frontier and BROXEELE respectively Amtn. Column at LE SART near MERVILLE.	
	4th		"G" Battery R.H.A. marched to ST MOMEZIN remaining under orders of V Army.	
	5th		Tactical Scheme with troops 8th Cav Bde & 7th Cav. Bde. K Battery R.H.A took part	
	6th		"C" Battery R.H.A. marched to ST MOMEZIN area.	
	8th		Concentration of Division in STEENBEQUE. ST VENANT MERVILLE area ordered. this was afterwards cancelled.	
	10th		"K" Battery R.H.A. with 7th Cav. Bde marched to LE CORNET MALO near HINGES.	
	17th		3rd Cav Div commenced move to DOMART-EN-PONTHIEU area. H.Q. R.H.A to PERNES, Amtn Column to FIEFS.	

(A7092). Wt. W12839/M1293. 750,000. 1/17. D. D. & L., Ltd. Forms/C.2118/14.

Instructions regarding War Diaries and Intelligence Summaries are contained in F. S. Regs., Part II. and the Staff Manual respectively. Title pages will be prepared in manuscript.

WAR DIARY
or
~~INTELLIGENCE SUMMARY.~~
(Erase heading not required.)

Army Form C. 2118.

OCTOBER 1917 H.Q. IV Bde R.H.A. (3)

Place	Date	Hour	Summary of Events and Information	Remarks and references to Appendices
	22nd		H.Q. R.H.A marched to HOUVIN HOUVIGNEUL	
			K Battery R.H.A with 7th Cav Bde to VALHUON	
	23rd		Amm Column moved to BONNIERES under orders of 7th Cav Bde	
			HQ R.H.A to LA HAIE Farm near DOMART	
			K Battery R.H.A to PETIT & GRAND BOURET.	
	24th		Amm Column to GORENFLOS and ERGNIES - K Battery to FRANSU	
			The Amm Column sent a party of 1 officer and 29 O.R. to work in PERONNE area at end of month.	
			Weather was generally wet Billets in new area comfortable for all units. Horses very well off	
			Capt H.M. BRYANS posted from K Battery to 59th Div. A.G.	
			Lieut R.H. CLARKE " " " " " R.F.C	
			Lieut H.A. BAKER " " C " " K Battery as a/Captain	
			Lieut M.E.S. Thompson " " Amm Column to K Battery R.H.A	
			2Lieut P.L. Hutchins " " " " to C " "	
			Lieut HINDLE " to " " from Base.	

E. I. Boylan Capt R.H.A
Adjt. for O.C. IV Bde R.H.A.

(A7092). Wt. W12839/M1293. 750,000. 1/17. D. D. & L., Ltd. Forms/C.2118/14.

3rd Cav Dv

Army Form C. 2118.

Instructions regarding War Diaries and Intelligence Summaries are contained in F. S. Regs., Part II. and the Staff Manual respectively. Title pages will be prepared in manuscript.

WAR DIARY
~~or~~
~~INTELLIGENCE SUMMARY.~~

(Erase heading not required.)

4th Bde RHA

NOVEMBER 1917

1/ Vol 34

Place	Date	Hour	Summary of Events and Information	Remarks and references to Appendices
	1st		Bde distributed as follows H.Q. LA HAIE Fm near DOMART EN PONTHIEU } in billets K/RHA FRANSU under 1st Cav Bde Ammn Column GORENFLOS C/RHA } ST MOMEZIN Area training RFA personnel under G/RHA } V Army.	
	9th		C and G Batteries rejoined Division from V Army C billeted at AILLY-LE-HAUT-CLOCHER under 1 Cav Bde. G " " BOURDON " 8 " "	
	12th		IV Bde RHA marched detached from Division H.Q to VIGNACOURT. AmtnCol to VIGNACOURT. C/RHA to FLESSELLES. K/RHA to " G/RHA remains BOURDON.	
	13th		Bde marched to CORBIE AREA HQ to CORBIE C/RHA to SAILLY LE SEC G/RHA to HAMEL K/RHA to VAUX Ammn Col to BONNAY C.R.H.A and B.C.s went on to 51st Div to [illegible]	

(A7092). Wt. W12839/M1293 750,000. 1/17. D. D. & L., Ltd. Forms/C.2118/14.

WAR DIARY

~~or~~

~~INTELLIGENCE SUMMARY.~~

(*Erase heading not required.*)

Instructions regarding War Diaries and Intelligence Summaries are contained in F. S. Regs., Part II. and the Staff Manual respectively. Title pages will be prepared in manuscript.

Army Form C. 2118.

4th Bde RHA

November 1917

2/

Place	Date	Hour	Summary of Events and Information	Remarks and references to Appendices
	14th		Bde to MOISLAINS marched from CORBIE 5pm. Reached MOISLAINS 7am 15th. Bivouac at MOISLAINS.	
	15th		Bde marched to camp at LE MESNIL EN ARROUAISE arriving 8pm.	
	16th		Reconnaissance of Positions by BCs & O [illegible]	
	17th		Guns and limbers sent up to HAVRINCOURT WOOD [illegible] there.	see Append A
	19th		Batteries went into action after dark at Q 10 d (ref 1/40000 57C) under orders of 51st Div Art. No registration to be carried out. H.Q. to Q 21 b near METZ EN COUTURE.	
	20th		ZERO hour 6.20 am 4 Bde RHA fired Barrages as in Appendix B. Ceased firing Zero + 4 hours. ~~[illegible]~~ Guns did not fire again on 20th. Advance of Tanks & Infantry successful. 1st Cav Division passed through METZ, we [illegible] to [illegible]	

(A7092). Wt. W12839/M1293. 750,000. 1/17. D. D. & L., Ltd. Forms/C.2118/14.

Instructions regarding War Diaries and Intelligence Summaries are contained in F. S. Regs., Part II. and the Staff Manual respectively. Title pages will be prepared in manuscript.

WAR DIARY or ~~INTELLIGENCE SUMMARY.~~

(*Erase heading not required.*)

Army Form C. 2118.

Nov 1917 — 4th Bde RHA [?] 3

Place	Date	Hour	Summary of Events and Information	Remarks and references to Appendices
	20th		3rd Cav Div: Still under orders of 51st Div Arty.	
	21st		Ordered to fire a barrage from 7am onwards to support an attack. See Appendix C	
			2.30pm Bde marched back to LE MESNIL Camp & joined up with Amm. Column & wagon lines who had remained there.	
	to 29th		Remained at LE MESNIL. Received ~~[illegible]~~ orders that 152 [?] should go into line South of EPEHY & positions reconnoitred by O.C. Brigade	
	30th		BC's & advanced parties went on to take over to HERVILLY [?]	
			About 11.30 am orders received from 4th Corps to stand to ready to move. Germans having broken our line about VILLERS GUISLAIN.	
			12 noon Ordered to move to LIERAMONT. O.C. Bde to report to 55th Div. at VILLERS FAUCON as soon as possible.	
			Bde marched from LE MESNIL about 12.45 pm	
			Colonel reconnoitred position for Bde West of EPEHY.	
			Bde under Major Scarlett DSO received separate orders	

(A7092). Wt. W12839/M1293. 750,000. 1/17. D. D. & L., Ltd. Forms/C.2118/14.

Instructions regarding War Diaries and Intelligence Summaries are contained in F. S. Regs., Part II. and the Staff Manual respectively. Title pages will be prepared in manuscript.

WAR DIARY
or
INTELLIGENCE SUMMARY.
(*Erase heading not required.*)

Army Form C. 2118.

Nov 1917 4 Bde RHA 4

Place	Date	Hour	Summary of Events and Information	Remarks and references to Appendices
	30th		to join 24th Div & go into action about TEMPLEUX LE GUERARD	
			All Batteries in action by 10 pm as follows. Ref 1/40000 62c	
			C/RHA 3 guns L2b6.7 } Wagon Lines HAMELET	
			3 guns L2d3.9 } Ammn Col MARQUAIX	
			G/RHA 2 guns L26d6.0 }	
			" 2 guns L2a99.95 }	
			K/RHA 5 guns K26a3.6 }	
			HQ L7b91 }	
			Attack expected gun limbers drew up to guns at 5 am.	
			Quiet night.	
			Capt E H MANN MC left C Battery RHA to join 59 Div Art	
			Following joined Bde during month.	
			Lieut HINDLE RFA	
			2Lieut V.C. HOLLAND R.F.A.	
			11/12/17	A. W. Mainwaring Lt Col 4 Brigade RHA.

(A7092). Wt. W12839/M1293. 750,000. 1/17. D. D. & L., Ltd. Forms/C.2118/14.

Instructions regarding War Diaries and Intelligence Summaries are contained in F. S. Regs., Part II. and the Staff Manual respectively. Title pages will be prepared in manuscript.

WAR DIARY
or
INTELLIGENCE SUMMARY.
(Erase heading not required.)

Army Form C. 2118.

4 Bde R.H.A.

DECEMBER 1 9 1 7.

Place	Date	Hour	Summary of Events and Information	Remarks and references to Appendices
	1st		Batteries in action as follows - Reference 1/40,000, 62c	
			"C" Battery, R.H.A. 3 guns L.2.b.6.7. / 2 guns L.2.d.3.9.	
			"G" Battery, R.H.A. 2 guns F.26.d.6.0. / 2 guns L.2.a.99.95. — Wagon Lines HAMELET.	
			"K" Battery, R.H.A. 5 guns F.26.d.3.6.	
			Covering 73rd Infantry Brigade consisting of the following Battalions -	
			9th Royal Sussex. 7th Northants. 13th Middlesex. 2nd Leinsters.	
			Zones of Batteries were -	
			"C" Battery, R.H.A. - CAT POST - Spur East of BENJAMIN POST.	
			"K" Battery, R.H.A. - Spur East of BENJAMIN POST - tp MALAKOFF Farm inclusive.	
			"G" Battery, R.H.A. - G.1.b.6.6. to RUBY WOOD inclusive.	
	2nd		Wagon Lines moved to VRAIGNES.	

A7092). Wt. W12839/M1297 750,000. 1/17. D. D & L., Ltd. Forms/C2118/14.

Instructions regarding War Diaries and Intelligence Summaries are contained in F. S. Regs., Part II. and the Staff Manual respectively. Title pages will be prepared in manuscript.

WAR DIARY
or
INTELLIGENCE SUMMARY.
(Erase heading not required.)

Army Form C. 2118.

Place	Date	Hour	Summary of Events and Information	Remarks and references to Appendices
	9		On night 9/10th one Section of each Battery was relieved, see appendix 'A' and took up new positions as under - "C" Battery, R.H.A. - L.32.b.0.3. "G" Battery, R.H.A. - L.27.d.9.1. "K" Battery, R.H.A. - L.26.c.5.8.	
			Headquarters 4th Brigade, R.H.A. formed Headquarters of Cavalry Divisional Artillery Group consisting of - SCARLETT'S GROUP (Chestnut Troop, "C", "G", and "K" Batteries, R.H.A.). STIRLING'S GROUP ("N" & "U" Batteries, R.H.A., "A" & "B" Batteries, R.C.H.A., D/311 (Howitzer) Battery, R.F.A.). MELLOR'S GROUP ("D" "E" "J" and "Q" Batteries, R.H.A.). Headquarters at R.8.a.5.8.	
			The Group covered the 3rd Cavalry Dismounted Division which held from L.18.a.0.0. to river L'OMIGNON, with 5th French Division on the right and 24th (British) Division on the left.	
			Policy entirely defensive.	
	16		Lieutenant Colonel A.R. WAINEWRIGHT, R.H.A. took over command of 24th Divisional Artillery during the absence of Brigadier General E.S. HOARE NAIRNE. Lieutenant Colonel W. STIRLING, D.S.O., R.H.A. took over command of Cavalry Divisional Artillery Group.	
	16		Mobile Sections were posted to Batteries. (Appendix 'B').	
	27		Lieutenant H.R. BENNETT, R.H.A. went to Headquarters 24th Divnl. Artillery as Reconnaissance Officer to Dismounted Divisions Artillery.	

A7092). Wt. W12859/M1297 750,000. 1/17. D. D & L., Ltd. Forms/C2118/14.

Instructions regarding War Diaries and Intelligence Summaries are contained in F. S. Regs., Part II. and the Staff Manual respectively. Title pages will be prepared in manuscript.

WAR DIARY
or
INTELLIGENCE SUMMARY.
(Erase heading not required.)

Army Form C. 2118.

Place	Date	Hour	Summary of Events and Information	Remarks and references to Appendices
	30		Cavalry Division Artillery Group was broken up . Headquarters 4th Brigade,R.H.A. took over Headquarters of SCARLETT'S GROUP, (which remained the same except that THE CHESTNUT TROOP was transfered to MELLOR'S GROUP), under command of Major H.G. YOUNG,D.S.O.,R.H.A. Lieutenant Colonel WAINEWRIGHT took over command of Dismounted Divisions Arty:	
			During the month -	
			Major (The Hon) H.R. SCARLETT,D.S.O.,R.H.A. was posted from "C" Battery, R.H.A. to 40th Division. Lieutenant J.P. DASHWOOD,R.H.A. from "K" Battery,R.H.A. to Guards Division. Lieutenant W.G. DEAKIN, R.F.A. from "K" Battery,R.H.A. to 61st Division.	
			the following officers joined the Brigade -	
			2ndLieutenant O.L. BOORDS,R.F.A. from WOOLWICH to "C" Battery,R.H.A. 2ndLieutenant V.StG. KNAGGS,R.F.A. from 62nd Division to "K" Battery,R.H.A. 2ndLieutenant S.B. RAWLINS,M.C.,R.H.A. from 307th Brigade,R.F.A.	
			Appointments. Captain E.T. BOYLAN,R.H.A. from Adjutant to 2nd in command of "C" Battery, Lieutenant H.G. MORRISON,R.H.A. appointed Adjutant and posted from "C" Battery,R.H.A.	
			[signature] Major, R.H.A. Commanding 4th Brigade,R.H.A.	

A7092). Wt. W12839/M1295 750,000. 1/17. D. D & L., Ltd. Forms/C2118/14.

'A'

R. H. A. GROUP - ORDER No.3

1. 1 Section per Battery will be relieved tonight by 1 Section per Battery of 7th Brigade, R.H.A., relief will commence about 4-30 p.m.

2. Section on relief will proceed direct to new position. They will be accompained by 4 Q.F. Wagons so that 176 rounds per gun may be dumped at new position.

3. All ammunition will be left at old position.

4. O.C. 7th Brigade, R.H.A. will take over command of Group on completion of relief of Section on night 9/10th.

5. 1 empty G.S. Wagon from Ammunition Column party at forward Dump will accompany each Battery, this wagon to be at Battery position at 4 p.m.

6. 7th Brigade,R.H.A. will take over forward Dump on 10th instant when 4th Brigade,R.H.A. party will return to VRAIGNES.

7. Batteries will make their own arrangements to guide their teams back to VRAIGNES from new positions.

8. Remainder of 4th Brigade,R.H.A. will be relieved on night 10/11th and will proceed to new positions.

9. Completion of relief each night will be wired to Group Headquarters by code word "SAFE".

Headquarters, E.T. BOYLAN, Captain, R.H.A.

9th December,1917. Adjutant R. H. A. Group.

'B'

O.C. "C" Battery, R.H.A.

O.C. "G" Battery, R.H.A.

O.C. "K" Battery, R.H.A.

O.C. Ammunition Column.

Reference attached Brigade Order -

1. In future when out of the line Mobile Sections will normally live with their Batteries. When in the line the Mobile Sections will stay with the Ammunition Column and one Officer per Battery will be sent to look after them. This Officer will be changed from time to time.

2. The Officers at present with the Ammunition Column will come up to do a tour of duty <u>forthwith</u> and Officers sent to replace them.

16th December, 1917.

H.G. MORRISON, Captain, R.H.A.
Adjutant 4th Brigade, R. H. A.

Army Form C. 2118.

Instructions regarding War Diaries and Intelligence Summaries are contained in F. S. Regs., Part II. and the Staff Manual respectively. Title pages will be prepared in manuscript.

WAR DIARY
or
INTELLIGENCE SUMMARY

(*Erase heading not required.*)

JANUARY 1918.

4 Bde R HA
Vol 36

Place	Date	Hour	Summary of Events and Information	Remarks and references to Appendices
			Reference 1/40,000, Sheet 62.c.	
			Headquarters and Batteries in action as follows -	
			Headquarters - L.32.a.4.0.	
			"C" Battery, R.H.A. L.32.b.0.3.	
			"G" Battery, R.H.A.	
			3 guns L.27.d.9.1.	
			2 guns L.27.b.8.8.	
			1 gun L.29.c.1.9.	
			"K" Battery, R.H.A. L.26.c.5.8.	
			On night 24th/25th 3 guns "G" Battery, R.H.A. moved from L.29.d.9.1. to L.26.d.5.3.	
			Wagon Lines at VRAIGNES.	
			The Brigade acting as SCARLETT'S Sub-Group under Left Group, Cavalry Divisional Artillery covering the front G.7.b.6.7. - L.18.c.9.0. which was held during the month by 2nd Dismounted Division and 4th Dismounted Division.	
			Policy - Defensive.	
			4-1-1918. - Lieutenant H.R. BENNETT, R.H.A. (Orderly Officer) died.	
			Lieutenant F.C. MOORE, R.F.A. joined the Brigade during the month.	
			[signature] Capt. for Major, R.H.A. Commanding 4th Brigade, R. H. A.	

(A7092). Wt. W12839/M1293 750,000. 1/17. D. D. & L., Ltd. Forms/C.2118/14.

Instructions regarding War Diaries and Intelligence Summaries are contained in F. S. Regs., Part II. and the Staff Manual respectively. Title pages will be prepared in manuscript.

WAR DIARY
or
INTELLIGENCE SUMMARY.
(Erase heading not required.)

Army Form C. 2118.

4 Bde R.H.A.

Vol 37

4th BRIGADE, R.H.A. FEBRUARY, 1918.

Place	Date	Hour	Summary of Events and Information	Remarks and references to Appendices
			Reference 1/40,000, Sheet 62.c.	
			Headquarters and Batteries in action as follows -	
			Headquarters ... L.32.a.4.0.	
			"C" Battery, R.H.A. ... L.32.b.0.3.	
			"G" Battery, R.H.A. ... L.26.d.5.3. (4 guns). L.27.b.8.8. (1 gun). L.29.c.1.9. (1 gun).	
			"K" Battery, R.H.A. ... L.26.c.5.8.	
			Wagon Lines at VRAIGNES.	
			The Brigade acting as Scarlett's Sub-Group under Cavalry Divisional Artillery 24th Divisional Arty: and 66th Divisional Arty: in turn, covered 4th Dismounted Division, 72nd Infantry Brigade and 199th Infantry Brigade respectively.	
			Policey - Defensive.	
			During the month -	
			2ndLieutenant A.E.J. CLARK, R.F.A. joined the Brigade from 24th Divisional Artillery and was posted to "K" Battery, R.H.A.	
			Lieutenant F.C. MOORE, R.F.A. was posted from 4th Brigade R.H.A. Ammunition Column to 58th Brigade, R.F.A.	

[illegible] Capt
for Major, R.H.A.
Commanding 4th Brigade R.H.A.

A7092). Wt. W12839/M1297 750,000. 1/17. D. D & L., Ltd. Forms/C2118/14.

2/8

Army Form C. 2118.

WAR DIARY
or
~~INTELLIGENCE SUMMARY~~.

Instructions regarding War Diaries and Intelligence Summaries are contained in F. S. Regs., Part II. and the Staff Manual respectively. Title pages will be prepared in manuscript.

4th BRIGADE, R.H.A. (Erase heading not required.) MARCH, 1918.

Vol 38

Place	Date	Hour	Summary of Events and Information	Remarks and references to Appendices
			Reference 1/40,000, Sheets 62,c. and 62,d.	
			Units in action as follows :-	
	1st		Headquarters ... L.32.a.4.0.)	
	to		"C" Battery, R.H.A. ... L.32.b.0.3.)	
	13th		"G" Battery, R.H.A. (3 Guns) L.27.d.9.1.) (2 Guns) L.27.b.8.8.) (1 Gun) L.29.c.1.9.) LEANCOURT AREA.	
			"K" Battery, R.H.A. L.26.c.5.8.)	
			Ammunition Column ... VRAIGNES.	
			Covering 66th Division.	
	13th		"G" Battery, R.H.A. was transfered to 17th Brigade, R.H.A.	
			Royal Canadian Horse Artillery Brigade was transfered from ~~17th Brigade~~, R.H.A. [5th Cav Div] to ~~4th Brigade, R.H.A.~~ [3rd Cav Div]	
			Attached appendix I account of operations from 21/3/1918 to 10/4/1918.	
			[signature] Lieutenant Colonel, R.H.A. Commanding 4th Brigade, R.H.A.	

A7092). Wt. W12839/M1297 750,000. 1/17. D. D & L., Ltd. Forms/C2118/14.

[Handwritten: Ref. 1/40000 62C 62D 66E]

APPENDIX I.

to

WAR DIARY - MARCH, 1918.

OPERATIONS CARRIED OUT BY 4th BRIGADE, R.H.A. BETWEEN 21st MARCH AND 10th APRIL, 1918.

21st. Units were in action as follows:-

"C" Battery, R.H.A.	(5 guns)	L.32.b.0.3.	JEANCOURT.
"K" Battery, R.H.A.	(6 guns)	L.26.c.5.8.	

Covering 66th Division.

"C" Battery had one Tank gun at L.29.c.1.9.
This gun was captured during the day and was reported by the infantry to have killed a lot of Germans over open sights, shooting up to the last moment.

Headquarters 4th Brigade, R.H.A. re-established in JEANCOURT at 4 p.m. acting as a Sub-Group under R.H.A. Group consisting of the Chestnut Troop, "Q" and "U" Batteries, R.H.A. and commanded by Lieutenant Colonel J. ALLARDYCE, D.S.O., R.H.A.

Both "C" and "K" were heavily shelled in the preliminary bombardment both with gas shell and H.E..

At 6 p.m. "C" retired to position in R.1.b. and then on to position in Q.12.a. where it was joined by "K" at about 7-30 p.m.. Headquarters also in Q.12.a. (South of VENDELLES).

22nd. At about 12 noon batteries, after shooting [handwritten: over] JEANCOURT, moved to position West of BERNES, "C" to Q.3.c., "K" to Q.2.d..

At 3 p.m. batteries moved to positions North of BOUVINCOURT in P.18.a. Headquarters at BEAUMETZ.

7 p.m. batteries moved to positions S.E. of CATELET in P.9.d.

23rd. At 12-15 a.m. owing to the obscure situation batteries were ordered to move up to the positions they had occupied on 22nd in P.18.a., but as the Germans were discovered to have advanced, batteries were again withdrawn at 1 a.m. to positions in ST. CREN ~~at~~ [handwritten: C to P21C, K to P21D] Headquarters in ST. CREN.

Batteries were still covering the 66th Division.

After dawn the Infantry had orders to retire and came back slowly, fighting, batteries staying in their positions till 10 a.m. and then withdrawing across country [handwritten: C] to positions close to PRUSLE cross roads O.30.a. ~~and b.~~ [handwritten: K to O31A]

At 11 a.m. enemy infantry were reported to be entering MON-EN-CHAUSSEE ~~and batteries were withdrawn across the river at BRIE to positions on the forward slope. "C" at O.25.c., "K" at O.31.a. (VILLERS-CARBENNEL) to cover the high ground in O.29.~~

[Handwritten: C was withdrawn across the river at BRIE to O25C. Both (VILLERS CARBONNEL) Both batteries being in a position to cover the high ground in O.29.]

At 1-30 p.m. as batteries were about to withdraw to positions under cover West of VILLERS CARBONNEL the advancing enemy were observed coming over the high ground in O.29., batteries engaged the enemy over open sights checking their advance.

Meanwhile 7 German aeroplanes unmolested circled over the batteries and teams, which were about 400 yards behind the guns, machine gunning the teams and gun detachments. One of these aeroplanes was brought down by rifle fire. At the same time teams and guns were heavily shelled by 77 m.m.. Batteries withdrew under heavy shell fire at 2 p.m. to positions in T.5.B and c., Headquarters in T.5.a. (about 1000 yards South of HORGNY).

24th. Batteries stayed in these positions until 5 p.m. on 24th when 4th Brigade, R.H.A. commanded by Major A.S. BARNWELL, D.S.O., R.H.A. came under direct command of 66th Divisional Artillery and moved to position between BARLEUX and ASSEVILLERS via ESTREES. "C" to position N.15.b. "K" to advance position N.11.d. Headquarters N.15.b..

25th. At 10 a.m. "K" was withdrawn to a position alongside "C" in N.15.b.

At 4-30 p.m. the enemy were seen advancing over high ground in O.19.a. and b. and engaged by "C" and "K".

At 5 p.m. the infantry having orders to retire to a line through Eastern edge of ASSEVILLERS. Batteries were withdrawn to position in ASSEVILLERS to cover this retirement, "C" to N.14.c., "K" to N.7.d.. Batteries stayed in these positions until dusk (having a good target of German infantry in the open just before dusk) when they were withdrawn to position at Sucrerie West of DOMPIERRE, "C" to M.10.b., "K" to M.10.a. to cover the line running through ASSEVILLERS.

26th. The 66th Divisional Artillery was withdrawn at dawn to positions at HARBONNIERRES and 4th Brigade, R.H.A. had orders to cover the retirement of the 66th Division, who, when driven out of their positions at ASSEVILLERS were to march on route ASSEVILLERS-ESTREES Road thence down main road to FOUCEAUCOURT to a line approximately RAINECOURT-FRAMERVILLE-VAUVILLERS.

This retirement commenced at about 10 a.m.

"C" from its position in M.10.b. covered the 66th Division, who marched in fours down ASSEVILLERS-ESTREES Road, from ASSEVILLERS to N.19.a., firing a defensive barrage about 700 yards East of the road. In N.19.a. the column turned right handed off the road avoiding ESTREES which was being shelled. And from this point "K" took on the defensive barrage, having moved at 10 a.m. to a position N.W. of FAY at M.16.d., to do this. The column moving across country to M.29.c. when it continued on the main road. "K" then covered it on the South (which was the flank from which interference was most expected) as far as SOYECOURT, meanwhile "C" moved to a position near PROYART in R.15.b. and covered the column until it reached its line of defence, when both batteries were withdrawn about 4 p.m. to positions at HARBONNIERES in W.6.c..

"G" Battery, R.H.A. then came under orders of 4th Brigade, R.H.A. and came into position in W.6.c. along side "C" and "K".

27th. At about 1 p.m. the enemy heavily shelled the batteries particularly "G" Battery who had numerous casualties and at 2 p.m. enemy infantry were seen to have reached cross roads HERBONNIERES-PROYART main AMIENS road in Q.30.d.. Batteries were withdrawn to positions in W.5. and engaged the ~~enmy~~ enemy on main AMIENS Road in R.25 and 26.

About 2-30 p.m.

About 2-30 p.m. "K" seeing a counter-attack developing from R.31. went forward independantly to a position in W.6.c. and opened fire in co-operation with the counter-attack, which was sucessful. "K" then moved to a position in W.5.b. and about dusk batteries were withdrawn to positions "K" and "G" to W.4.c., "C" to W.10.a.

Throughout this fighting zone of Brigade was FRAMERVILLE-VAUVILLERS both inclusive.

At 10 p.m. Lieutenant Colonel A.R. WAINEWRIGHT, D.S.O., R.H.A. took command of 4th Brigade, R.H.A. (from leave).

28th. At 4 a.m. the enemy was reported to be in BAYONVILLERS and Brigade withdrew before dawn to CAYEUX, where "K" came into action at V.30.a., "C" and "G" in D.5. where "K" joined them shortly after.

Batteries covering GUILLAUCOURT-WIENCOURT both inclusive.

At about 2 p.m. "G" and "K" were withdrawn to DEMUIN in D.1.c. "C" stayed in its position till 6-30 p.m. when it was withdrawn to D.1.d.. During this time the enemy had advanced towards MEZIERES from S.E. and at 7-30 p.m. batteries were again withdrawn across the river to HANGARD, "G" to U.29.d. "C" and "K" to U.29.b..

29th. At about 12 noon 4th Brigade, R.H.A. was transfered to 50th Divisional Artillery and moved via CACHY to positions S. of VILLERS BRETONNEUX, "C" to O.36.c., "G" and "K" to U.5.b., Headquarters in VILLERS BRETINNEUX.

Brigade stayed in this position till 4th April, covering 66th Division (MARCELCAVE) until 2nd April, and then 18th Division. Under orders of 50th Divisional Artillery. On 3rd Lieutenant Colonel A.R. WAINEWRIGHT proceeded to join 9th Division as C.R.A., Major BARNWELL taking over command of 4th Brigade, R.H.A.

On 4th April the enemy bombarded the battery areas and VILLERS BRETONNEUX with 77 m.m., 4.2, 5.9, and gas shell from 5-30 a.m. to 7-30 a.m when he attacked but was repulsed. All three batteries having a lot of casualties. He continued desultory fire allmday until 4 p.m. when he again commenced a counter-battery shoot on to the battery areas, and particularly on to "C" whose casualties were very heavy (having only 2 Officers and 11 men left). At about 5-30 p.m. the enemy attack commenced and our infantry retired, the enemy getting as far as the Chateau in U.6.a at 6 p.m., mounting a machine gun in the top storey and shooting at 400 yards at "G" Battery as it was withdrawing, "C" and "K" were also withdrawn over the ridge to positions North of CACHY, "C" U.3.a., "G" and "K" to U.1.a. and at dusk "C" to U.1.b..

An Australian Battalion however counter-attacked at once and drove the enemy back. "C" and "K" were accordingly moved up at 4 a.m. to positions "K" to U.3.a., "C" to U.2.a., "G" was relieved by "A" and "B" Batteries, R.C.H.A. who moved to U.3.a. at 4 a.m.

5th. At this time the 4th Brigade, R.H.A. came under command of Lieutenant Colonel ELKINS, D.S.O., R.C.H.A. with Headquarters at house N.35.b. and consisted of "C" and "K" Batteries, R.H.A., "A" and "B" Batteries, R.C.H.A..

At 8 p.m. the Brigade again came under orders of 66th Divisional Artillery covering Australian troops, shooting on the line MARCALCAVE.

On 7th "C" moved to position in O.27.d..

On 8th "B" Battery, R.C.H.A. having no guns left went out of action and "K" and "A" R.C.H.A. moved to position in O.28.a..

The Brigade

The Brigade covered 35th Australian Battalion from 5th to 6th and then 18th Australian Battalion until 10th instant, coming under orders of 58th Divisional Artillery on 9th instant.

On 9th instant Lieutenant Colonel R.H. LASCELLES, D.S.O., R.H.A. took over command of 4th Brigade, R.H.A.

At 7-30 p.m. on 10th instant frontage of 4th Brigade, R.H.A. was taken over by batteries of 8th Divisional Artillery and 4th Brigade, R.H.A. was withdrawn to Wagon Lines at CAGNY, coming under orders of 3rd Cavalry Division.

Total casualties from 21st March to 10th April, 1918 :-

			OFF	O.R	HORSES
"C" Battery, R.H.A.	...	68.	5	63	49
"K" Battery, R.H.A.	...	60.	2	58	58

MOVES OF AMMUNITION COLUMN.

21-3-1918 - VRAIGNES.
22-3-1918 - At 2 p.m. moved to LE MESNIL-BRUNTEL.
23-3-1918 - Moved about 3 a.m. to North of VILLERS CARBONNEL, moved about 1 p.m. to FOUCAUCOURT.
24-3-1918 - FOUCAUCOURT, moved about 2 p.m. to PROYART.
25-3-1918 - Moved from PROYART 7-30 a.m. to VILLERS BRETONNEUX.
26-3-1918 - Moved just West of VILLERS BRETONNEUX.
27-3-1918 - Moved about 6 a.m. to MOREUIL leaving there about 4 p.m. and marched to SAINS-EN-AMIENOIS.
28-3-1918 - Moved about 10 p.m. to BOVES.
29-3-1918 - Moved at 1 p.m. to CAGNY.
30-3-1918 to 10-4-1918 - CAGNY.

R. Lascelles

Lieutenant Colonel, R.H.A.
Commanding 4th Brigade, R. H. A.

3rd Cav.Div.

WAR
DIARY

Headquarters,

4th BRIGADE, R.H.A.

A P R I L

1 9 1 8

4th BRIGADE, R.H.A.

Army Form C. 2118.

Instructions regarding War Diaries and Intelligence Summaries are contained in F. S. Regs., Part II. and the Staff Manual respectively. Title pages will be prepared in manuscript.

~~WAR DIARY~~ or INTELLIGENCE SUMMARY.

APRIL (Erase heading not required.) 1918.

Vol 39

Place	Date	Hour	Summary of Events and Information	Remarks and references to Appendices
			Operations from 1st to 10th April are included in Appendix 'A' to War Diary for March.	
	4th		Lieutenant Colonel A.R. WAINEWRIGHT, D.S.O.,R.H.A. was appointed C.R.A. 9th Division.	
	8th		Lieutenant Colonel R.H. LASCELLES, D.S.O.,R.H.A. joined to command Royal Horse Artillery, 3rd Cavalry Division.	
	11th		4th Brigade, R.H.A. and R.C.H.A. Brigade marched to LA CHAUSSEE; R.C.H.A. Ammunition Column to TIRANCOURT.	
	12th		Marched again - "C" and "K" Batteries,R.H.A. to BEALCOURT, "A" and "B" Batteries,R.C.H.A. to BEAUVOIR - RIVIERE, Headquarters R.H.A. and R.C.H.A. and the two Ammunition Columns to MAIZICOURT.	
	13th		Continued march - Headquarters R.H.A. and R.C.H.A. to PERNES. Remainder of R.C.H.A. Brigade to OSTREVILLE, 4th Brigade,R.H.A. Ammunition Column to TROISVEAUX, "C" Battery,R.H.A. to BETHONVAL, "K" Battery,R.H.A. to BELVAL.	
	14th		Batteries came under orders of their affiliated Brigades. "C" Battery,R.H.A. moved to FIEFS remaining there 3 hours and then moved on to SBACHIN.	
	15th		"K" Battery, R.H.A. moved with 7th Cavalry Brigade to MANQUEVILLE. Ammunition Column moved to PRESSY-LES-PERNES.	
	16th		"K" Battery, R.H.A. returned to PERNES. Whole of R.C.H.A. Brigade including Headquarters moved to EPS.	
	27th		R.C.H.A. Brigade moved to VERCHIN.	

A7092). Wt. W12859/M1297 750,000. 1/17. D. D & L., Ltd. Forms/C2118/14.

Army Form C. 2118.

Instructions regarding War Diaries and Intelligence Summaries are contained in F. S. Regs., Part II. and the Staff Manual respectively. Title pages will be prepared in manuscript.

WAR DIARY
or
INTELLIGENCE SUMMARY.
(Erase heading not required.)

Place	Date	Hour	Summary of Events and Information	Remarks and references to Appendices

From 14th onwards to end of month Batteries were on short notice to move.

Refitting was carried out from 14th onwards and batteries and column were practically complete by the end of the month.

The following officers joined the Brigade during the month :-

Lieutenant J. W. STOBART, R.F.A.
Lieutenant B. McLACHLAN, M.C., R.F.A.
2ndLieutenant E. F. MAUDE, R.F.A.
2ndLieutenant G. RENOUF, R.F.A.
2ndLieutenant C. H. BRUNKER, R.F.A.
2ndLieutenant D. W. LILLEY, R.F.A.
2ndLieutenant W. HEXTALL, R.F.A.

Lieutenant Colonel, R.H.A.

Commanding 4th Brigade, Royal Horse Artillery.

A7092). Wt. W12839/M1297 750,000. 1/17. D. D & L., Ltd. Forms/C2118/14.

Army Form C. 2118.

Cmdg R.H.A. + 4 Bde R.H.A.

WAR DIARY
or
INTELLIGENCE SUMMARY.

Instructions regarding War Diaries and Intelligence Summaries are contained in F. S. Regs., Part II. and the Staff Manual respectively. Title pages will be prepared in manuscript.

R.H.A. 3rd Cavalry Divn: *(Erase heading not required.)* MAY, 1918.

Vol 40

Place	Date	Hour	Summary of Events and Information	Remarks and references to Appendices
	1st		Units billetted as follows :- Headquarters R.H.A. ... ... PERNES. "C" Battery, R.H.A. ... ... SACHIN. "K" Battery, R.H.A. ... ... PERNES. Divn'l: Ammn: Column. ... ... PRESSY-LES-PERNES. R.C.H.A. Brigade (less Section of Column) VERCHIN.	
	4th		The Division moved to an area East of HESDIN - Headquarters R.H.A. to WAIL. "C" Battery, R.H.A. to CONCHY-SUR-CANCHE. "K" Battery, R.H.A. to HARAVESNES. Divn'l: Ammn: Column to OEUF. R.C.H.A. Brigade. to VIEIL - HESDIN.	
	5th		March continued to an area East and South-East of AUXI-LE-CHATEAU. Headquarters R.H.A. to YVRENCH. "C" Battery, R.H.A. to WAVANS. "K" Battery, R.H.A. to MONTIGNY-LES-JONGLEURS. Divn'l Ammn: Column. to YVRENCHEUX. R.C.H.A. Brigade. to MESNIL-DOMQUEUR.	
	6th		March concluded - Headquarters R.H.A. to CONTAY. "C" Battery, R.H.A. to CONTAY. "K" Battery, R.H.A. to CONTAY. Divn'l Ammn: Column. to BEHENCOURT. R.C.H.A. Brigade to BEHENCOURT.	

A7092). Wt. W12839/M1297 750,000. 1/17. D. D & L., Ltd. Forms/C2118/14.

Army Form C. 2118.

PAGE 2.

WAR DIARY
or
INTELLIGENCE SUMMARY.
(Erase heading not required.)

Instructions regarding War Diaries and Intelligence Summaries are contained in F. S. Regs., Part II. and the Staff Manual respectively. Title pages will be prepared in manuscript.

R.H.A. 3rd Cavalry Division — MAY, 1918.

Place	Date	Hour	Summary of Events and Information	Remarks and references to Appendices
	17th		4th Brigade, R.H.A. moved as follows :- Headquarters R.H.A. to BELLOY-SUR-SOMME. "C" Battery, R.H.A. -ditto- "K" Battery, R.H.A. to ST. OUEN. 4th Brigade, R.H.A. Amm: Col: BETHENCOURT - ST OUEN.	
	24		R.C.H.A. Brigade remained complete at CONTAY until 24th when it was relieved by "K" Battery, R.H.A. and a Section of the 4th Brigade, R.H.A. Ammunition Column. R.C.H.A. Brigade less Canadian Section of Ammunition Column moved to ST OUEN. Canadian Section of Ammunition Column rejoined Divisional Ammunition Column.	
	31st		"C" Battery, R.H.A. and 1 Section of Divisional Ammunition Column relieved "K" Battery, R.H.A. and 1 Section Divisional Ammunition Column. "K" Battery, R.H.A. moving to BELLOY-SUR-SOMME and relieved-section of Ammunition Column rejoining Divisional Ammunition Column.	
			The following Officers joined during the month - Major D. SCOTT, M.C., R.H.A. 2/Lieutenant J.F. SMEE, R.F.A. 2/Lieutenant H.A. MACONOCHIE, R.F.A. The following Officers left the Brigade during the month - Lieutenant J.W. STOBART, R.F.A. to Australian Artillery Reinforcement Camp. 2/Lieutenant W. HEXTALL, R.F.A. to 7th Brigade, R.H.A. Lieutenant Colonel, R.H.A. C. R. H. A., 3rd Cavalry Division.	

A7092). Wt. W12839/M1297 750,000. 1/17. D. D & L., Ltd. Forms/C2118/14.

Instructions regarding War Diaries and Intelligence Summaries are contained in F. S. Regs., Part II. and the Staff Manual respectively. Title pages will be prepared in manuscript.

WAR DIARY
or
INTELLIGENCE SUMMARY.
(Erase heading not required.)

Army Form C. 2118.

4 Bde RHA

Vol 41

R.H.A. 3rd Cavalry Division. JUNE, 1918.

Place	Date	Hour	Summary of Events and Information	Remarks and references to Appendices
	1st to 13th		Reference Sheets - AMIENS & LENS, 1/100000. Units billetted as follows - Headquarters R.H.A. — BELLOY-SUR-SOMME. "C" Battery, R.H.A. (& 1 Section D.A.C.) — BEHENCOURT. "K" Battery, R.H.A. — BELLOY-SUR-SOMME. R.C.H.A. Brigade. — ST OUEN. Divn'l: Ammn: Column. (less 1 Section) — BETHENCOURT-ST. OUEN.	
	14th		"K" Battery, R.H.A. and 1 Section Divn'l: Ammunition Column relieved "C" Battery, R.H.A. and 1 Section Divn'l: Ammn: Column in the forward area at BEHENCOURT. "C" Battery, R.H.A. moved back to BELLOY-SUR-SOMME and Section of D.AMC. rejoined Divisional Ammunition Column.	
	22nd		R.C.H.A. Brigade and R.C.H.A. Section of Divn'l: Ammn: Column relieved "K" Battery, R.H.A. and 1 Section D.A.C. in forward area at BEHENCOURT. "K" Battery moved to ST. OUEN and Section of D.A.C. rejoined Div: Ammn: Column.	
	26th		Owing to an outbreak of fever "C" Battery, R.H.A. moved with 6th Cavalry Brigade to RIENCOURT.	

Page 2.

A7092). Wt. W12839/M1291 750,000. 1/17. D. D & L., Ltd. Forms/C2118/14.

Instructions regarding War Diaries and Intelligence Summaries are contained in F. S. Regs., Part II. and the Staff Manual respectively. Title pages will be prepared in manuscript.

WAR DIARY
or
INTELLIGENCE SUMMARY.
(Erase heading not required.)

Army Form C. 2118.

Place	Date	Hour	Summary of Events and Information	Remarks and references to Appendices
			On night 29th/30th The Royal Horse Artillery (less S.A.A. Sections) (Divisionalised) marched to POULAINVALLE where they came under orders of the Australian Corps.	
			Reference Sheet - 62.d. 1/40,000.	
			On night 30th/31st Batteries came into action in J.14 and J.15., Wagon Lines H.24.a.2.3., Divisional Ammunition Column H.12.	
			R.C.H.A. H.Q. remained back at PONT NOYELLES and took command of Divisionalised Wagon Lines.	
			Headquarters R.H.A. were in J.14.	
			"C" and "K" Batteries, R.H.A. and "A" and "B" Batteries, R.C.H.A. under R.H.A. H.Q. acted as a Sub-Group under Left Group 3rd Australian Divisional Artillery covering a front on the North bank of the River SOMME - J.35.d.9.0. to J.35.d.55.40.	
			The undermentioned Officer left the Brigade during JUNE -	
			Lieutenant M.E.S. THOMPSON, R.F.A. to 69th (Army) Brigade, R.F.A.	
			W. A. P. [illegible] Lt Col. for Lieutenant Colonel, R.H.A. C. R. H. A., 3rd Cavalry Division.	

A7092). Wt. W12839/M1291 750,000. 1/17. D. D & L., Ltd. Forms/C2118/14.

4 Bde R HA

Army Form C. 2118.

Vol 42

WAR DIARY
or
INTELLIGENCE SUMMARY.

Instructions regarding War Diaries and Intelligence Summaries are contained in F. S. Regs., Part II. and the Staff Manual respectively. Title pages will be prepared in manuscript.

R.H.A. 3rd Cavalry Division. *(Erase heading not required.)* JULY, 1918.

Place	Date	Hour	Summary of Events and Information	Remarks and references to Appendices

Reference Sheet 62.D., 1/40,000.

Units in action as follows :-

Headquarters R.H.A.	J.14.
"C" Battery, R.H.A. "K" Battery, R.H.A. "A" Battery, R.C.H.A. "B" Battery, R.C.H.A.	J.14. and J.15.
Wagon Lines	H.24.
Divisional Ammn: Column.	H.12.
R.C.H.A. Headquarters	PONT NOYELLES.

All 4 Batteries under Headquarters R.H.A. acting as a Sub-Group under Left Group, 3rd Australian Divisional Artillery covering a front on North bank of River SOMME - J.35.d.9.0. - J.35.d.55.40.

On 4th July at 3-10 a.m. 6th, 4th and 11th Australian Infantry Brigades attacked and reached their final objectives without any hitch whatever.

During this operation Batteries fired a barrage to the North of the attacking troops.

Page 2.

A7092). Wt. W12839/M1297 750,000. 1/17. D. D & L., Ltd. Forms/C2118/14.

Army Form C. 2118.

Instructions regarding War Diaries and Intelligence Summaries are contained in F. S. Regs., Part II. and the Staff Manual respectively. Title pages will be prepared in manuscript.

WAR DIARY
or
INTELLIGENCE SUMMARY.
(Erase heading not required.)

Place	Date	Hour	Summary of Events and Information	Remarks and references to Appendices
			On night 8th/9th Batteries were withdrawn to POULAINVILLE and on night 9th/10th the Divisional Artillery moved to DAILY MAIL Woods - T.29.a.& b. (reference 57.D.,1/40,000).	
			The Divisional Artillery stayed in these woods until end of the month acting as IIIrd Corps Artillery Reserve.	
	31st		3rd Cavalry Divisional Artillery Sports. ~~Programme attached~~.	
			Following casualties occurred during month :-	
			2/Lieutenant E. F. MAUDE, R.F.A. - Wounded in action 1st JULY, 1918.	
			4 Other Ranks Killed in action, 1 Other Rank wounded in action 4th JULY, 1918.	
			Lieutenant E. A. MITCHELL, R.H.A. joined the Brigade 18th JULY, 1918.	
			[signature] Lieutenant Colonel, R.H.A.	
			C. R. H. A. 3rd Cavalry Division.	

A7092). Wt. W12839/M1297 750,000. 1/17. D. D & L., Ltd. Forms/C2118/14.

Instructions regarding War Diaries and Intelligence Summaries are contained in F. S. Regs., Part II. and the Staff Manual respectively. Title pages will be prepared in manuscript.

WAR DIARY
or
~~INTELLIGENCE SUMMARY.~~

(Erase heading not required.)

Army Form C. 2118.

4 Bde R HA

R.H.A.3rd Cavalry Division.

August 1918.

18 43

Place	Date	Hour	Summary of Events and Information	Remarks and references to Appendices
			Reference AMIENS LENS MAP 1/100,000 62 D 66E " 1/40,000	
	1.st/5th		R.H.A. 3rd Cavalry Division in Mobile Reserve in 3rd Corpd area.	
	6th		R.H.A. moved to an Area W.of AMIENS : H.Q. R.H.A.and D.A.C. to Pont De Metz. "C" Battery R.H.A. to RENANCOURT. "K"Battery R.H.A. to MONTIERES. R.C.H.A. to gardens just west of AMIENS in R.3.d. & R.4.c. Here R.H.A.joined 3rd Cavalry Division and C.K.& R.C.H.A. came under the orders of their Affiliated Cavalry Brigades. (see War Diarys of 6th,7th ,and Canadian Cavalry Brigades)	
	Night 7/8th		H.Q. R.H.A. moved with H.Q.3rd Cavalry Division to Cross Tracks T.3.b.2.4.(62,D 1/4o,000	
	8th		Throughout Operations during 8th 9th and 10th,H.Q. R.H.A. moved with H.Q. 3rd Cavalry Division, moves being as follows- times approximate. Reference AMIENS 1/1oo,ooo To CACHY 6.am. Wood ½ mile N.of A of AUBERCOURT 9 am. High Ground E.of BEAUCOURT -- DEMUIN Road 12 noon. CayEUX Wood 3.pm. Cross Roads CAIX) -BEAUCOURT CAYEUX -- Le QUESNEL 5 pm. Road junction ½ mile S of CAYEUX on CAYEUX--Le QUESNEL Road 7-30 pm.	
	9th		Point 93. on CAYEUX--CAIX Road 9 am.	

(A7092). Wt. W12839/M1293. 750,000. 1/17. D. D. & L., Ltd. Forms/C.2118/14.

SHEET 2.

Instructions regarding War Diaries and Intelligence Summaries are contained in F. S. Regs., Part II. and the Staff Manual respectively. Title pages will be prepared in manuscript.

WAR DIARY
or
INTELLIGENCE SUMMARY.

(Erase heading not required.)

Army Form C. 2118.

Place	Date	Hour	Summary of Events and Information	Remarks and references to Appendices
	10th		Point 95 1 mile South of CAIX 9-0 am. Windmill 1 mile S.W.of VRELY 12-noon N.outskirts of BEAUFORT 2.pm. Point ½ mile South of B.of BEAUFORT 4-pm. Point 96 ½ mile N of BEAUFORT. 6-30 pm.	
	11th		To F.M.1 mile W.of C. of COTTENCHY 5- pm. H.Q.R.H.A. stayed here until 13th when it moved to SAINS EN AMIENOIS. Moves of D.A.C. and S.A.A.Section from night 7/8th to 13th as below;- D.A.C. 8th Assembled Sheet 62 D N.31.a. at 5-30 am. Left for " T.2.a. 6-0 am. Left for " U.2.d. 11-0 am. Left for 66E C.4.c. 12-15 pm. 9th Left for 62D V.28.b. 12-30 pm. 10th Left for 66E E.3.a. 9-0 am. Left for " E.30 a. 2-45 pm. 11th Left for REMIENCOURT 5.pm. S.A.A.Section 8th Assembled Sheet 62 D T.2.c. at 4-0 am. Left for " T.3.a. 9-0 am. Left for " U.2.a. 11-0am Left for " U.27.d. 2 pm. Left for 66E C.3.d. 5.pm. 9th Left for 62D V.23.c. 4.pm. 10th Left for 66E E.7.b. 12-30 pm. Left for " E.30.c. 4-0 pm. 11th Left for REMIENCOURT 5.pm.	

(A7092). Wt. W12839/M1293. 750,000. 1/17. D. D. & L., Ltd. Forms/C.2118/14.

SHEET 3.

Instructions regarding War Diaries and Intelligence Summaries are contained in F. S. Regs., Part II. and the Staff Manual respectively. Title pages will be prepared in manuscript.

WAR DIARY
or
INTELLIGENCE SUMMARY.

(Erase heading not required.)

Army Form C. 2118.

Place	Date	Hour	Summary of Events and Information	Remarks and references to Appendices
			While at E.30.a. (66 E) D.A.C. where shelled and bombed, 9 horses being hit.	
	Night 15/16th		H.Q. R.H.A. Moved to YZEUX D.A.C. moved to BETHENCOURT St OUEN.	
	17th		H.Q. R.H.A. moved to BELLOY.	
	Night 25/26th		H.Q. R.H.A. and D.A.C. moved to CAUMONT.	
	26th		H.Q. R.H.A. and D.A.C. moved to WILLEMAN.	
	~~[illegible]~~		~~Mobile sections of D.A.C. attached permanently to Batteries.~~	

H Johnson Capt
Lieutenant Colonel R.H.A.
C. R. H. A. 3rd Cavalry Division.

(A7092). Wt. W12839/M1293. 750,000. 1/17. D. D. & L., Ltd. Forms/C.2118/14

Army Form C. 2118.

4 Bde RHA
Sept '18

WAR DIARY
or
~~INTELLIGENCE SUMMARY.~~
(Erase heading not required.)

Instructions regarding War Diaries and Intelligence Summaries are contained in F. S. Regs., Part II. and the Staff Manual respectively. Title pages will be prepared in manuscript.

Place	Date	Hour	Summary of Events and Information	Remarks and references to Appendices
			September War Diary	
			Reference :- LENS) AMIENS) 1/100,000	
	1st		H.Q. R.H.A. and D.A.C. at WILLEMAN.	
	10th		H.Q. R.H.A. and D.A.C. ~~&&~~ to CAUMONT.	
	15th		H.Q. R.H.A.and S.A.A.Section D.A.C. carried out the following moves while engaged in Cavalry Corps September Manoeuvres:- 16th to ESTRUVALLE CHATEAU. 17th H.Q.R.H.A. to CHATEAU DE BEAUVOIN S.A.A.Section D.A.C.to WAVANS. 18th H.Q. R.H.A. to EQUIERIE S.A.A.Section to VACQUERETTE.	
	17th		Heavy Section D.A.C. moved to VACQUERETTE.	
	19th		D.A.C. to FILLIEVRES.	
	20th		H.Q.R.H.A. to VACQUERETTE.	
	Night 25/26TH		H.Q.R.H.A.to VAUCHELLES LES AUTHIE. D.A.C. to AUTHIEULE.	
	Night 26/27th		D.A.C. to ALBERT-DERNANCOURT ROAD.	
	Night 27/28th		H.Q. R.H.A.to CLERY SUR SOMME. D.A.C. to CURLU.	
	29th		H.Q. R.H.A. to POEUILLY. D.A.C. to CAULAINCOURT.	
			During the month Lieut. R.L.Hutchins R.F.A. and Lieut O.L.Boord M.C.R.F.A.joined R.H.A. 3rd Cavalry Division from England + posted to "C" Battery R.H.A.	

Lieut Col.RHA.
C.R.H.A. 3rd Cavalry Division

9/52/44

Army Form C. 2118.

Instructions regarding War Diaries and Intelligence Summaries are contained in F. S. Regs., Part II. and the Staff Manual respectively. Title pages will be prepared in manuscript.

WAR DIARY
or
~~INTELLIGENCE SUMMARY.~~
(Erase heading not required.)

HQ RA
4th Bde RHA
Vol 40

Place	Date	Hour	Summary of Events and Information	Remarks and references to Appendices
			OCTOBER 1918	
			Reference Sheets 1/40,000 62b. 57 b 62c 57c.	
	1st		H.Q.R.H.A. at POEUILLY - D.A.C. at CAULAINCOURT.	
	2nd		The Division moved to a position of readiness at BELLENGLISE in support of Infantry attack. H.Q. R.H.A. at TUMULUS M.1.d.(62b) and later to H.19.(62b), but eventually returned to POEUILLY at night.	
	8th		The Division moved forward in support of 1st Cavalry Division. H.Q.R.H.A. moving to H.19. thence to B.22. and returning to H.19 at night(62b) D.A.C.moved to BELLINGLISE.	
	9th		3rd Cavalry Division moved forward ,direction- main ESTREES-LE-CATEAU road. H.Q.R.H.A. moved in bounds to C.7.(62b),U.26.(57b),U.12.a.(57b),P.26.(57b) and stayed there for the night. D.A.C. moved up the main LE-CATEAU road (keeping roughly 4-5 miles behind the fighting line), and stayed the night at U.12.a (57b).	
	10th		H.Q.R.H.A. moved to P.4.(57b).At 3.pm.the Artillery of theDivision came under the orders of the C.R.H.A. and with D/23 Battery R.F A. came into action in J.25 (57b) and fired a barrage for the support of the 33rd Division who pushed forward to Cross R SELLE between NEUVILLY and MONTAY. On Conclusion of Barrage Batteries rejoined their Brigades and H.Q.R.H.A. moved to U.11.b.	
	Night 10/11th		D.A.C. moved to P.7.	
	12th		H.Q. R.H.A. moved to BERTRY and thence to ELINCOURT.	
	13th		H.Q.R.H.A. moved to MANANCOURT (57C) D.A.C. moved to HONNECOURT (57B).	
	14th		D.A.C. moved to LECHELLE (57C). D/23 Battery R.F.A. was attached to R.H.A. 3rd Cavalry Division on 6.10.18 and remained with 3rd Cavalry Division till 12.10.18	

D. D. & L., London, E.C. (A8041) Wt W1771/M2031 750,000 5/17 Sch. 52 Forms/C2118/14

Instructions regarding War Diaries and Intelligence Summaries are contained in F. S. Regs., Part II. and the Staff Manual respectively. Title pages will be prepared in manuscript.

WAR DIARY

or

~~INTELLIGENCE SUMMARY.~~

(Erase heading not required.)

Army Form C. 2118.

Place	Date	Hour	Summary of Events and Information	Remarks and references to Appendices
			During these operations this Battery moved with Divisional Troops on a line with H.Q.R.H.A. until 12 noon when it was attached to Canadian Cavalry Brigade for an attack on MAUROIS HONNECUY, and REUMONT . It remained with Canadian Cavalry Brigade during the night 9/10th(when it fired on River crossing at MONTAY). On morning 10th it was attached to 7th Cavalry Brigade until it came under the orders of C.R.H.A. for the Barrage for 33rd Division. On 13.10.18 it rejoined 23rd Brigade R.F.A. Remained in above Billet till end of month. Casualties during month:- Major R.L.Palmer D.S.O. M.C. R.H.A. Wounded Lieut. A.A.Bontor M.C.R.H.A. Wounded. Lieut. B. Maclaghlan M.C. Died of Wounds. Major J.N.Diggle R.H.A. ,2/Lieut M.H.Cooper R.F.A., 2/Lieut J.G.Murdock R.F.A. Lieut J.N.Neville R.F.A. Posted to R.H.A. 3rd Cavalry Division. Lieut E.A.Mitchell to England sick. 2/Lieut J.F.Smee Struck off Strength. (to RFA) Lieut R.L.Hutchins.R.F.A. Lieut D.C.Fergusson R.F.A. Lieut E.L.Vale Pope R.F.A. Lieut. G.Renouf R.F.A. Lieut D.W.Lilley R.F.A. Appointed to R.H.A. 4 O.R's Killed and 37 O.R's wounded. [signature] Lieutenant Colonel R.H.A. C. R. H. A. 3rd CavalryDivision.	

D. D. & L., London, E.C.
(A8104) Wt W1771/M2031 750,000 5/17 Sch. 52 Forms/C2118/14

Army Form C. 2118.

HQ 4 Bde R H A

WAR DIARY
or
~~INTELLIGENCE SUMMARY~~
(Erase heading not required.)

Instructions regarding War Diaries and Intelligence Summaries are contained in F. S. Regs., Part II. and the Staff Manual respectively. Title pages will be prepared in manuscript.

November 1918.

9846

Place	Date	Hour	Summary of Events and Information	Remarks and references to Appendices
			November War Diary.	
			Reference LENS) VALENCIENNES) BRUSSELS) TOURNAI) 1/100,000	
	1st		H.Q. R.H.A. at HENNOIS WOOD . D.A.C. at LECHELLE.	
	6th		H.Q. R.H.A. and D.A.C. moved to INCHY-EN-ARTOIS.	
	7th		H.Q. R.H.A. and D.A.C.moved to Western Suburb of DOUAI. Reference TOURNAI 1/100000	
	8th		H.Q. R.H.A. SAINGHIN D.A.C. PETIT ATTICHES	
	10th		H.Q. R.H.A. ANTOING	
	11th		H.Q. R.H.A. moved ~~XX~~ with Divisional H.Q. to 500 yds N.of "C" of CORON (TOURNAI.1/100000) and returned to ANTOING the same night after the declaration of the Armistice.	
	13 th		D.A.C. moved to BURY.	
	17 th		H.Q. R.H.A. moved to BASSILY D.A.C. to BOURLON.	
	18 th		H.Q. R.H.A. moved to ENGHIN D.A.C. to COQUAINE (Reference Brussels 1/100000).	
	21st		H.Q. R.H.A. moved to WATERLOO D.A.C. to ROUSSART & JOLI-BOIS.	
	22nd		H.Q. R.H.A. moved to PERWEZ D.A.C. to LE MONT.	
	24th	~~XXXX~~	H.Q. R.H.A. moved to THOREMBAIS ST TROND.	
			During the Month 2/Lieut COOPER R.F.A. left to join 35th Divisional Artillery. Lieut E.A.Mitchell R.H.A. rejoined from England.	

[signature]
Lieutenant Colonel R.H.A.
C. R. H. A. 3rd Cavalry Division.

D. D. & L., London, E.C. (A7034) Wt. W1771/M2031 750,000 5/17 Sch. 52 Forms C2118/14

Instructions regarding War Diaries and Intelligence Summaries are contained in F. S. Regs., Part II. and the Staff Manual respectively. Title pages will be prepared in manuscript.

WAR DIARY
or
INTELLIGENCE SUMMARY.
(Erase heading not required.)

Army Form C. 2118.

HQ 3 Cav Div RHA

Vol 47

Place	Date	Hour	Summary of Events and Information	Remarks and references to Appendices
			Dec 18	
			WAR DIARY for December 1918	
			Reference BRUSSELS, LIEGE, NAMUR, MARCHE 1/100,000	
	1st		H.Q. R.H.A. at THOREMBAIS ST TROND D.A.C. at LE MONTE	
	15th		H.Q. R.H.A. and D.A.C. WARET L'EVEQUE.	
	16th		H.Q. R.H.A. at SCRY D.A.C. ST VITU and ABEE (Permanent Winter Billets)	

Mitchell RHA

Lieutenant Colonel R.H.A.
C. R. H. A. 3rd Cavalry Division.

D. D. & L., London, E.C.
(A7001) Wt. W1771/M2031 750,000 5/17 Sch. 52 Forms C2118/14

Instructions regarding War Diaries and Intelligence Summaries are contained in F. S. Regs., Part II. and the Staff Manual respectively. Title pages will be prepared in manuscript.

WAR DIARY
or
~~INTELLIGENCE SUMMARY.~~
~~(Erase heading not required.)~~

Army Form C. 2118.

VR 48

Place	Date	Hour	Summary of Events and Information	Remarks and references to Appendices
			1919	
			JANUARY - WAR DIARY.	
			Reference Sheet No. 9 MARCHE 1/100000.	
	1st.		H.Q., R.H.A. Chateau TILTESSE (SCRY). D. A. C. do. ST. VITU.	
	to 31st		During the month the following Officers have joined:- Lieut. A.A.Bontor, M.C., R.H.A. (Posted to "C" Battery, R.H.A. Lieut. the Hon. A.M.A.Baillie, R.F.A. ditto [illegible] been demobolised:- The [illegible] Murdock, R.F.A.	

[signature]

Lieutenant Colonel, R.H.A.,

C.R.H.A. 3rd Cavalry Division.

D. D. & L., London, E.C. (A5001) Wt. W1771/M2031 750,000 5/17 Sch. 52 Forms C2118/14

Army Form C. 2118.

Instructions regarding War Diaries and Intelligence Summaries are contained in F. S. Regs., Part II. and the Staff Manual respectively. Title pages will be prepared in manuscript.

WAR DIARY

or

~~INTELLIGENCE SUMMARY.~~

Vol 49

Place	Date	Hour	Summary of Events and Information	Remarks and references to Appendices
			FEBRUARY WAR DIARY.	

Reference MARCHE 1/100000. HQ RHA at SCRY – ... at ST VITU

The following Officers left during the month:-

Lieutenant Colonel R.H.Lascelles, D.S.O., R.H.A.,
Deceased 16.2.19. (whilst on leave to U.K.)

Major J.Diggle D.S.O., R.H.A.,
Demobolised 13.2.19 (on expiration of Leave)

Lieut. G. Renouf R.H.A.
To report to War Office.

Captain H.A.Baker, M.C., R.H.A.,
To England Sick.

[signature]
Captain, R.H.A.
for C.R.H.A., 3rd Cavalry Division.

H.Q. R.H.A.
3RD
CAVALRY DIVISION.
No. ......
Date. ......

D. D. & L., London, E.C.
(A7093) Wt. W1:71/M2031 750,000 5/17 Sch. 52 Forms C2118/14

Army Form C. 2118.

Instructions regarding War Diaries and Intelligence Summaries are contained in F. S. Regs., Part II. and the Staff Manual respectively. Title pages will be prepared in manuscript.

WAR DIARY
or
INTELLIGENCE SUMMARY.
(Erase heading not required.)

Place	Date	Hour	Summary of Events and Information	Remarks and references to Appendices
			WAR DIARY - MARCH 1919.	
			Reference:- LIEGE 1/100000.	
	11.3.19.		H.Q., R.H.A., moved from Chateau Siltesse to Chokier.	
	do.		D. A. C. moved from Chateau St.Vitu to Chokier.	
			The following transfers took effect during the month:-	
			Capt.EATG Boylan D.S.O.,R.H.A. posted to "E" Battery, R.H.A.	
			Capt. F.James, M.C., R.H.A., posted to 7th Bde. Amm. Col.	
			Lieut. F.Westrop e R.F.A. evacuated to Hospital.	
			Lieut. E.A.Mitchell R.H.A. do do.	
			Lieut. CHM Brunker R.H.A. to command D.A.C.	
			Lieut. O.L.Boord M.C., R.H.A. to D.A.C. from "C" Battery.	
			Lieut. R.L.Hutchins R.H.A. posted to "K" Battery from "C" Battery, R.H.A.	

Captain, R.H.A.,
for ~~C.R.H.A.~~, 3rd Cavalry Division.

D. D. & L., London, E.C. (A7023) Wt. W1771/M2031 750,000 5/17 Sch. 52 Forms C2118/14

Instructions regarding War Diaries and Intelligence Summaries are contained in F. S. Regs., Part II. and the Staff Manual respectively. Title pages will be prepared in manuscript.

12

WAR DIARY
or
INTELLIGENCE SUMMARY.
(Erase heading not required.)

Army Form C. 2118.

Vol 51

Place	Date	Hour	Summary of Events and Information April 1919	Remarks and references to Appendices
			Reference LIEGE 1/100,000	
CHOKIER	1st		H.Q. 4th Brigade and 4th Brigade R.H.A. Ammunition Column remained at CHOKIER.	
			During month following changes in Officers :-	
			Lieutenant O.L.BOORD R.F.A. took over duties of Adjutant. Captain H.G.Morrison R.H.A. to England to report to War Office. Lieutenant E.A.Mitchell R.H.A. to Report to War Office. Lieutenant H.A.Maconochie R.F.A. from "C"Battery R.H.A. to Ammunition Column.	
			30.4.19 — O.L. Boord. Lieutenant R.F.A. for Commanding 4th Brigade R.H.A.	

(A7001) Wt. W1171/M2031 750,000 5/17 D. D. & L., London, E.C. Sch. 52 Forms C2118/14

Army Form C. 2118.

4 Bde RHA

Instructions regarding War Diaries and Intelligence Summaries are contained in F. S. Regs., Part II. and the Staff Manual respectively. Title pages will be prepared in manuscript.

WAR DIARY
or
INTELLIGENCE SUMMARY.
(Erase heading not required.)

Place	Date	Hour	Summary of Events and Information	Remarks and references to Appendices
			War Diary. May 1919	
CHOKIER	1st		H.Q. 4th Brigade R.H.A. and 4th Brigade R.H.A. Ammunition Column at CHOKIER	
			No change during month	
CHOKIER	31st		Both units still at CHOKIER.	

M. Boyd.
Lieut. RFA
for Commanding 4th Bde RHA.

D. D. & L., London, E.C.
(A5934) Wt. W1771/M2031 750,000 5/17 Sch. 52 Forms C2118/14

Army Form C. 2118.

Instructions regarding War Diaries and Intelligence Summaries are contained in F. S. Regs., Part II. and the Staff Manual respectively. Title pages will be prepared in manuscript.

WAR DIARY
or
INTELLIGENCE SUMMARY.
(Erase heading not required.)

JUNE 1919.

Headquarters 4th Bde R.H.A. & Amm. Col.

53

Place	Date	Hour	Summary of Events and Information	Remarks and references to Appendices
			War Diary.	
CHOKIER.	1st		H.Q. & Ammunition Column 4th Brigade R.H.A. at CHOKIER.	
	6th		H.Q. & Amm. Col. handed in equipment to Ordnance at ENGIS.	
	7th		" " " " loaded their vehicles on a train for them to go to the Vehicle Reception Park at BEAUMARAIS.	
	10th		The remaining men of both units. H.Q. 4. Am. Col. 38. } proceed to CONCENT at MARCHIENNE-AU-PONT for demobilisation.	
	10th.		Units cease to exist as such. From the 10th Officers attached to 3rd Cav. Div. Cadre Bde. for reposting. viz. Lieut's. BOORD, BRUNKER, and MACONOCHIE.	
			H. Boord Lieut. R.F.A. for Commanding 4th Bde R.H.A.	

D. D. & L., London, E.C. (A8093) Wt. W1771/M2031 750,000 5/17 Sch. 52 Forms C2118/14

www.ingramcontent.com/pod-product-compliance
Lightning Source LLC
Chambersburg PA
CBHW080534250426
43668CB00052B/2158